"While it focuses on the Brown Church [...] of Brown experience and theology, this book is about much more than the Brown Church. It is about church, gospel, truth, and justice. It is about me who is brown but also about you who are not. This is an important read for any who wish to be faithful Christians in today's context."

Justo L. González, historian and theologian

"Passionate, theological, and formational! This is a book that redefines the social identity of the Brown Church, breaking away from religious stereotypes of the Latina/o community and uncovering a rich legacy and discussion of Latina/o faith and identity. Chao Romero tells the bold, proud history of advocacy and the work of social justice across the centuries of the Brown Church, including scriptural and theological foundations, so that the children of the Brown Church and those seeking to understand her may clearly see her spiritual light and the costly marks of faithful, creative courage and sacrifice."

Elizabeth Conde-Frazier, coordinator of relations for theological entities at the Association of Hispanic Theological Education, coauthor of *Latina Evangélicas: A Theological Survey from the Margins*

"Brown is the color of the blood of slathered communities for five hundred years crying to God from the lands of the Americas (Gen 4:10). It is the color that symbolizes both the pride and oppression of those sacrificed to the voracity of colonial modernity, depredatory capitalism, and civilizing Christian missions. But *Brown Church* is also an embedded witnessing to Jesús of Aztlán, walked in pain and hope by border communities in the power of the decolonial Spirit outside the gate. *Brown Church* showcases recovered history of Christian activism, uncovered human dignity, and above all, the ecclesial imagination called home by a Latinx generation of Christians that for too long have lived stripped of their own faith and sense of mission as decolonial justice. Readable, well documented, passionately evangélico, Robert Chao Romero's work may very well be his new manual of 'church for revolutionaries.'"

Oscar García-Johnson, author of *Spirit Outside the Gate* and associate professor of theology and Latinx studies, Fuller Theological Seminary

"Here is a sweeping and fascinating account of the vital theologies and prophetic witness of the Brown church in the Americas. Weaving together stories of oppressed Latin American and US Latina/o communities, Robert Chao Romero tells of faithfulness to Christian calling, commitment to biblical justice, and collaborative theologies that challenge injustice and transform society. *Brown Church* is a story for the entire church as it seeks to fulfill its callings in the twenty-first century."

Edwin David Aponte, executive director of the Louisville Institute

"*Brown Church* is a truly significant book, filling a unique and critically important niche at this historic juncture. For emerging Latinx generations, this book offers *consuelo y animo* (comfort and inspiration)—a way to connect roots and wings. For scholars, activists, and church leaders, this book translates wisdom and integrates worlds, bringing us all together to a place of common understanding and mutual enrichment. As professor and pastor, I will use and recommend this book; it is a treasure."

Alexia Salvatierra, ecclesial faculty, Centro Latino and School of Intercultural Studies, Fuller Theological Seminary

"As a historian, lawyer, and pastor, Dr. Chao Romero integrates disciplines to clearly argue that the Brown Church has played and will continue to play a critical role in Christianity. The Latina/o community has not only survived church- and state-sanctioned oppression and injustice, we are thriving in the midst of it. Latina/o churches' integrated understanding of the gospel is demonstrated in the way that our Spirit-filled worship is not separated from our Spirit-empowered pursuit of justice. *Brown Church* is a book not only for Latinas/os; it is a book for all Christians to grasp the power and depth of what the Brown Church offers Christians who seek to understand the whole gospel."

Sandra Maria Van Opstal, founding executive director of Chasing Justice

"Written by a scholar and pastor, Chao Romero's *Brown Church* breaks new ground in Christian evangelical studies. This work traces the experience, praxis, and contribution of Latina/o Christians to a conception of the Christian faith that sees and enacts the relationship of the Gospel and societal transformation as necessarily interdependent. We find in this account how historically marginalized church communities sustained their Christian faith while pursuing justice and political conditions conducive to the social and spiritual well-being of Latinas/os, even as they were ignored by many a majority-culture Christian. With an original methodology, *Brown Church* highlights the study of Latina/o spirituality by using tools from sociology, critical theory, history, and theology to center the longstanding presence of a suffering and joyous part of the body of Christ for the sake of the Gospel."

Jules A. Martinez Olivieri, assistant professor of faith and culture at Trinity Evangelical Divinity School, author of *A Visible Witness: Christology, Liberation, and Participation*

BROWN CHURCH

FIVE CENTURIES OF LATINA/O SOCIAL JUSTICE, THEOLOGY, AND IDENTITY

ROBERT CHAO ROMERO

ivp
Academic
An imprint of InterVarsity Press
Downers Grove, Illinois

InterVarsity Press
P.O. Box 1400, Downers Grove, IL 60515-1426
ivpress.com
email@ivpress.com

InterVarsity Press® is the book-publishing division of InterVarsity Christian Fellowship/USA®, a movement of students and faculty active on campus at hundreds of universities, colleges, and schools of nursing in the United States of America, and a member movement of the International Fellowship of Evangelical Students. For information about local and regional activities, visit intervarsity.org.

Scripture quotations, unless otherwise noted, are from the New Revised Standard Version of the Bible, copyright 1989 by the Division of Christian Education of the National Council of the Churches of Christ in the USA. Used by permission. All rights reserved.

While any stories in this book are true, some names and identifying information may have been changed to protect the privacy of individuals.

Cover design and image composite: David Fassett
Interior design: Jeanna Wiggins
Images: abstract pattern: © Annykos / iStock / Getty Images Plus
  worn paper background: © billnoll / iStock / Getty Images Plus
  postage stamp border: © troyek / E+ / Getty Images

ISBN 978-0-8308-5285-7 (print)
ISBN 978-0-8308-5395-3 (digital)

Printed in the United States of America ∞

InterVarsity Press is committed to ecological stewardship and to the conservation of natural resources in all our operations. This book was printed using sustainably sourced paper.

Library of Congress Cataloging-in-Publication Data
A catalog record for this book is available from the Library of Congress.

P	23	22	21	20	19	18	17	16	15	14	13	12	11	10	9	8	7	6	5	4	3	2	1
Y	39	38	37	36	35	34	33	32	31	30	29	28	27	26	25	24	23	22	21	20			

CONTENTS

DEDICADO A LA MEMORIA DE MI ABUELITA,

Doña Luz Torres de Romero

Nos enseñó a amar a Jesus

Le extrañamos mucho

ACKNOWLEDGMENTS

I NEVER EXPECTED to write this book. When I started as a professor at UCLA in 2005, my research was on a totally different subject—the Chinese people of Mexico. At that time I felt called to be a professor of all things "Asian-Latino," and I felt a separate vocation to minister in issues of race and justice when off campus—but I never imagined that my academic and pastoral callings would merge into a single project of engaged scholarship. This book, *Brown Church*, is the result.

I am grateful to my UCLA colleague Susan Plann for nudging me in this direction. Six years ago, at our department graduation ceremony, I shared with her (with much fear and trembling) my nascent inclination to pursue a new research project in Chicana/o religion. She encouraged me to do so, and I haven't looked back since. To prepare myself for the task, I pursued my dream of seminary education and took classes at Fuller Theological Seminary while on sabbatical. Not too long after that, my family and I began attending La Fuente Ministries at Pasadena First Church of the Nazarene. The world of Latina/o theology then opened up to me. I am indebted to Pastor Marcos Canales for curating my introduction to Latina/o theology, Liberation Theology, and Misión Integral. More than any church I know, La Fuente Ministries embodies the values of these important biblical theologies. La Fuente is a quintessential "Brown Church."

Others have also helped me make the transition to professor of religious history and faith-rooted community organizer. Though I grew up in the Latina church, I spent two decades away from her, learning from other parts of the Body of Christ, and these past five years have been a story of return, of *volver*, to my spiritual roots. Thank you Rev. Dr. Alexia Salvatierra, Rev. Dr. Melvin Valiente, and Rev. Ada Valiente for shepherding me back as a pastor and community organizer of the Matthew 25 Movement in Southern California. Thanks are also owed to Professors Oscar García-Johnson and Juan Martínez for their encouragement and invitation to be a part of the intellectual life of Centro Latino at Fuller Seminary. Professors Hak Joon Lee and James Bradley also offered helpful advice at the outset of this project. I am grateful to Professor Roberto Sirvent and the editors of *Perspectivas*, the Latina/o theology journal of Princeton Theological Seminary, for their support of my research on the spiritual praxis of César Chávez. I am also indebted to Rev. Michael Mata for his mentorship and *apoyo* for *Jesus for Revolutionaries*—my initial popular foray into this genre of writing—and to the late Pastor Faye Newman, who saw my spiritual calling and ordained me one decade ago in South Los Angeles.

Special thanks to my colleagues of the César E. Chávez Department of Chicana/o studies at UCLA who have embraced my new line of religious and theological research. The worlds of ethnic studies and theology have rarely heretofore met, but my colleagues have supported my new scholarship with grace, sincerity, and an open mind. *Gracias*.

An enormous debt of gratitude is owed to Dr. Edwin Aponte and the Louisville Institute for their support of this project. A Sabbatical Grant for Researchers for the 2017–2018 academic year gave me the time and space to write *Brown Church*. I could not have done it otherwise. I am also grateful for the invitation to participate in the IVP Latino/a consultation. It was there that I first aired these ideas in earnest, and there where this book first took formal shape. Special thanks is owed to the anonymous reviewers of my draft manuscript. Their helpful questions and suggestions made this a stronger book.

I have been so privileged to write *Brown Church*. A central tenet of Latina/o theology is *teología en conjunto*—communal theological reflection. My great honor in the following pages is simply to share of the spiritual communal treasure that the Brown Church has amassed over the past five hundred years in Latin America and the United States. This spiritual treasure has been largely overlooked, and yet is a central component of Latina/o history and community cultural wealth. It is born of centuries of hard-fought struggle, perseverance, and deep fellowship with Jesus Christ. My privilege is to lift up these voices of our spiritual community to new audiences—to forge an intellectual bridge with the world of Chicana/o and Latina/o studies, to raise awareness of this history within the vibrant, multigenerational Latina/o church of the United States, and to sound a prophetic call to majority culture Christian seminaries and universities. *Brown Church* just scratches the surface of this monumental history and theological trove, but hopefully it will be enough to inspire some to begin a journey of exploration. Many thanks to Rev. Dr. Raymond Rivera, Rev. Dr. Liz Ríos, and Rev. David Ramos of the Latino Pastoral Action Center for believing in this project and launching the Brown Church Conference.

Finally, I dedicate this book to the memory of my *abuelita*, Doña Luz Torres de Romero. She was the spiritual rock of the Romero family, and she taught us to love Jesus. She is sorely missed, and I look forward to one day seeing her again. *Este libro también está dedicado a mi familia— mi esposa Erica y nuestros hijos Robertito y Elena.*

INTRODUCTION

Brown Church

ROSA WAS EXCITED about attending her first college lecture. She was the first of her family to attend college and was the valedictorian of Roosevelt High School. Her 4.2 grade point average had earned her a full ride to Pitzer College, one of the best liberal arts college in the United States according to *U.S. News and World Report*.

Rosa's Mom and Dad were deacons in their local church and had brought her up to be a Christian. They told many stories of how God had taken care of them when they made the dangerous journey to the United States across the Sonoran desert. Her dad worked two jobs—as a short order cook during the week and a gardener during the weekend. He also collected cardboard to raise extra money for the family. Her mom was a nanny to a rich family in San Marino and also managed their family of four kids. Church provided one of the few spaces of social respect for Rosa's parents. They had *dignidad* (dignity) when they walked into church, and were addressed as deacons, and *hermano* (brother) and *hermana* (sister) Ramos.

Rosa's first class was a Chicana/o history class, and her professor began his lecture by saying, "Christianity is the white man's religion." The professor went on to detail how the Spaniards used Christianity to colonize the Aztecs and the millions of indigenous people of the Americas. Rosa also learned about how the Bible was used to justify ethnic genocide, murder, and the oppression of women. Rosa left class devastated. She didn't know what to do. Who was right about Christianity? Was it her working class, immigrant parents who loved and followed Jesus? Or was it her professor who had his PhD from Harvard and had written many famous books over the past twenty years?

As the first few weeks of classes continued, Rosa felt lonely because most of her classmates came from affluent backgrounds and she could not relate to them. She was also one of the few Latinas on campus. To try and find friends Rosa went to a meeting of the Chicana/o activist group on campus. She met great friends there—peers from South Los Angeles, Long Beach, and East LA who also grew up in working class immigrant communities. She felt a special solidarity with them. There was one problem: whenever the topic of religion came up, most of her friends repeated the same things they heard in class—"Why are you a Christian? Christianity is the colonizer's religion!"

When I met Rosa, she was in her second year of college and undergoing clinical depression. She had been seeing a psychiatrist to help her with the deep loss and the emotional conflict she was experiencing trying to reconcile the faith of her youth with the perspectives of Christianity she was learning in her classes and from her Chicana/o friends.

Carlos was a transfer student at UC Berkeley. He grew up with learning disabilities and most of his teachers didn't think he was smart. Carlos was raised in La Puente and came from a tough family background. His dad was an alcoholic and left the family when Carlos was fourteen years old. After his dad left, Carlos's mom, Lupe, worked two jobs to try and keep the family afloat. Although she didn't earn much money from her part-time jobs at Walmart and McDonald's, somehow she always managed to put enough food on the table. She credited it all to God. Lupe, you see, was a strong Catholic. She never missed a Sunday at church and was a leader for charismatic Catholic retreats where people worshiped God and spoke in tongues. And she was always praying: for Carlos and his brothers and sisters. Although Carlos wouldn't consider himself too religious, he had turned to God throughout his childhood for strength in the midst of all his family's troubles. If asked, he would say he was "spiritual" and, if push came to shove, he'd say "Catholic."

The drive up to the Bay Area from La Puente was like a dream for Carlos. He had taken a few road trips to Tijuana and San Diego, but other than that he hadn't journeyed outside of LA. He decided to take the scenic route on the Pacific Coast Highway, and on the way up he stopped at beautiful Carmel and Monterey Bay. He loved it so much. It was like a new world opening up. While walking around the town of Carmel, he got a few weird stares from white people, but for the most part it was an amazing trip.

As an ethnic studies major at Berkeley, Carlos learned about Chicana/o history in the United States. His professor taught him about the "unjust" Mexican American war, which was justified by the strange idea of "Manifest Destiny." According to Manifest Destiny, many Anglo Americans in the nineteenth century believed that God had ordained them to conquer the Native Americans and Mexicans who lived in what is now Texas, California, New Mexico, Arizona, Colorado, Nevada, and Utah. God's destiny for them was to seize these western territories so that they could spread their version of democracy and Christianity. Carlos also read about the segregation of Mexicans in housing, education, juries, parks, and pools during the era of Jim Crow segregation. He was inspired to learn about the many ways in which Mexican Americans successfully challenged segregation as part of cases such as *Mendez v. Westminster* and *Hernandez v. Texas*. He was especially inspired to read about the Chicana/o civil rights movement of the 1960s and such civil rights heroes as Dolores Huerta, César Chávez, and Corky Gonzalez. Like Rosa, however, he was told that Christianity was one of the main sources of historical oppression of

Chicanas/os. Also like Rosa, he didn't know what to do with it all, so he stopped attending Mass and declared himself a Marxist and atheist.

□ □ □

Edwin was a "PK" (pastor's kid).[1] His parents immigrated to the United States from Central America to escape gang violence and the poverty that has eclipsed El Salvador in the wake of its brutal civil war. Edwin's dad was the pastor of a Pentecostal church in Pico Union, and Edwin grew up playing piano on the church worship team. Wanting to shield Edwin from some of the "worldly" teachings that he might encounter at a public university, Jorge instead decided to enroll him in the local Christian college. Arriving in the freshman dorms, Edwin felt a little uncomfortable because none of his roommates were Latino and they all came from fairly privileged middle-class backgrounds. They were nice though, and after a short while they started hanging out in the cafeteria and going to the movies, and they became friends.

The first year was going pretty well until one tragic day in May 2019. Edwin had been up late studying for finals one night when he received a phone call that would change his life forever. It was his fourteen-year-old sister Angelica. In tears, she reported to him that their mother and father had just been arrested by ICE, Immigration and Customs Enforcement, and they were going to be deported. Edwin's family had fled to the United States as refugees because the *maras* (gangs) in El Salvador had targeted Jorge for recruitment, shot their uncle, and burned his grandfather's house down. Because they did not have enough money to hire an immigration lawyer, however, they were unable to prove to ICE that they qualified for asylum. As a result, they were being deported according to President Trump's draconian immigration policies.

---

[1]Adapted from the essay "Toward a Perspective of 'Brown Theology'" by Robert Chao Romero, from *Evangelical Theologies of Liberation and Justice*, edited by Mae Elise Cannon and Andrea Smith (Downers Grove, IL: IVP Academic, 2019), 75-95.

After hearing the terrible news, Edwin fell to his knees and prayed to God for strength and for the safety of his parents. A million questions raced through his mind: Would his mom and dad be safe while in custody with ICE? Could he talk to them? Did they have any legal recourse to block their deportation? When would he see them again? Who would take care of his young sister?

Fortunately, when the raid occurred, Angelica was at their aunt's house and was not apprehended by ICE. Where would she now live? How would he support her? Would he be able to stay in college? Because their family's asylum application had been denied, Edwin and Angelica were also both subject to deportation.

After a restless and sleepless night, Edwin stumbled into his political science class the next morning. The topic of the presidential elections came up. One of his classmates said, "I support Donald Trump because he tells it like it is. He doesn't care about political correctness. He wants to build 'the wall.' He wants to deport all of those 'illegals' and 'rapists' that are taking our jobs and causing crime to go up." Edwin was stunned. He didn't know what to say or how to respond. The most painful part was that he felt rejected by his Christian peers he had come to know and respect.

As reflected in these critical race counterstories, Latinas/os who care about faith and justice occupy a "spiritual borderlands."[2] In many institutional religious spaces, we feel out of place because our concern for

---

[2]Counterstories involve composite characters drawn from social science data, interviews, and personal experience. Daniel Solórzano and Tara Yosso, "Critical Race Methodology: Counter-Storytelling as an Analytical Framework for Education Research," *Qualitative Inquiry* 8, no. 1 (2002): 33. Rosa, Carlos, and Edwin are composite characters drawn from my interaction with many Latina/o students throughout the United States over the past decade. The concept of "in between," "borderlands" identity was developed in Chicana/o studies through the writings of Gloria Anzaldua in her famous book, *Borderlands/La Frontera: The New Mestiza* (San Francisco: Aunt Lute Books, 2012).

social justice issues is not understood. When we share our concerns about issues of educational inequity or comprehensive immigration reform we are met with blank stares or even outright opposition. We are told, "Those are political issues that are separate from faith." As a result, we often walk away from church and formal religious institutions. We may cling tenuously to a personal faith, but our activism becomes divorced from institutional Christianity.

At the same time, in the world of Chicana/o studies and activism, our faith is usually discouraged or criticized. We are told, "You can't be a Christian and care about issues of racial and gender justice. Christianity is the white man's religion, and it's a tool of settler colonialism. It's racist, classist, and sexist." As a result of such hostility, many Chicanas/os keep silent about their faith in activist circles for fear of persecution or ostracization. Others lose their faith. Some tenuously cling to a personal relationship with God but abandon institutionalized Christianity altogether. In the words of Gloria Anzaldúa, Christian Chicanas and Chicanos are "left out or pushed out" of existing Christian and Chicana/o categories.[3]

This negative perspective on religion within Chicana/o studies is understandable. It is grounded in centuries of historical and contemporary misrepresentation of the teachings of Jesus. In a very real sense, the history of Latinas/os in the Americas is one of systemic racism perpetuated by white individuals claiming to be Christian. From the Spanish Conquest, to nineteenth-century Manifest Destiny in the United States, to Jim Crow segregation and Operation Wetback, to the present day "Make America Great Again" movement, many individuals continue to perpetuate the stereotype that Christianity is a racist, classist, and sexist religion. And so, understandably, the Chicana/o movement continues to reject Christianity as part of its party platform.

---

[3]Gloria Anzaldua, "Haciendo Caras, una Entrada," in *Making Face, Making Soul: Creative and Critical Perspectives by Women of Color*, ed. Gloria Anzaldua (San Francisco: Aunt Lute Books, 1990), xv-xxviii.

CONSEQUENCES

There are a number of harmful consequences that result from the wholesale rejection of Christianity in Chicana/o studies and Latina/o studies. First, as expressed in Rosa's counterstory, many students experience severe emotional damage. In fact, the character of Rosa, and her experience of clinical depression, is based on a true-life story. The following is a common trajectory for Latina/o students like Rosa, Carlos, and Edwin: They come to know God through their families and are raised in what Latina/o theologians call "Abuelita Theology."[4] As top students, they then come to the university and learn about systemic justice but also get exposed to negative perspectives on Christianity in their classes; this leads to a period of deep spiritual and emotional wrestling. They feel like they are forced to choose between faith and activism; between their families and Chicana/o studies; between being Chicana/o and a person of faith. Deep emotional turmoil, even depression, is the result.

Another consequence is that thousands of potential students are unnecessarily turned away from the discipline of Chicana/o studies. If asked to choose between the faith of their family and Chicana/o studies, they reject Chicana/o studies. I can understand this decision, and it keeps thousands of Chicanas/os and Latinas/os from coming to study Chicana/o studies at the university level.

A third painful consequence is that objective research about faith and activism, and the role of faith in Chicana/o and Latina/o communities, is squelched. Even though the founding document of the Chicana/o movement, *El Plan Espiritual de Aztlán*, asserts freedom of religious expression within its membership, Latinas/os of Christian background have been historically marginalized by the academic discipline of Chicana/o studies.[5] Microaggressions against Christianity and Christian Chicanas/os

---

[4] Because formal religious instruction is often lacking among Latinas/os, the best theologians of the Mexican American community are often grandmothers, or, abuelitas. Moises Sandoval, *The Mexican American in the Church: Reflection on Identity and Mission* (New York: Sadlier Books, 1983), 125.

[5] According to the founding document of the Chicana/o movement, El Plan Espiritual de Aztlán, or The Spiritual Manifesto of Aztlán, "Nationalism as the key to organization transcends all re-

are common in the context of various academic settings, including the classroom, disciplinary conferences, and faculty gatherings. As an example, I vividly remember attending one National Association of Chicana and Chicano Studies Conference on a Good Friday and hearing Christianity blasted by the keynote speaker. I have also personally experienced discrimination as a professor based on my Christian convictions; indeed, I fear intellectual and professional backlash for the publication of this book. In its most insidious forms, religious microaggressions take the form of viewpoint discrimination and violate highly held principles of academic freedom.

This common rejection of Christianity by Chicana/o studies is regrettable, because it ignores not only the contemporary religious landscape of the Latina/o community, but also the central role that Christianity has played in social justice movements among Latin Americans and US Latinas/os. From Bartolomé de Las Casas, to Dolores Huerta and César Chávez, to the Sanctuary Movement of the 1980s, to contemporary organizing among undocumented Latinas/os, faith has been at the center. Despite the central role played by faith in the life of César Chávez and the broader Chicana/o civil rights movement, the role of religion as a motivating factor for social change has been largely neglected by the field of Chicana/o studies.

Because of the inherent bias against Christianity in Chicana/o studies, the objective study of religion is squelched despite the fact that faith is central to our families and communities and has been a key source of community organizing for centuries. Although Latinas/os are transforming the landscape of religion in the United States,[6] Chicana/o scholarship on this topic is severely lacking. With few notable exceptions, including the work of Mario García, Jacqueline Hidalgo, Gaston Espinoza, David Carrasco, and Elisa Facio, few academic studies examine the Mexican American religious experience. As professor of Chicana/o studies at the University

---

ligious, political, class, and economic factions or boundaries. Nationalism is the common denominator that all members of La Raza can agree upon." clubs.arizona.edu/~mecha/pages /PDFs/?ElPlanDeAztlan.pdf.

[6]Pew Research Center: Religion and Public Life, "The Shifting Religious Identity of Latinos: Nearly One in Four Latinos Are Former Catholics," May 7, 2014, www.pewforum.org/2014/05/07 /the-shifting-religious-identity-of-latinos-in-the-united-states.

of California, Santa Barbara, Mario García has pioneered the field of Chicana/o religious studies in recent years. His books, *Católicos: Resistance and Affirmation in Chicano Catholic History* (2010) and *Mexican American Religions: Spirituality, Activism, and Culture* (2008), have laid the academic groundwork for the examination of religion in Chicana/o studies.[7] According to García, "Despite the fact that the vast majority of U.S. Latinos claim to be religious or spiritual, little has been written on Mexican American/Chicano religions from a multidisciplinary perspective."[8] In addition to being an understudied topic in Chicana/o and Latina/o studies, the topic of Chicana/o religions and spirituality has also been largely overlooked by the broader field of religious studies.[9] Jacqueline Hidalgo stands out as one of the few Latina/o scholars to explicitly bridge the fields of ethnic studies and biblical studies.[10]

As further evidence of this dearth of spiritual scholarship, a review of all publications from the flagship Chicana/o studies journal, *Aztlán: A Journal of Chicano Studies*, revealed very few articles directly dealing with religion as the main topic of examination.[11] Some articles mentioned religion, but very few focused exclusively on the subject. A significant number discussed religion with a negative connotation. Several essays called for a reclaiming of indigenous spirituality and the rejection of Christianity as a western religion.

Curricular and textbook offerings on the role of religion in Chicana/o communities are also generally quite limited. In my own department of Chicana/o studies, for example, only two permanent course offerings exist with respect to religion. The classic Chicana/o history text *Occupied America: A History of Chicanos* by Rudy Acuña leaves out discussion of

---

[7]Mario García, *Católicos: Resistance and Affirmation in Chicano Catholic History* (Austin: University of Texas Press, 2010); Gastón Espinoza and Mario García, eds., *Mexican American Religions: Spirituality, Activism, and Culture* (Durham: Duke University Press, 2008).

[8]Espinoza and García, *Mexican American Religions*, 1.

[9]García, *Católicos*, 17.

[10]Jacqueline Hidalgo, *Revelation in Aztlán: Scriptures, Utopias, and the Chicano Movement* (Palgrave Macmillan, 2016).

[11]*Aztlán* is the flagship journal of Chicana/o studies. I have been privileged to publish in it and serve on its editorial board.

the role of faith in Chicana/o history.[12] A more recent text, *Crucible of Struggle: A History of Mexican Americans from the Colonial Period to the Present Era*, likewise tells the history of Chicanas/os in a way that is detached from the faith life of the community.[13]

COMMUNITY CULTURAL WEALTH

In what follows, I seek to engage the study of Latina/o spirituality utilizing the critical race theory (CRT) framework of community cultural wealth. CRT scholars Tara Yosso and Danny Solórzano developed the concept of community cultural wealth in the context of urban educational studies.[14] Instead of approaching Latina/o educational achievement in terms of "cultural deficit" models, which depict Latina/o students as deficient insofar as they are unlike white suburban students, Yosso and Solórzano argue that scholarly analysis should begin with an understanding of the unique community cultural wealth possessed by Chicanas/os or Latinas/os. Building on this approach, Lindsay Pérez Huber found that "spiritual capital" was a major component of the community cultural wealth of undocumented student activists.[15] Her interviews with Dreamers revealed that faith served as critical "spiritual capital" for their educational success.

Drawing on the important theories of my colleagues Yosso, Solórzano, and Pérez Huber, I assert that spiritual capital has served as a crucial component of Latina/o community cultural wealth from Latin American colonial times to the present. From Juan Diego, to Guáman Poma de Ayala, Garcilaso de la Vega el Inca, and Las Casas, to the iconic civil rights movement of Dolores Huerta and César Chávez, to the Sanctuary

---

[12]Rudy Acuña, *Occupied America: A History of Chicanos* (London: Pearson, 2014).

[13]Zaragosa Vargas, *Crucible of Struggle: A History of Mexican Americans from the Colonial Period to the Present Era* (Oxford: Oxford University Press, 2010). Ironically, this text is published as part of the American Academy of Religion Aids for the Study of Religion Series.

[14]Tara J. Yosso, "Whose Culture Has Capital? A Critical Race Theory Discussion of Community Cultural Wealth," *Race Ethnicity and Education* 8, no. 1 (2005): 69-91, doi: 10.1080/1361332052000341006.

[15]Lindsay Pérez Huber, "Challenging Racist Nativist Framing: Acknowledging the Community Cultural Wealth of Undocumented Chicana College Students to Reframe the Immigration Debate," *Harvard Educational Review* 79, no. 4 (2009).

Movement of the 1980s, and the contemporary immigration reform movement, spiritual capital has been a central component of Latina/o community cultural wealth. As such, it merits significant study within the field of Chicana/o and Latina/o studies.

THE "BROWN CHURCH" AND "BROWN THEOLOGY"

It is my contention that these many Latina/o Christian social justice pioneers form what may be called the Brown Church: a prophetic ecclesial community of Latinas/os that has contested racial and social injustice in Latin America and the United States for the past five hundred years. As such, Brown Church is a multivalent category, encompassing ethnic, historical, theological, spiritual, and sociopolitical dimensions. In every instance of racial and social injustice in Latin America and the United States over the centuries, the Brown Church has arisen to challenge the religious, socioeconomic, and political status quo. Collectively, the Brown Church has challenged such great evils as the Spanish conquest and Spanish colonialism, the *sistema de castas* (caste system), Manifest Destiny and US settler colonialism in the Southwest, Latin American dictatorships, US imperialism in Central America, the oppression of farmworkers, and the current exploitation and marginalization of undocumented immigrants. The Brown Church has done all of this in the name of Jesus. It's also worth noting that the Brown Church has comprised an ecumenical body of Roman Catholic and Protestant followers of Christ who have worked both in cooperation with, and in prophetic witness to, official ecclesiastical authorities and institutions.[16]

As a natural outgrowth of its prophetic advocacy efforts and praxis, the Brown Church has developed a unique and consistent body of theology based upon the Christian Scriptures. I call this Brown Theology. Brown Theology rejects the narrow presentation of Christianity as eternal "fire

---

[16]Paragraph adapted from the essay "Toward a Perspective of 'Brown Theology'" by Robert Chao Romero, from *Evangelical Theologies of Liberation and Justice*, edited by Mae Elise Cannon and Andrea Smith, 75-95.

insurance" that leaves most of life untouched by God's love and redemption. According to this narrow conception of Christianity, which has been around in Latin America since colonial times, we believe in Jesus so that we can be forgiven and so that we can go to heaven after we die. Notwithstanding the critical importance of heaven and forgiveness, this shortsighted version of Christianity presented during the conquest of the Americas ignores the biblical value of justice and the social dimensions of Jesus' redemption. It thereby allowed for the genocide and dehumanization of native and African communities, and the presentation of a corrupt and distorted gospel: "It's okay for us to decimate and enslave millions of 'Indians' and thousands of African slaves because we are saving their souls by sharing Christianity with them. Without us they'd just go to hell."

Brown Theologians throughout the centuries—Bartolomé de Las Casas, Archbishop Oscar Romero, Gustavo Gutiérrez, Justo González, Ada María Isasi-Díaz, Elizabeth Conde-Frazier, E. René Padilla and Samuel Escobar, to name a few—have challenged this narrow and unbiblical view of the gospel and have proclaimed that Jesus came to save, redeem, and transform every aspect of our lives and the world. His salvation extends over all of God's good creation, which has become twisted and corrupted as a consequence of sin. This includes everything distorted and broken in our world—whether personal, familial, social, or global. Nothing is left out. It includes our personal emotional brokenness and dysfunctional family relationships, but also poverty, racism, slavery, human trafficking, oppression of immigrants, warfare, lack of clean water, AIDS, gang violence, and lack of educational opportunity. In the language of Padilla and Escobar, the gospel imperative is one of *misión integral*.[17] In fact, from a biblical standpoint, although God loves all people equally, he also shows unique concern for immigrants, the poor, and all who are socially marginalized. In the words of Latino theologian Gustavo Gutiérrez, God expresses a "preferential option for the poor."[18]

---

[17]"Integral" or "holistic" mission.
[18]Gustavo Gutiérrez. *A Theology of Liberation* (Maryknoll: Orbis Books, 2012).

Jesus' salvation also encompasses our fractured human family. Because we have turned our backs against God, we have turned our backs against each other. Women and men are separated by sexism and machismo; ethnic groups are divided by selfishness, materialism, and pride; mixed-race individuals are divided against others because of the social construction of monoracial identities; the church turns its back on the LGBTQ+ community; and, the so-called documented are divided against those without papers because our country desires cheap labor but does not want to recognize the full humanity of immigrants. Jesus came to reconcile all human beings to himself and to one another. This is also Brown Theology.

The framework of Brown Theology and the Brown Church is my attempt to articulate a new social identity for Latina/o Christians who are socially conscious and passionate about God's heart for social justice. In the words of Gloria Anzaldúa, my goal is to present a framework "that will rewrite history using race, class, gender, and ethnicity as categories of analysis, theories that cross borders, that blur boundaries—new kinds of theories with new theorizing methods . . . new positions in the 'in between,' Borderlands worlds of ethnic communities and academies . . . new categories for those of us left out or pushed out of existing ones."[19] This book invites readers to explore the five-hundred-year history of the Brown Church, investigate the rich tradition of Brown Theology that undergirds it, and join the contemporary movement of Brown Christians in the United States.

A NOTE ON "BROWN"

Latinas/os are *Brown*. Not necessarily literally and phenotypically Brown, but Brown in terms of our racial and social positioning in United States history. Some, like myself, are literally Brown, but we Latinas/os come in all colors and hues—some are *moreno* (dark-skinned), some are *güeritos* (light-skinned), some are subtle in-between shades, and quite a few, like

---

[19]Gloria Anzaldúa, "Haciendo caras, una entrada," in *Making Face, Making Soul: Creative and Critical Perspectives by Women of Color,* ed. Gloria Anzaldua (San Francisco: Aunt Lute Books, 1990), xv-xxviii.

myself, are even Asian.[20] In this sense, *Brown* is symbolic of the cultural and biological *mestizaje*, or, mixture, in Latin America. In the US context, Brown also symbolizes the racial liminality experienced by Latinas/os as betwixt and between that of white and black.[21] According to Asian American theologian Sang Hyun Lee, liminality "is the situation of being in between two or more worlds, and includes the meaning of being located at the periphery or edge of a society."[22]

Historically, most Latinas/os have lived on the margins of white American society and have experienced de jure and de facto racial segregation and discrimination. A few of us have always been granted token acceptance by white majority culture (think Ted Cruz), but in the language of settler colonialism theory, most of us have been excluded as the "exogenous other."[23] At the same time, our marginalization has often been less than that of our Black brothers and sisters. Our experience has been neither white nor black—*It has been Brown.*

As a metaphor for racial, cultural, and social liminality, Brown should be considered a fluid "space" as opposed to any body of static, essentialized cultural characteristics. In this sense, *Brown* is an apt descriptor for many cultural and ethnic groups in the United States—such as Asian Americans, South Asians, Pacific Islanders, Middle Easterners, and the fast-growing mixed race community—who also find themselves in the liminal space somewhere between that of black and white. Brown is also a process, and certain cultural groups such as Italians, Greeks, Poles, Ashkenazi Jewish migrants, and Irish who have historically occupied this intermediate racial space have subsequently transitioned into whiteness and mainstream cultural membership, to one degree or another.

---

[20]Robert Chao Romero, *The Chinese in Mexico, 1882–1940* (Tucson: University of Arizona Press, 2010).
[21]For an excellent discussion of racial liminality in the Asian American context, see Sang Hyun Lee, *From A Liminal Place: An Asian American Theology* (Minneapolis: Fortress Press, 2010). For a theoretical discussion of the "brown commons" within Latina/o studies, see Iván A. Ramos, "Muñoz, José Esteban," *Oxford Research Encyclopedia of Literature*, June 2018, doi: 10.1093/acrefore/9780190201098.013.356.
[22]Hyun Lee, *From a Liminal Place*, x.
[23]Lorenzo Veracini, *Settler Colonialism: A Theoretical Overview* (Palgrave Macmillan, 2010), 26.

Brownness is a liminal social, legal, political, and cultural space that US Latinas and Latinos have inhabited since the US-Mexico War and the Treaty of Guadalupe-Hidalgo of 1848. In exchange for the benefits of land (nearly half of Mexico), the Treaty of Guadalupe-Hidalgo reluctantly granted US citizenship to former Mexicans, and with it, an implied "whiteness." At the same time however, through legal and social convention ever since, the United States has denied full and equal membership to Latinas/os within the American polity. We have been wanted for our land and labor, while at the same time rejected for our cultural and ethnic difference. When economic times get tough, we become the disposable "illegal alien," and are scapegoated and deported. We are wanted and unwanted. Necessary, yet despised. We are Brown.

In the era of Jim Crow, though we were legally defined as white, and therefore technically exempt from segregation, our families and communities were nonetheless still segregated and rendered unequal through legal loopholes and unwritten social conventions. Our Puerto Rican sisters and brothers have experienced this social and political liminality for more than a century. Though officially US citizens, Puerto Ricans cannot vote for president and have no equitable representation in Congress. Their political fate lies in the hands of a Congress in which they have no vote. They are Brown. Wanted and unwanted at the same time.

In the present moment, though many of our families have lived in the United States for multiple generations, or even long before this land was the United States, we are painted by politicians and the media as a "Latino threat," "unwilling or incapable of integrating, of becoming part of the national community. Rather, [we] are part of an invading force from south of the border that is bent on reconquering land that was formerly theirs (the U.S. Southwest) and destroying the American way of life."[24] According to the Latino threat narrative, we are perpetual foreigners, even if we were born in this country, and regardless of our citizenship

---

[24]Leo R. Chavez, *The Latino Threat: Constructing Immigrants, Citizens, and the Nation* (Stanford: Stanford University Press, 2008), 3.

status. This hateful narrative fuels white nationalist violence, and it inspired the El Paso massacre of August 3, 2019—the worst mass slaughter of Latinas/os in modern times.[25]

As the Brown Church, we take solace in knowing that Jesus, our Lord, was also Brown. As a working class, young adult, Jewish man living in the colonized territory of Galilee, he also occupied a space of social, political, cultural, and religious liminality.[26] Geographically, Galilee was a borderlands region where Jewish, Greek, and Roman worlds collided. As a sign of their cultural mestizaje, Galileans like Jesus spoke with an accent and were bilingual. Politically, they were ruled by the Roman Empire, subject to oppressive tribute, and dehumanized by imperial laws that made them second class citizens in their own historic land. Even among his own people, Jesus and other Galilean Jews were looked down as *jíbaro*, as backwards *campesinos*, who lived far from the center of religious and economic power in the capital of Jerusalem.[27] When God chose to dwell among us, to take on human flesh, and to make our suffering his own, he chose to be *Brown*.

LIMITATIONS AND A NOTE ON POSITIONALITY

This book offers a macro-history of the Brown Church in Latin America and the United States. It is not intended to be exhaustive, and as such, no doubt overlooks many important stories of the Brown Church that remain to be documented, or have already been told in other places. This

---

[25]Jenny Jarvie, David Montero, Suhauna Hussain, "The El Paso Shooting Victims: What We Know," *Los Angeles Times*, August 6, 2019.

[26]Virgilio Elizondo, *Galilean Journey: The Mexican-American Promise* (Maryknoll: Orbis Books, 2005), 50-53, 91; Ched Myers, *Binding the Strongman: A Political Reading of Mark's Story of Jesus* (Maryknoll: Orbis Books, 2012), 49, 53.

[27]*Jíbaro* refers to those who are like "country bumpkins"; *campesinos* are farmworkers. Elizondo, *Galilean Journey*, 50-53; Orlando Costas, "Hispanic Theology in North America," in *Struggles for Solidarity: Liberation Theologies in Tension*, ed. Lorine M. Getz and Ruy O. Costa (Minneapolis: Fortress, 1992), 72; Orlando Costas, "Evangelism from the Periphery: A Galilean Model," *Apuntes* 2, no. 3 (1982): 52-54; Loida I. Martell-Otero, "From *Satas to Santas: Sobrajas* No More. Salvation in the Spaces of the Everyday," in *Latina Evangélicas: A Theological Survey from the Margins*, ed. Loida I. Martell-Otero, Zaida Maldonado Pérez, and Elizabeth Conde-Frazier (Eugene: Cascade Books, 2013), 78.

book is indebted to scholars such as Justo González, Edwin Aponte, Mario García, Gaston Espinoza, Arlene Sánchez-Walsh, Daniel Ramírez, Miguel De La Torre, J. Daniel Salinas, and Juan Martínez, who have preserved and recounted the history of the Brown Church already for many years. I hope that many others will rise up to share the many unknown stories of the Brown Church that remain to be told.

I develop the notion of the Brown Church/Brown Theology through a historical analysis of key moments of social injustice in Latina/o history. Specifically, I examine the ways in which the Latina/o community has responded to such injustices through the lens and empowerment of faith. This history is told from a Brown Latina/o perspective. In the words of Latino theologian Michael Jiménez, it is a history written "from the underside of modernity."[28]

It is also important to note that *Brown Church* is neither a comprehensive history of Latinas/os in the United States, nor a systematic theological treatise. As such, it risks leaving academic readers of both Latina/o history and theology dissatisfied. For Chicana/o and Latina/o studies readers, much of the history shared will be familiar, but the role of religion and theology in that history will be largely new; for mainstream Protestant, evangelical, and Catholic theologians, almost all of it will be new. For my colleagues in Latina/o Theology, what may be new is the application of critical race theory and ethnic studies paradigms to the study of Latina/o religious history.[29] The unique contribution of *Brown Church*, I believe, is bringing together the largely disparate literatures of Latina/o history, ethnic studies, critical race theory, and theology into a new type of academic "Brown jazz." The meaning comes in the intersection—in the

---

[28]Michael Jimenez, *Remembering Lived Lives: A Historiography from the Underside of Modernity* (Eugene: Cascade Books, 2017).

[29]Michelle A. González states, "Latino/a theology's emphasis on the theological academy as the primary, and often exclusive conversation partner limits its scope. It is curious that Latino/a theologians do not enter into dialogue with area studies, ethnic studies, critical race theory, and the social sciences in a more explicit manner to enrich their discussions of Latino/a identity and faith life." Michelle A. Gonzalez, *A Critical Introduction to Religion in the Americas: Bridging the Liberation Theology and Religious Studies Divide* (New York: New York University Press, 2014), 91.

Brown. As is common with the development of new musical styles, some disciplinary purists might not like the sound of the fusion—of the *menudo*.[30] I am hopeful, however, that many readers will resonate with this new style of historical, theological, and ethnic studies Brown jazz, and find their story within it.

A word on my positionality. I am an Asian-Latino or "Chino-Chicano," historian, lawyer, and evangélico pastor (in the Latin American tradition, and to be fiercely distinguished from American evangelicalism). I was born in East Los Angeles to a Mexican immigrant father and Chinese immigrant mother. I was raised in the small San Gabriel Valley town of Hacienda Heights. I was called "beaner" as a child and denied access to gifted learning programs in the recently desegregated public schools of Los Angeles. In sharing my ambition to become a lawyer, I was told in high school, "I'd never hire a Mexican lawyer." I was also told by my high school counselor that I should consider the local state school instead of UCLA. I went on to receive my PhD in Latin American history from UCLA and my JD from UC Berkeley, and I have been a professor of Chicana/o studies and Asian American studies at UCLA since 2005. I was ordained "in the hood" by black and Latino multidenominational Christian pastors of South Los Angeles, and, together with my wife, Erica, I've been a pastor to activist students for more than a decade as part of our Jesus 4 Revolutionaries ministry.[31] Over the years I have experienced racial microaggressions by professors, church congregants, activists of the left and right, hateful internet trolls, realtors, and police. I have been on the inside and the outside of ethnic studies, Chicana/o studies, Asian American studies, American evangelicalism, Latina/o and Asian American churches, and even my own Mexican and Chinese families. I have lived my life in the in-between. This book flows from my Brown experience of living *entre* these various racial, ethnic, religious, and academic categories.

---

[30]Menudo is a rich Mexican soup comprising a mixture of beef tripe, hominy, onion, oregano, and rosemary.

[31]See www.jesus4revolutionaries.com.

Brown Church is most deeply shaped by my belief in Jesus and firm commitment to the traditional tenets of orthodox Christianity. As such, I view the history of Brown Theology through the lens of a double-insider: I am Brown by my lived experience, and also a follower of Jesus. As a result, I have certain "cultural intuition" about the topic, as my critical race theory colleagues would say.[32] No doubt, I have some biases too.

OVERVIEW OF CHAPTER CONTENTS

Chapter one situates the Brown Church, and the chapters to come, within the radical "good news" of Jesus Christ. It is critical to reframe the biblical message of Christianity for Latina/o academics and activists because most of us have previously only heard a colonized gospel, what Dallas Willard calls "the gospel of sin management."[33] According to this limited view of Christianity, the gospel means, "Believe in Jesus so that you will be forgiven and go to heaven when you die. Don't worry about trying to change the oppressive socioeconomic and political systems of the United States and Latin America. That's political and not the gospel. Suffer through this life and your reward will come after."

Unbeknownst to most, the expression "good news" carried insurgent undertones when used by Jesus and the early disciples. In the Roman context, the expression was reserved for the emperor Caesar who also claimed titles such as "Son of God," "Lord," and "Savior of the world."[34] In proclaiming the "good news" of the arrival of the kingdom of God, and in revealing himself as Jewish Messiah, and therefore Lord of the world, Jesus presented a direct challenge to the authority of Caesar and arguably the most powerful empire of human history. Drawing on this forgotten historical context, chapter one reframes the good news of Jesus

---

[32]Dolores Delgado Bernal, "Using a Chicana Feminist Epistemology in Educational Research," *Harvard Educational Review* 68, no. 4 (1998): 555-79.

[33]Dallas Willard, *The Divine Conspiracy: Rediscovering Our Hidden Life in God* (New York: Harper-Collins, 1998), 35-37.

[34]N.T. Wright, *Simply Jesus: A New Vision of Who He Was, What He Did, and Why He Matters* (New York: Harper One, 2011), 29-30.

Christ as a radical manifesto, as *El Plan Espiritual de Galilee*.[35] According to El Plan Espiritual de Galilee, Jesus came as Lord, Savior, and King, to save, redeem, and transform every aspect of our lives and the world. Beginning in the historical margins of Nazareth of Galilee, he came to reconcile to himself all things, and to make all things new.

With the important theological context of chapter one in place, chapter two examines the birth and development of the Brown Church in colonial Latin America. The Brown Church was born in 1511 in protest to Spanish imperialism and the exploitation of the indigenous peoples of modern-day Cuba, Puerto Rico, Haiti, and the Dominican Republic. Under the guidance of Dominican Friars Antonio de Montesinos and Bartolomé de Las Casas, the Brown Church first developed a unique body of social justice teachings that may be called Brown Theology. The writings of Las Casas represent the earliest theological challenge to colonial notions of race and racism.

Montesinos and Las Casas not only founded Brown Theology and the Brown Church—they also gave birth to the racial social justice movement of the Americas! They were the first to speak of racial and social injustice as we know it today, and they were the first pastors and theologians to question the military conquest and colonization of people of color. Their powerful advocacy, moreover, prompted what was called "The Great Debate" in which, for the first time in recorded human history, an entire nation paused to reflect on the moral injustice of war and colonization. As a final note of reflection, this chapter explores the important role played by La Virgen de Guadalupe as a symbol of racial and gendered justice for the Brown Church over the centuries.

Chapter three examines the history of the Spanish caste system in Latin America and examines its role in shaping contemporary racial attitudes among US Latinas/os. Unbeknownst to most, out of the ashes of Spanish racial imperialism and the sistema de castas, God raised up multicultural, mestizo, black, indigenous, female, male, Spanish, and Asian

---

[35]The Spiritual Plan, or Manifesto, of Galilee.

voices to challenge the perverted racial and sexist logic of the Spanish colonial project. This chapter examines the lives and voices of three central leaders of the Brown Church during the colonial period—Garcilaso de la Vega el Inca, Guaman Poma de Ayala, and Sor Juana Inés de la Cruz—and uplifts them as examples of the diversity of the Brown Church and of those who struggled for racial and gender equality in seventeenth-century Latin America.

Chapter four follows the prophetic trail of the Brown Church into the United States in the nineteenth century. Buttressed by theological notions of Manifest Destiny, in 1848, Anglo Americans seized nearly half of Mexican territory as part of what Abraham Lincoln and Ulysses Grant called the "unjust" US-Mexico War. The subsequent Treaty of Guadalupe-Hidalgo granted reluctant citizenship to the erstwhile Mexicans of the Southwest, and established a legal and social framework which positioned us somewhere betwixt and between that of black and white. Since then, we have been Brown. The most notable religious challenge to life under the new American regime was waged by Father Antonio José Martínez, "El Cura de Taos." Padre Martínez was clergyman, seminary professor, canon lawyer, and state legislator, and out of his public protests to religious colonization the Brown Church of the United States was born.

Although César Chávez is revered as the most famous Latino civil rights icon of the 1960s, most scholars and activists overlook the profound role played by Christian spirituality in his personal life and the farm workers movement. Chapter five explores the spiritual formation and praxis of César Chávez. It examines his early familial upbringing in popular Mexican Catholicism and his later mentorship in Catholic social teachings by white clergyman Father Donald McDonnell. Building on this spiritual foundation and the skills gained as community organizer under Saul Alinsky, Chávez founded the United Farm Workers of America in 1962. The UFW fused popular Mexican religious symbols and practices such as the Virgin of Guadalupe, *peregrinación* (pilgrimage), and fasting, with Catholic social teaching, leading to the first successful unionization of farm workers in United States history.

Chapter six returns to Latin America during the late 1960s and examines another watershed moment for the Brown Church in Latin America—the birth of the Liberation Theology and Misión Integral movements. Confronted with the ravages of poverty, oppression, and a decade of failed programs of economic modernization, Latin American priests gathered at Medellín, Colombia, in 1968 to frame a biblical response. In one unified voice they declared, "The Latin American bishops cannot remain indifferent in the face of the tremendous social injustices existent in Latin America."[36] The result was the launching of the Liberation Theology movement and the reminder to the world of the biblical "preferential option for the poor"—that God takes the side of the poor in their oppression. Stirred by the same milieu of poverty, militarism, and oppression as their Roman Catholic Liberation Theology counterparts, Latin American "radical evangélicos" of the 1960s and '70s wrestled with creating a movement and a theology that was faithful to their contextualized experience and distinct theological commitments. The second half of chapter eight explores the development of the distinct evangélico theology of misión integral, or holistic mission. Closely associated with E. René Padilla and Samuel Escobar, the misión integral movement understood that the theological approaches and ministry methods of North America were insufficient for the contextual needs of Latin America. They were "tired of the evangelical power centers in North America telling us how to think, who to read, and what it meant to be evangelical," and they rejected existing theological models in which the "racist can continue to be a racist, [and] the exploiter can continue to be an exploiter."[37] In response to these

---

[36]Conference of Latin American Bishops, "Medellin 1968 (excerpts)," Poverty of the Church I.1, www.geraldschlabach.net/medellin-1968-excerpts/#poverty.

[37]Michael Clawson, "Misión Integral and Progressive Evangelicalism: The Latin American Influence on the North American Emerging Church," *Religions* 3 (2012): 791; Ruth Irene Padilla DeBorst, "Integral Mission Formation in Abya Yala (Latin America): A Study of the Centro de Studios Teológicos Interdisciplinarios (1982–2002) and Radical Evangélicos" (PhD diss., Boston University, 2016), 46.

extreme blind spots of Western Protestant Christianity, Padilla and Escobar, together with Orlando Costas, Pedro Arana, Emilio Antonio Nuñez, Orlando Gutiérrez, and Peter Savage, founded the *Fraternidad de Teólogos Latinoamericanos* (Fraternity of Latin American Theologians) and developed the theological model of misión integral.

Chapter seven offers two concrete examples of the embodiment of Liberation Theology in Latin America and the United States, and it moves the story of the Brown Church forward into the 1980s. The first is the *testimonio* of saint and martyr Archbishop Oscar Romero of El Salvador. Like Las Casas four centuries before, Romero's story is one of *concientización* and conversion to the poor, and a transformed understanding of Christ's teaching that the gospel must be "good news" to the poor and all who are marginalized.[38] Through weekly sermons broadcast over national radio, pastoral letters, and public talks, Romero challenged the torture, murders, and disappearances of the El Salvadoran totalitarian state. For his prophetic support of the poor of El Salvador and his public condemnation of US military intervention, Romero was gunned down on March 24, 1980, while administering Mass.

Romero's lived example of "the preferential option for the poor" inspired many from *el otro lado*.[39] Among those touched by his message was Father Luis Olivares and the hundreds of thousands of Central American migrants, clergy, and allies who formed the Sanctuary Movement in the United States during the 1980s. The inspiring message of Liberation Theology, coupled with the life example of César Chávez, led to the second conversion of Father Luis Olivares and the creation of the Sanctuary Movement in Los Angeles. With Latino leadership at the helm, this movement confronted the racist refugee policies of the Reagan era and helped forge the beginnings of a new pan-Latina/o identity in the United States.

Chapter eight introduces readers to the rich but little-known field of Latina/o theology. Unbeknownst to most within the worlds of both

---

[38]*Concientización* is "conscientization," or the process of developing a consciousness, or awareness, of social justice issues.
[39]Or, "the other side," referring to the United States.

mainstream evangelical theological education and Chicana/o and Latina/o studies, Latina/o theologians such as Justo González, Ada María Isasi-Díaz, Orlando Costas, Virgilio Elizondo, Elizabeth Conde-Frazier, Juan Martínez, and Oscar García-Johnson have developed a powerful corpus of race and social justice theology since the 1980s. Almost without exception, however, most mainstream theology textbooks ignore even a cursory discussion of Latina/o theology.[40] For Latina/o Christians it makes us feel as if we have had no meaningful theological contributions to offer the church in the United States over the past 150 years. When we do get a mention, moreover, our theology is called "contextual," as opposed to the "objective" theology of white seminaries and European theologians.

A central aim of *Brown Church* is to spread awareness of the Latina/o theology movement to new audiences, especially to the academic world of Chicana/o and Latina/o studies and the millions of young Latina/o Christians in the United States who seek an authentic, cultural theological voice for themselves. Chapter eight introduces readers to some of the main themes and thinkers of Latina/o Theology. Themes include mujerista and Latina evangélica theology, Latina/o hermeneutics, the Galilee principle, and pneumatology of liberation. Featured authors include Justo Gonzalez, Virgilio Elizondo, Ada Maria Isasi-Díaz, Elizabeth Conde-Frazier, Loida I. Martell-Otero, Zaida Maldonado-Pérez, Edwin Aponte, Miguel De La Torre, Orlando Costas, Eldin Villafañe, Sammy Alfaro, Oscar García-Johnson, and Jules Martínez-Olivieri.

Chapter nine concludes this book by reflecting on the persecution of the Latina/o community in the United States today. In the face of increasing family separations, children being held in cages at the border, and all manner of racial injustice unseen for decades, the Brown Church is rising up to stand against the injustices of modern-day Pharaohs like President Donald Trump. We are doing so in the name of Jesus, the Savior from

---

[40]For example, see Alistair E. McGrath, *Historical Theology: An Introduction to the History of Christian Thought* (Oxford: Blackwell Publishers, 1998).

Galilee, who takes the side of the oppressed and most vulnerable, and who has walked with us for five hundred years through the evils of conquest, colonialism, segregation, exploitation in the fields, and violent military interventions in the lands of our mothers and fathers. This time is no different.

Chapter nine also asks the question ¿Quién soy yo?, or, "Who am I?" As discussed in the introductory chapter, thousands of Latina/o millennials and Gen Zs live their lives in the "Christian-Activist Borderlands" and are caught between the social identities of Christ-follower, Latina/o, and activist. They crave a social identity that encompasses their love for Jesus, their rich, God-given cultural heritage, and their passion for social justice. As a source of shalom to the many Latinas/os trapped in the borderlands of these identities, chapter ten invites readers into a "Brown Christian" identity and articulates the basic tenets of a Brown Christianity.

The following poem expresses the history and identity of the Brown Church in its multivalent complexity:[41]

I am the Brown Church
God calls me mija/mijo[42]
Brown, black, white, even yellow, are all within me
When Black and White come to talk, my voice is not heard,
I am not invited to the table
I share much with my Black sisters and brothers, yet my voice is distinct
I long, I cry out to be heard for who I am
THE BROWN CHURCH

Yo soy Montesinos, gritando, in 1511, "The Conquest is opposed to
    Christ!"[43]
y Bartolomé de Las Casas, whose eyes like Moses were opened to the
    suffering of his
people and never looked back

---

[41]"The Brown Church" (2016) by Robert Chao Romero. This poem was inspired by the Chicana/o movement poem "I Am Joaquín" (1967) by Corky Gonzáles.
[42]Or, "daughter/son."
[43]"I am Montesinos, shouting, in 1511, 'The Conquest is opposed to Christ!'"

Yo soy Sor Juana Inés de la Cruz,

My heart burns for the treasures of wisdom which are hidden in Christ

Though machísmo assails me, aunque está bloqueado el camino, I do
      not relent[44]

Yo soy Catarina de San Juan, "La China Poblana"

Stolen from Asia, enslaved by Spanish masters, I find freedom as the
      Bride of Christ

I too hold the keys of the Kingdom

Yo soy Padre Antonio Martínez de Nuevo México

Aunque robaron a Aztlán, I know no nation holds a manifest destiny to
      decimate the people[45]

of another, also beloved of God

In the time of Jim Crow, they called me "wetback," "beaner," "spic," and
      sent me to

"Mexican schools"

Yet, I am Méndez, Bernal, Perales, Calleros

My children are not cows; you cannot place them in a barn

Yo soy Mama Leo y Santos Elizondo, MUJERES, forged in tongues of
      fire[46]

Nadie me detendrá; El Espíritu del Señor está sobre mi[47]

I am Dolores Huerta and César Chávez

I was raised in the bosom of Abuelita Theology

And know that the cries of the harvesters have reached the ears of God

Unos años despues, mis primos huyeron la tierra madre[48]

The land of the Savior, Guatemala, Nicaragua, Honduras, Centroamérica

Argentina, Peru, Bolívia, Brasil, y al resto del Sudamerica,

Empujada por el huracán de violencia[49]

---

[44]"Though sexism assails me, although my path is blocked, I do not relent."

[45]"Although they stole Aztlán, I know no nation holds a manifest destiny to decimate the people."

[46]"I am Mama Leo and Santos Elizondo, WOMEN, forged in tongues of fire."

[47]"No one will stand in my way; the Spirit of the Lord is upon me."

[48]"Some years later, my cousins fled from the motherland."

[49]"Argentina, Peru, Bolivia, Brazil, and the rest of South America, pushed by the hurricane of violence."

Guerillas, Reagan, priest, all vied for me
Yet on Christ my eyes were fixed

I am Gutiérrez, Boff y Romero
Yo sé que el Reino de Díos trae liberación
Que el Espiritu nos libera[50]

Como Protestantes, we also protested—

Porque "la ropa anglo-sajon" strangled
la Buena Nueva
Soy Padilla y Escobar,
Recobrando la misión integral del Señor[51]

Yo soy los dos alas del mismo pájaro,
Puerto Riqueño, Neyorican, Cubano, y Dominicano también[52]
Though the colonizers have changed, the cries of Las Casas still ring
        strong in my ears

I am a Dreamer; indocumentado; sin papeles
No human being is illegal. Jesús es mi refugio. I am a child of God.[53]

I now seek my voice, thoughts of God my own
I also am among the 12
God calls me mija/mijo
I AM THE BROWN CHURCH

---

[50]"I know that the Kingdom of God brings liberation, that the Spirit frees us."
[51]"As Protestants, we also protested—Because the 'Anglo raiment/cultural trappings' strangled the
    Good News. I am Padilla and Escobar, recovering the holistic mission of God."
[52]"I am the two wings of the same bird, Puerto Rican, Neyorican, Cuban, and Dominican also."
[53]"I am a Dreamer; undocumented; without papers. No human being is illegal. Jesus is my refuge.
    I am a child of God."

1

EL PLAN ESPIRITUAL DE GALILEE

EL PLAN ESPIRITUAL de Aztlán is the historic manifesto of the Chicana/o movement. First promulgated in 1969 during the height of the civil rights era, it declares:

> In the spirit of a new people that is conscious not only of its proud historical heritage but also of the brutal "gringo" invasion of our territories, *we,* the Chicano inhabitants and civilizers of the northern land of Aztlán from whence came our forefathers, reclaiming the land of their birth and consecrating the determination of our people of the sun, *declare* that the call of our blood is our power, our responsibility, and our inevitable destiny. . . .
>
> Once we are committed to the idea and philosophy of El Plan de Aztlán, we can only conclude that social, economic, cultural, and political independence is the only road to total liberation from oppression, exploitation, and racism. Our struggle then must be for the control of our barrios, campos, pueblos, lands, our economy, our culture, and our political life.[1]

El Plan was revolutionary because it articulated a bold, new "Chicano" social identity that recognized the flagrant history of racism against Mexicans in the United States and sounded a clarion call to social justice activism. Chicanas and Chicanos understood that the United States had seized half of Mexico's territory in 1848 as part of what even Abraham

---

[1] El Plan Espiritual de Aztlán was adopted by the First National Chicano Liberation Youth Conference in Denver, Colorado, in March 1969. "El Plan Espiritual de Aztlán," MECha of Central Washington University, accessed September 18, 2018, www.cwu.edu/~mecha/documents/plan_de_aztlan.pdf.

Lincoln had called an unjust war. The Treaty of Guadalupe-Hidalgo, which ended the US-Mexico War, granted erstwhile Mexicans the rights of US citizens in theory, but denied these rights in practice through legislative and judicial chicanery. Chicanas/os also knew that Mexicans and other Latinas/os had been segregated in housing, education, and public spaces during the era of Jim Crow, and that the Méndez, Bernal, and López families fought these injustices in the courts and won.[2] Chicanas/os were also familiar with so-called Americanization programs that sought to erase Latina/o culture and force assimilation, as well as with having their mouths taped and their hands slapped with rulers for speaking Spanish in public schools. More than that, they lived the dismal reality of socioeconomic and political marginalization. The median income of a Mexican American family in the 1960s was 62 percent of the general population. One-third of all Mexican American families lived below the federal poverty line ($3,000/year). Four-fifths were concentrated in unskilled or semiskilled jobs, and one in three of this number was employed in agriculture. The vast majority of Chicanas and Chicanos attended segregated schools. Seventy-five percent of students dropped out before high school graduation. In 1968, only one Mexican American served in the United States Senate and three in the House of Representatives. Not a single Mexican American was elected to the California state legislature.[3]

Armed with an understanding of this history and the consciousness of their lived realities, young Mexican Americans created a new, politicized cultural identity that they called Chicano. As reflected in El Plan and the famous poem "I Am Joaquin,"[4] Chicana/o identity comprised three main components: (1) pride in the dual indigenous and Spanish cultural heritage of Mexican Americans; (2) recognition of the historic

[2]See Mendez v. Westminster, 161 F.2d 774 (9th Cir. 1947); Doss v. Bernal et al. (1943), Superior Court of the State of California, Orange County, no. 41466; Lopez v. Seccombe, 71 F. Supp. 769 (S.D. Cal. 1944).
[3]Zaragoza Vargas, *Crucible of Struggle: A History of Mexican Americans from Colonial Times to the Present Era* (New York: Oxford University Press, 2011), 306.
[4]Rodolfo Corky Gonzales, "I Am Joaquin," 1967, www.latinamericanstudies.org/latinos/joaquin.htm.

structural and systemic racism experienced by the Mexican descent community; (3) commitment to a lifestyle of social justice aimed at remedying the socioeconomic and political inequalities experienced by the Mexican American community.[5] Beyond a new social identity, Chicanas and Chicanos throughout the United States developed a multifaceted movement known as "La Causa," which fought for labor rights for farmworkers, educational reform, and women's rights.

Because of the deep persistence of racial and structural inequality in the Latina/o community, the Chicana/o social identity continues to thrive among millennials and Generation Z today. They will not stay silent in the face of a US presidency that declares that they and their family members are rapists, drug dealers, and criminals, unjustly arrests and deports their mothers and fathers, and separates children from their parents at the border and locks them in cages. They cannot sit back as supporters of the status quo when 27 percent of all Latina/o children still live in poverty, only 8 percent will graduate from college, and less than one in one hundred go on to earn a doctorate.[6] Nor will they stand silent when thousands of beautiful Brown youth are treated by law enforcement as guilty until proven innocent, and dozens are gunned down as part of unjust systems of policing. Nor can they turn a blind eye to the physical suffering experienced by themselves and their family members for lack of healthcare, and an inequitable health care system in which 39 percent of Latina/o immigrants, and 25 percent of all Latinas/os, have no health insurance.[7] In the wake of the bloody El Paso Massacre, they understand

---

[5] Aída Hurtado and Patricia Gurin, *Chicana/o Identity in a Changing U.S. Society* (Tucson: University of Arizona, 2004).

[6] National Center for Children in Poverty, "Poverty by the Numbers By Race, White Children Make Up the Biggest Percentage of America's Poor," accessed September 18, 2018, www.nccp.org/media/releases/release_34.html; Tara J. Yosso and Daniel G. Solórzano, "Leaks in the Chicana and Chicano Educational Pipeline," *Latino Policies and Issues Brief* 13 (March 2006), www.chicano.ucla.edu/files/LPIB_13March2006.pdf.

[7] Jens Manuel Krogstad and Mark Hugo Lopez, "Hispanic Immigrants More Likely to Lack Health Insurance Than U.S.-Born," Pew Research Center, September 26, 2014, www.pewresearch.org/fact-tank/2014/09/26/higher-share-of-hispanic-immigrants-than-u-s-born-lack-health-insurance.

that we live in a turning point of United States history.[8] In the face of this lived reality, thousands of young Latinas/os continue to find personal and cultural validation and empowerment in the Chicana/o identity. Where they struggle, however, is in finding connection between the Christian (Protestant, Catholic, Pentecostal, Evangelical) faith of their families and these social justice concerns that weigh so heavily on their hearts.

There is good news, however, because what most young Latinas and Latinos have never heard is that Jesus had a "plan," too, and his manifesto arose out of a shared experience of socioeconomic, political, and cultural colonization and marginalization.

Like Latinas/os in the United States, Jesus and his Jewish sisters and brothers lived as colonized peoples in what was once their own land. Roman soldiers sieged Jerusalem in 63 BC and made Judea a client state of the empire.[9] From then, and on to the days of Jesus, Rome ruled the ancestral Jewish homeland through puppet governments and stripped the Jews of their socioeconomic, political, and religious sovereignty. Similar to the concept of Manifest Destiny, which undergirded the unjust US-Mexico War, Rome and its various emperors believed that they possessed a divine destiny to bring peace and prosperity to the ancient world. The Caesars in fact claimed for themselves titles like "Son of God," "Lord," "King of kings," and "Savior of the world," and the poet Virgil praised Rome for birthing global renewal and "a new order of the ages." Convinced of a similar universal calling, the authors of the United States Constitution would later borrow this phrase for the Great Seal of the United States and the dollar bill.

As a *fronterizo* from the northern borderlands of Galilee, Jesus lived a doubly marginalized life.[10] In addition to the general weight of oppression experienced by all Jews under Roman colonization, Galilee was relegated

[8]Jenny Jarvie, David Montero, and Suhauna Hussain, "The El Paso Shooting Victims: What We Know," *Los Angeles Times*, August 6, 2019.
[9]N. T. Wright, *Simply Jesus: A New Vision of Who He Was, What He Did, and Why He Matters* (New York: Harper One, 2011), 29-30, 62.
[10]*Fronterizo* means "Someone who lives in the borderlands of two nations."

to a secondary status within the larger Jewish community itself.[11] Because of Galilee's distinct cultural mixture and geographic distance from the capital city of Jerusalem, Jews from Galilee were looked down on by their compatriots in Judea of the south. Like many Latinas/os, Galileans were bilingual (speaking Aramaic and Greek) and also spoke with an accent. Their frequent contact with Gentiles (non-Jews) threatened standards of cultural and religious purity. Similar to many Latinas/os, Galileans were shunned as mixed race and "half breeds"—mestizos. Galilee was also far away from the center of Jewish religious and political power in Jerusalem, which was embodied by the temple there. Galilee was the borderlands, the margins, the "hood"; Jerusalem was the seat of political, religious, and economic power, the "big city." And Jesus was a Galilean. Not only that, Jesus was from Nazareth, a small town of several hundred people that was marginalized even within Galilee itself. "Can anything good come from Nazareth?" one of his early disciples famously quipped (John 1:46). If Jesus lived in California today, he would come from South LA, East LA, the Inland Empire, or the Central Valley.

Most Galileans were peasant farmers. In fact, Galilee was known as the breadbasket of the plains because it supplied important agricultural products for its surrounding neighbors.[12] Although Galilean farmers were subsistence farmers, they were also forced to grow extra crops for Roman tribute and temple tithes and taxes. They also paid up to half their harvest in rent to elite Jewish landlords. These extra burdens were often crushing, and led to great economic insecurity for most Galileans. Many Galilean peasants lost their lands to large landholders due to increasing debt.

Just as Latinas/os have been historically pressured to assimilate through Americanization programs and English-only movements, the Jewish residents of Galilee faced strong pressure to adopt foreign cultural, economic, and political practices and identities through what

---

[11] Virgilio Elizondo, *Galilean Journey: The Mexican-American Promise* (Maryknoll: Orbis Books, 2005), 50-53.

[12] Ched Myers, *Binding the Strongman: A Political Reading of Mark's Story of Jesus* (Maryknoll: Orbis Books, 2012), 49, 51-53.

was known as Hellenization. Similar to the unrelenting economic forces of gentrification currently experienced by Latina/o communities in Los Angeles such as Boyle Heights, Highland Park, and Pico Union, Jesus and his Galilean family were encroached upon on all sides by the dual economic and cultural forces of Hellenistic urbanization. In fact, like Los Angeles, Galilee was known to be a cultural melting pot and a geographic borderlands where Jews, Greeks, and Romans all came together—sometimes in hostility.

In Jesus' day, there were three major responses to the oppression of Roman cultural, political, and economic colonialism.[13] The first was compromise. This approach was characterized by the Sadducees and the Herodians. These ruling religious and political elites secured for themselves a place of socioeconomic comfort and stability in imperial society by colluding with the Romans. The Sadducees were the priestly class, and the high priest was appointed by the Roman governor.[14] The Herodians supported the puppet political rule of Rome.[15] These were the "sellouts."

The second approach of Jesus' day was that of withdrawal. The Essenes, of Dead Sea Scrolls acclaim, embodied this approach. They felt that the best response to the oppression and religious impurity of the day was to move out into the desert and live a holy life in isolation and community. In God's time, God would act as he saw fit.[16]

The Zealots represent the third approach common in Jesus' day. Largely overlapping with the Pharisees of the time, Zealots prayed hard and sharpened their swords.[17] They felt that the best way to respond to Roman oppression was to draw close to God, live highly religious lives, and prepare for war. Their approach was to counterstance, to stand on the opposite side of the river bank locked into a duel between oppressor

---

[13]N. T. Wright, *The Challenge of Jesus: Rediscovering Who Jesus Was and Is* (Downers Grove: Inter-Varsity Press, 1999), 37.

[14]E. Mary Smallwood. "High Priests and Politics in Roman Palestine," *The Journal of Theological Studies* 13, no. 1 (1962): 14.

[15]Myers, *Binding the Strongman*, 56; N. T. Wright, *The Challenge of Jesus*, 37.

[16]N. T. Wright, *The Challenge of Jesus*, 37.

[17]N. T. Wright, *The Challenge of Jesus*, 37, 39.

and oppressed.[18] The Zealots believed that as long as they remained close to God, God would give them military victory over their enemies and reestablish his kingdom.

In the twenty-first century, we see these three basic approaches reflected in the Latina/o community of the United States. We have our Sadducees—religious leaders who compromise, partnering with the ruling political establishment to maintain the status quo. Think of the numerous Latina/o clergy who stood in alliance with Donald Trump for the US presidency, and who downplayed the squalid conditions of border asylum camps. We have our Herodians—Latina/o politicians who assimilate into the American mainstream and pass laws and policies with little regard for the devastating impact on the lives of most Latinas/os. Think Ted Cruz.

Latina/o Essenes, those who withdraw, are probably the most common within the Latina/o religious community. Modern day Latina/o Essene churches do a good job of connecting their members with personal Christian spirituality and relationship with Jesus. Their great blind spot, however, is that they tend to dismiss legitimate and pressing issues of social justice as "liberal" and "worldly." To make matters worse, many modern day Latina/o Essenes and Sadducees have formed a partnership with Latina/o Herodians in support of the status quo and modern day empire. Chicana/o activists are the secular Zealots of our day, seeking the liberation of La Raza "by any means necessary," but often without a spiritual foundation.

In response to these limited options, many Latina/o millennial and Gen Z Christians today feel trapped in what Gloria Anzaldúa calls "a constant state of mental nepantilism."[19] *Nepantla* is an Aztec word meaning "torn between ways." It captures the experience of the Christian-Activist Borderlands and is another word for Brown. In the twenty-first century, millions of young Latinas/os find themselves torn between the worlds of contemporary Latina/o Essene spirituality and the activism of

---

[18]Gloria Anzaldúa, *Borderlands/La Frontera: The New Mestiza* (San Francisco: Aunt Lute Books, 2007), 100.

[19]Anzaldúa, *Borderlands/La Frontera*, 100.

modern day secular Chicana/o Zealots. Like Carlos in chapter one, they enter the Christian faith and personal relationship with Jesus through the Latina/o Essene church. In fact, many grow deeply in their spiritual life as Latina/o Essenes. After going to college or getting involved in the world of activism, they come to understand the history of racism in the United States against Latinas/os, and they get "woke." Most Latina/o Zealots are hostile to Christian faith, however, and condemn Christianity as the religion of the modern day Roman colonizers—i.e., white Republican males. Confused, many Latina/o millennials and Gen Zs go back to their home churches and look for answers from their pastors and parents about how to reconcile their newfound social consciousness with the Essene faith of their youth. In response, they hear one typical Latina/o Essene response: "Don't get involved with the Zealots—that is, activist Chicanas/os. They're liberals who don't know God. We're called by God to obey the government. Our president is chosen by God, and to challenge him is to challenge God. The gospel is about a personal relationship with Jesus and doesn't concern itself with social justice."

As social justice–minded Latina/o Christians, we can find great hope in the example of Jesus. Like Chicana/o activists of the 1960s, Jesus also had a "Plan," and he developed a *movimiento* that has lasted more than 2,000 years.[20] Born into a borderlands context of imperialism and cultural nepantla, Jesus declared a fourth way: *El Plan Espiritual de Galilee.*[21]

> Jesus went into Galilee, proclaiming the good news of God. "The time has come," he said. "The kingdom of God has come near. Repent and believe the good news!" (Mk 1:14-15 NIV)

Galilee. Jesus began his movement in Galilee. As we've discussed, Galilee was a borderlands region and symbol of cultural mestizaje and multiple rejection. Jesus was a young adult, working class, mestizo from the "hood." He was conceived to a single mom. God became flesh and launched his movimiento among those who were despised and rejected

---

[20]*Movimiento* means "movement."
[21]"The Spiritual Manifesto of Galilee."

by both their Roman colonizers and the elite of their own people. Jesus didn't go to the big city and seek recruits among the religious, political, and economic elite. He didn't go to the Beverly Hills or Harvard or the Upper East Side of Manhattan of his day. He didn't go to a modern day Latina/o Beverly Hills like South Florida or Hacienda Heights. He started in what today would be East LA, the Artesia Community Guild, or Spanish Harlem. To change the system, Jesus had to start with those who were excluded from the system. This also reveals the intentionality and inclination of God's heart toward the poor and marginalized of every society. In fact, from a biblical standpoint, although God loves all people equally, he shows unique concern for immigrants, the poor, and all who are socially marginalized. One Brown theologian calls this the Galilee principle: "What human beings reject, God chooses as his very own."[22]

Kingdom of God. In the context of deep longing for liberation by his own colonized people, and against the backdrop of centuries-old biblical expectations, Jesus proclaimed that he was king and Lord. As king, he came to establish the long-awaited rule and reign of God on the earth, which would transform every aspect of our lives and the world. The "good news" was that Jesus came to make us and the whole world new.

This includes everything messed up and broken in our world—whether personal, familial, social, or global. It includes our personal emotional brokenness and dysfunctional family relationships, but also poverty, colonialism, racism, white nationalism, slavery, human trafficking, oppression of immigrants, warfare, lack of clean water, AIDS, gang violence, and lack of educational opportunity. God wants to transform all of us and all things. Jesus came to reconcile all human beings to himself and to one another. There is no room for "oppositional identities"; the goal is the Beloved Community.[23]

---

[22]Elizondo, *Galilean Journey*, 91.

[23]AnaLouise Keating, "'I'm a Citizen of the Universe': Gloria Anzaldúa's Spiritual Activism as Catalyst for Social Change," *Feminist Studies* 34, no. 1/2, The Chicana Studies Issue (2008): 53-69. Martin Luther King Jr. popularized the concept of the Beloved Community through his speeches, writings, and activism.

This holistic focus of the good news is referred to by Brown Theologians as *misión integral*.[24] In the words of Brown Theologian René Padilla, misión integral is "the mission of the whole church to the whole of humanity in all its forms, personal, communal, social, economic, ecological, and political."[25] This is Brown soteriology—a Latina/o view of salvation.

The apostle Paul articulated the holistic nature of El Plan Espiritual de Galilee in his letter to the Colossians:

> He is the image of the invisible God, the firstborn of all creation; for in him all things in heaven and on earth were created, things visible and invisible, whether thrones or dominions or rulers or powers—all things have been created through him and for him. He himself is before all things, and in him all things hold together. He is the head of the body, the church; he is the beginning, the firstborn from the dead, so that he might come to have first place in everything. For in him all the fullness of God was pleased to dwell, and through him God was pleased to reconcile to himself all things, whether on earth or in heaven, by making peace through the blood of his cross. (Col 1:15-20)

The spirit of misión integral is likewise communicated by John in *Apocalipsis*:

> El que estaba sentado en el trono dijo: «¡Yo hago nuevas todas las cosas!» (Apoc 21:5 NVI)

> And the one who was seated on the throne said, "See, I am making all things new." (Rev 21:5)

The multicultural vision of Christ's beloved community is cast in Revelation 7:9-10:

> After this I looked, and there was a great multitude that no one could count, from every nation, from all tribes and peoples and languages,

---

[24]"Integral" or "holistic mission." Ruth Irene Padilla DeBorst, "Integral Mission Formation in Abya Yala (Latin America): A Study of the Centro de Studios Teológicos Interdisciplinarios (1982-2002) and Radical Evangélicos" (PhD diss., Boston University, 2016), 364.

[25]Tetsunao Yamamori and C. René Padilla, eds., *The Local Church, Agent of Transformation: An Ecclesiology for Integral Mission* (Buenos Aires: Kairos Ediciones, 2004), 9.

standing before the throne and before the Lamb, robed in white, with palm branches in their hands. They cried out in a loud voice, saying,

"Salvation belongs to our God who is seated on the throne,
    and to the Lamb!"

Although the good news of Jesus is for the whole human family, it goes first to the poor and all who are marginalized. Like a loving father, God loves all his children equally, but shows special concern for those of his children who suffer most.[26] Immigrants, refugees, and the poor bear the brunt of a sinful and broken world, and they feel firsthand the destructive effects of sin most directly. God's unique concern for them is reflected in more than two thousand verses of sacred Scripture. It is clearly reflected in Jesus' "Nazareth Manifesto," as well as in his famous Beatitudes.[27]

According to the Gospel of Luke, Jesus launched his public career in his hometown of Nazareth by reading these words from the scroll of Isaiah:

The Spirit of the Lord is upon me,
    because he has anointed me
        to bring good news to the poor.
He has sent me to proclaim release to the captives
    and recovery of sight to the blind,
        to let *the oppressed* go free,
to proclaim the year of the Lord's favor. (Lk 4:18-19)

From this passage, we learn that the "good news" of God's kingdom was first proclaimed to the "poor," the "captives," the "blind" and the "oppressed"—the Nazarenes, Galileans, and Jewish underclass of Jesus' day. Riling under the double burden of Roman colonialism and economic and spiritual oppression by the elites of their own people, they

---

[26]Roberto Goizueta, *Caminemos Con Jesús: Toward a Hispanic/Latino Theology of Accompaniment* (Maryknoll, NY: Orbis, 1995), 176.

[27]Samuel Wells and others have referred to Luke 4:18-19 as Jesus' "Nazareth Manifesto" because it lays out his ministry mission statement centered on social engagement. Samuel Wells, *A Nazareth Manifesto: Being with God* (Hoboken: Wiley, 2015).

needed first to hear the announcement of God's liberation. Though they were seen as weaker in the eyes of the Pharisees, Sadducees, and ruling elite, Jesus considered them indispensable; though they were thought to be less honorable, Jesus gave them greater honor. Jesus gave greater honor to those who lacked it (1 Cor 12:22-25). He went first to those "outside the gate" of institutional power and authority.[28]

We find this same divine predilection towards the poor in Jesus' famous "blessings" and "woes" found in Luke chapter 6.

Then he looked up at his disciples and said:

> "Blessed are you who are poor,
>   for yours is the kingdom of God.
> "Blessed are you who are hungry now,
>   for you will be filled.
> "Blessed are you who weep now,
>   for you will laugh.

> "Blessed are you when people hate you, and when they exclude you, revile you, and defame you on account of the Son of Man. Rejoice in that day and leap for joy, for surely your reward is great in heaven; for that is what their ancestors did to the prophets.

> "But woe to you who are rich,
>   for you have received your consolation.
> "Woe to you who are full now,
>   for you will be hungry.
> "Woe to you who are laughing now,
>   for you will mourn and weep." (Lk 6:20-25)

As will be discussed in greater detail in chapter seven, Brown Theologians refer to God's unique concern for the socially and economically disenfranchised as "the preferential option for the poor." In the words of Gustavo Gutiérrez,

---

[28]Orlando Costas, *Christ Outside the Gate: Mission Beyond Christendom* (Maryknoll, NY: Orbis Books, 1982).

The entire Bible, beginning with the story of Cain and Abel, mirrors God's predilection for the weak and abused of human history. This preference brings out the gratuitous or unmerited character of God's love. The same revelation is given in the evangelical Beatitudes, for they tell us with the utmost simplicity that God's predilection for the poor, the hungry, and the suffering is based on God's unmerited goodness to us.[29]

God' preferential option for the poor, the weak, the least members of society runs throughout the Bible and cannot be understood apart from the absolute freedom and gratuitousness of God's love. . . . For God, therefore, "the last will be first, and the first will be last." . . . God's love, and therefore what God demands of us, leaps over these boundaries and goes out in a free and generous search of those whom society marginalizes and oppresses. . . . Universality and preference mark the proclamation of the kingdom. God addresses a message of life to every human being without exception, while at the same time God shows preference for the poor and the oppressed.[30]

It is also of paramount importance to note that the redemption and reconciliation of Jesus also includes a "preferential option for mujeres."[31] Men and women are both deeply loved by God, but, in a fallen world characterized by sexism, misogyny, and machísmo, women often bear the brunt of sinful gendered relationships. And when God sees one of his daughters abused or exploited by one of his sons, God does not stand idly back. Jesus desires his sisters to thrive in the full image of God in which they have been created, and for them to take their rightful place as spiritual leaders, *mujeristas*, within the church.[32] In the words of path-breaking mujerista theologian Ada María Isasi-Díaz:

---

[29]Gustavo Gutiérrez, *A Theology of Liberation* (Maryknoll, NY: Orbis Books, 1988), xxvii, in Goizueta, *Caminemos Con Jesús*, 175.
[30]Gustavo Gutiérrez, *The God of Life* (Maryknoll: Orbis Books, 1991), 116.
[31]Roman Catholic theologian Ada María Isasi-Díaz was the first to extend the biblical principle of God's preferential option for the marginalized to women.
[32]Mujeristas are "womanists" or "feminists."

In the mujerista God revindicates the divine image and likeness of women. The mujerista is called to gestate new women and men: a strong people. Mujeristas are anointed by God as servants, prophets and witnesses of redemption. Mujeristas will echo God's reconciling love; their song will be a two-edged sword, and they will proclaim the gospel of liberation.[33]

REPENT AND BELIEVE THE GOOD NEWS

"Repent." Greek: *metanoeite*. Have a new mind. Think differently. Concientización. Get "woke." Change the way you are thinking about how you are living your life and how you can change the world. El Plan Espiritual de Galilee calls us to follow Jesus and learn from him how to bring about liberation for ourselves and this broken world. We must stop thinking like an Essene. We are not going to change the world by withdrawing into the desert. Nor will we change the world through political compromise like the Herodians and Sadducees. Though it might seem romantic to some, we are also not going to find liberation from empire by mixing religiosity with violence as the Pharisees and Zealots attempted—that did not, and does not, end well.

No, if we want to change the world, we must do an about face, a change of direction, and believe the good news that Jesus is Lord and King, As Jewish messiah, and therefore Savior of the world, Jesus came to make us and the whole world new. Nothing and no one is left out!

When Jesus gives us eyes to see, and allows us to understand El Plan Espiritual de Galilee, it is *La Buena Nueva*![34] When we finally get it, it is "like treasure hidden in a field, which someone found and hid; then in his joy he goes and sells all that he has and buys that field," or "like a merchant in search of fine pearls; on finding one pearl of great value, he went and sold all that he had and bought it" (Mt 13:44-46). The scales fall from our eyes. We are made new. Nothing can contain our joy. We are ready to change the world!

---

[33]Ada María Isasi-Díaz, "Mujeristas: A Name of Our Own!!" Religion Online, accessed September 18, 2018, www.religion-online.org/article/mujeristas-a-name-of-our-own.
[34]"The Good News."

DISCIPLESHIP

After we hear and believe the good news of Jesus' kingdom announcement, the next step is to follow Jesus in discipleship. As Jesus called the Twelve, so he beckons us: "Come, follow me." To be a disciple of Jesus is to be his student or mentee.[35] And the goal of being Jesus' disciple is to become like him in both character and action. As we walk with him each day in the big and *lo cotidiano*, he teaches us, heals us, and transforms us from the inside out to make us more like him.[36] As we walk with Jesus, he sends us to where he has already been at work—among the poor, the suffering, the immigrant, and all who are cast aside. He even calls some of us to the "Joseph of Arimatheas" and religious and political elites of our day. Jesus acts through us to bring his kingdom to bear in every space of hurt so that God's kingdom might come on earth as it is in heaven. He sends us out in mision integral to serve as agents of God's reconciliation, redemption, and justice.

Jesus' offer of discipleship is extended to all. The revolutionary nature of discipleship is easy to miss without knowing the history of this word and practice. In the days of Jesus, the privilege of being the disciple of a rabbi was limited by ethnicity, gender, and formal academic achievement. Only Jewish boys were allowed to become disciples after successfully navigating a rigorous, three-tiered religious educational system.[37] The three levels of Jewish education were called Bet Sefer (House of the Book), Bet Talmud (House of Learning), and Bet Midrash (House of Study). Notwithstanding its exclusivity, it was an extraordinary educational system for its day. Bet Sefer lasted four years, and as part of its curriculum, students memorized the first five books of the Bible—Genesis, Exodus, Leviticus, Numbers, and Deuteronomy. Only those considered gifted were allowed to move on to the next level, Bet Talmud.

---

[35]See Dallas Willard, *The Divine Conspiracy: Rediscovering Our Hidden Life In God* (New York: Harper, 1998).

[36]"Lo cotidiano" refers to our daily lived experiences. Ada Maria Isasi-Díaz, *Mujerista Theology: A Theology for the Twenty-First Century* (Maryknoll, NY: Orbis Books, 2005).

[37]Rob Bell, *Velvet Elvis: Repainting the Christian Faith* (New York: Harper Collins, 2005), 124-134.

Bet Talmud consisted of the memorization of the remaining thirty-four books of the Jewish Old Testament. Bet Midrash, or House of Study, was the third and final level of study. Bet Midrash was restricted to the most elite students, for it involved becoming a "disciple" of a well-known rabbi, and eventually, becoming a rabbi oneself. Being a rabbi, in turn, was one of the most revered and well-respected positions one could hold. Those who did not make it up the educational ranks returned home to apprenticeships as farmers, fishermen, carpenters, shepherds, etc.

As part of the ritual of becoming a disciple, a successful student of Bet Talmud would approach a well-known rabbi and declare: "Rabbi, I want to be your disciple." A period of theological questioning would then ensue, and, if the test was passed, the rabbi would invite the student into the sacred bond of discipleship. The rabbi would say, "Come, follow me." At that point, the disciple would leave his father, mother, family, friends, and community to follow the rabbi. From that point on, the disciple's main task was to learn from the rabbi and become like him. The main way this was accomplished was by spending every waking moment with the rabbi. In fact, we are told that disciples would follow their rabbis so closely that at the end of the day they would literally be covered in dust from their teacher's feet. A saying was even circulated among disciples that admonished them to "cover yourself with the dust of your rabbi's feet."[38] Following sixteen years of apprenticeship with a rabbi, Bet Midrash was completed and, at the age of thirty, one could begin their own career as a rabbi.

It is within this highly exclusive educational and religious context that Jesus called Andrew, James, and John to be his first disciples. He broke all the rules when he told these fishermen, these rabbinic school flunkouts to "Come, follow me." You could even say that Jesus invented affirmative action. But the revolutionary nature of El Plan Espiritual de Galilee did not stop with an expansion of discipleship among a broader category of Jewish men. Following his resurrection, Jesus commanded the remaining eleven disciples:

---

[38]Bell, *Velvet Elvis*, 130.

All authority in heaven and on earth has been given to me. Go therefore and make disciples of all nations, baptizing them in the name of the Father and of the Son and of the Holy Spirit, and teaching them to obey everything that I have commanded you. And remember, I am with you always, to the end of the age. (Mt 28:18-20)

In this passage, Jesus makes a dramatic and earth-shattering announcement to his earliest students: he tells them that the call to spiritual discipleship should no longer be limited to males, and that it was no longer the sole privilege of any particular ethnic or cultural group. Jesus, rabbi and Messiah, invites all people—male and female, from every nation of the world, and every socioeconomic background—to be his disciples. No one is left out. This is where El Plan Espiritual de Galilee becomes personal. Jesus is not only the King and Lord who came to make the whole world new, he is the Teacher and Mentor who calls us to walk so intimately with him that we are covered in the dust of his feet. As he teaches us, heals us, and transforms us, he sends us out among the Galilees—and Jerusalems— of the world to pronounce the good news of El Plan Espiritual de Galilee and to be agents of his redemption, justice and reconciliation. This is the message that Brown Christians have celebrated and lived out for the past five hundred years. This is the good news upon which the Brown Church stands and is called to embody. This is La Buena Nueva.

THE CROSS: A REBEL'S DEATH

The Brown Church also looks to the cross, for without the cross, the good news would not be possible. The cross was a symbol of multiple rejection. It was a rebel's death. Crucifixion was what Rome did to those who dared question the authority of Caesar and his ruthless Empire:

It said, loud and clear: we are in charge here; you are our property; we can do what we like with you. It insisted, coldly and brutally, on the absolute sovereignty of Rome, and of Caesar. . . . It said, in particular: this is what happens to rebel leaders.[39]

---

[39]N. T. Wright, *Jesus and the Victory of God* (Minneapolis: Fortress Press, 1996), 543.

Caesar was the false king who claimed to be Lord, Son of God, Prince of Peace, and the embodiment of "good news" to the world. It was a revolutionary political statement to say that Jesus was Lord, and Caesar was not; that Jesus was the King of the Jews and long-awaited Son of God, the Anointed One who would bring peace and transformation to the world. Jesus rightfully claimed for himself the titles of Caesar, and this led to his death on the cross. This is also what spurred persecution of the early church and the martyrdom of nearly all the apostles. And now, as then, Jesus tell us: "If any want to become my followers, let them deny themselves and take up their cross daily and follow me" (Lk 9:23).

The cross was also a symbol of rejection by the religious and political elite of his own people, of his own day. Those who seek to follow Jesus today should expect the same. In the words of the Master, "Remember the word that I said to you, 'Servants are not greater than their master.' If they persecuted me, they will persecute you; if they kept my word, they will keep yours also" (Jn 15:20).

On the cross, Jesus opened up the way for the kingdom of God to burst forth through all of humanity, and paid the price for our redemption and participation in El Plan Espiritual de Galilee. On the cross, Jesus, the incarnate Son of God, paid the price for your sins and mine, and for the sins of the world. This includes our personal sin, as well as the grievous social sins of racism and empire, which the Brown Church has struggled against for more than five centuries. On the cross, Jesus took it all on himself so that God's renewal might be opened up for the whole world. In the familiar words of the Gospel of John, which, in light of El Plan Espiritual de Galilee, hopefully take on new light to those who have only before heard the gospel of empire—

> For God so loved the world that he gave his only Son, so that everyone who believes in him may not perish but may have eternal life.
>
> Indeed, God did not send the Son into the world to condemn the world, but in order that the world might be saved through him. (Jn 3:16-17)

When Jesus rose on the third day, new creation sprung. The rebirth of the world, and the rebirth of all who would trust in him, follow from the lynchpin of the resurrection. When we place our faith in Christ and follow him in discipleship, we pass from spiritual death to life, and we experience the new creation of God (Jn 5:24; 2 Cor 5:17). We also become members of his body and the local and global church (Rom 12:4-5; 1 Cor 12:27). As we continue to follow him in discipleship, he makes us more and more like him, and he sends us out as agents of his new creation, agents of misión integral and El Plan Espiritual de Galilee. "Blessed be the God and Father of our Lord Jesus Christ! By his great mercy he has given us a new birth into a living hope through the resurrection of Jesus Christ from the dead, and into an inheritance that is imperishable, undefiled, and unfading" (1 Pet 1:3-4). *Así es.* Él nos llama. Él nos invita. Ven.[40]

If Jesus launched an empire-challenging, global transformative movement beginning with the poor and marginalized of Galilee, why does Christianity in the twenty-first century share such close association with five hundred years of European colonization, genocide, and white nationalism in the Americas? What happened between the time of Jesus and the present moment, such that the radical message of El Plan Espiritual de Galilee became co-opted by colonialism and half a millennium of white supremacy cloaked in the raiment of Christianity? The next two chapters explore the history of the hijacking of Christianity by Spanish colonists and the multicultural, multigendered resistance that gave birth to the Brown Church.

---

[40]"That's the way it is. He calls us. He invites us. Come."

LAS CASAS, LA VIRGEN DE GUADALUPE, AND THE BIRTH OF THE BROWN CHURCH

I'm Spanish.

My family is from Spain.

We're from Peru, but my husband is Italian.

I'm a *norteño*;[1] I'm not an Indian from southern Mexico.

She has "bad hair."

Marry someone lighter than you, *pa' que mejorar la raza*.[2]

Look at those "Chichimecas," those little Indians.

AS LATINAS/OS GROWING UP
in the United States, we hear these types of racial, and racist, remarks on
a regular basis. We hear them from our parents, family members, church
friends, and even random people we meet in the streets. Such insensitive
comments reflect a five-hundred-year history of racism and colonialism
in Latin America that is deeply imbedded within the psyche and social
institutions of Latinas/os in the United States.

---

[1]In this example, *norteño* refers to "someone from Northern Mexico" where most people, rightly
or wrongly, share a "white," "Spanish" identity.

[2]"Marry someone lighter than you, to improve the race."

When a Latina/o says in casual conversation, "I'm Spanish," it is not a neutral assertion of ethnic identity in the way that someone in Chicago might say, "My grandparents came from Sweden in the 1890s." No, when a Latina/o person says, "I'm Spanish," it is a claim of racial superiority and privileged socioeconomic status. Implicitly, they are saying, "I identify with the Spanish conquerors and the colonial society they created. I have a privileged status in this racial system because I descend from them and am not indigenous or black." Many Latinas/os make this claim even though no one from their family has stepped foot in Spain since the 1600s. Others do so even though it is unmistakable that they also possess indigenous or African ancestry. Such statements reinforce a racial caste system that has poisoned Latin American culture and society for five hundred years. To this day, the indigenous and African descent populations of Latin America are the poorest and most politically disenfranchised, while those of (mostly) Spanish ancestry remain in control of the economy and institutional power in its various forms. This racial legacy has led to an obsession with whiteness in virtually all aspects of Latina/o and Latin American society, including family, film, television, schools, business, politics, government, and churches.

Brown Christians reject the racist legacy of Latin America in all of its manifestations. As followers of Jesus, we condemn all racist attitudes and all forms of racial inequality that are found in the Latina/o community. One can be a faithful follower of Jesus, or a racist, but not both. As a fundamental aspect of El Plan Espiritual de Galilee, we seek the promotion of racial justice and the reconciliation of all peoples, of all cultural backgrounds, within the one Beloved Community of God. As Latinas/os, we take pride in our history of mestizaje (mixture between indigenous and Spanish), mulatez (mixture between African and Spanish), and various other forms of cultural blending, which include Chinese, Korean, Japanese, Indian, Taiwanese, Filipino, Lebanese, Arab, Syrian, Italian, German, Russian, Jewish, Armenian, and other cultural communities of the world. We honor our distinct multicultural mixture as a treasure from

God (Rev 21:26) and a proud source of our identity as children of God. We celebrate the different shades of our skin, our diverse body types, the curls and kinks and highlights of our hair, and the round, brown, green, and almond eyes that are all found in our tribe. *Estamos muy orgullosos de ser hijas e hijos de Díos. Somos Latinas/os.*[3]

As Brown Christians, we understand that the Spanish Conquest set in motion the fundamental racial inequalities that persist to the present day in Latin America and among US Latinas/os. We mourn the fact that as much as 95 percent of the indigenous population of Mexico died within the first one hundred years of the Spanish conquest and that millions more lost their lives as part of the various European conquests and colonization efforts in North and South America.[4] We lament the sistema de castas which officially governed Latin American colonial society for more than three hundred years, and which seared a racist imprint upon the Latina/o psyche that persists to the present moment. We deeply grieve the fact that the message of Jesus was twisted to justify murder, enslavement, and colonization, and that the Bible was perversely manipulated to construct colonial theologies of conquest and dehumanization.

As Brown Christians, however, we find solace in knowing that the Brown Church has challenged racism and colonialism in Latin America from the very beginning. This chapter and the next trace the origins of the Brown Church to the early sixteenth century and examine the multicultural Christian protests to the Spanish Conquest led by Antonio de Montesinos, Bartolomé de Las Casas, Garcilaso de la Vega el Inca, Guaman Poma de Ayala, and Sor Juana Inés de la Cruz. We celebrate the multicultural indigenous, African, Spanish, mestizo, black, and Asian backgrounds of the Brown Church, and in their lives and theology we find inspiration to fight the racial battles of the Brown Church today.

---

[3]"We are proud of being daughters and sons of God. We are Latinas/os."
[4]Michael Haines and Richard Steckel, eds., *A Population History of North America* (Cambridge: Cambridge University Press, 2000), 253.

MONTESINOS AND THE BIRTH
OF BROWN THEOLOGY (1511)

The Brown Church was born in 1511 on the Sunday before Christmas on the Island of Hispaniola.[5] On that day, in a straw-thatched church, Dominican Friar Antonio de Montesinos preached the first fiery sermon condemning the Spanish Conquest.[6] Invoking the prophetic words and ministry of John the Baptist, Montesinos declared,

> In order to make your sins against the Indians known to you I have come up on this pulpit, I who am a voice of Christ crying in the wilderness of this island, and therefore it behooves you to listen, not with careless attention, but with all your heart and senses, so that you may hear it; for this is going to be the strangest voice that ever you heard, the harshest and hardest and most awful and most dangerous that ever you expected to hear.[7]

He continued,

> This voice says that you are in mortal sin, that you live and die in it, for the cruelty and tyranny you use in dealing with these innocent people. Tell me, by what right or justice do you keep these Indians in such a cruel and horrible servitude? On what authority have you waged a detestable war against these people, who dwelt quietly and peacefully on their own land. . . . Are these not men. . . . Are you not bound to love them as you love yourselves?[8]

Montesinos' prophetic sermon did not go over well with his audience of Spanish colonists. Deeply angered, they met together in the house of Diego Columbus (governor, and son of the infamous Christopher Columbus) and condemned the sermon as a treasonous act against King Ferdinand of Spain. They also sent a delegation to the Dominican monastery of Montesinos and demanded an apology and recantation of the prophetic sermon. Undeterred, Montesinos returned the next Sunday to

---

[5]Hispaniola is the present-day Dominican Republic and Haiti.
[6]Lewis Hanke, *The Spanish Struggle for Justice in the Conquest of America* (Dallas: First Southern Methodist University Press, 2002), 17.
[7]Hanke, *The Spanish Struggle for Justice*, 17.
[8]Hanke, *The Spanish Struggle for Justice*, 17.

a crowded audience of leading Spanish officials and colonists, and preached another sermon even more infuriating than the last. He declared, "Suffer me a little, and I will show thee that I have yet to speak on God's behalf."[9] In this second sermon, Montesinos compared the colonists to highway robbers and told them that they would be denied confession and absolution unless they repented and ended their abuse of the native population.

The testimony of Montesinos proved persuasive, and a special council of lawyers and theologians was constituted by the Crown to examine the charges of abuse against the natives.[10] In response, however, the junta issued a series of policy recommendations that provided only nominal relief and left in place the unjust practice of Indian slavery. Although Montesinos was unsuccessful in ending the mistreatment of the indigenous peoples of the Caribbean, his protests brought to light, for the first time, the abuses of the Spanish conquest.

The sermons of Montesinos gave birth to the Brown Church and a movement of multicultural protest to Spanish imperialism that spanned the entire colonial period. These protesters included indigenous, Spanish, mestizo, and even Asian Christians who challenged the injustices of Spanish colonialism and sought to detangle the message of Jesus from the misrepresentations of racism and imperialism. Each, in their own way, challenged the racial logic of Spanish colonialism and called for a Christian spirituality that accurately reflected the teachings of Jesus and El Plan Espiritual de Galilee. The rest of this chapter continues the narrative of the Brown Church's protests against the cruelties of Spanish colonialism by examining the life and ministry of Bishop Bartolomé de Las Casas.[11] Through his ministry, advocacy, and writings, Las Casas did more than any other individual of the colonial period to battle racial

---

[9]Hanke, *The Spanish Struggle for Justice*, 18.
[10]Hanke, *The Spanish Struggle for Justice*, 23-24.
[11]Some may challenge the inclusion of Las Casas as an exemplary of the Brown Church because of his Spanish ancestry. As by definition a mixed race community, the Brown Church is inclusive of individuals of every ethnic and cultural background who stand for racial justice.

injustice and exploitation of the indigenous peoples of Latin America. Other than César Chávez and Sor Juana Inés de la Cruz, he is perhaps the most well-known leader of the Brown Church. He is the father of the Brown Church.

BARTOLOMÉ DE LAS CASAS (1484–1566)

Bartolomé de Las Casas was the central founder of the Brown Church and progenitor of Brown Theology in the Americas.[12] He has also been credited with founding the modern concept of social justice as we know it.[13] Las Casas was born in Seville, Spain in 1484, and, reflecting the diversity of the Brown Church, scholars believe he may have come from Jewish origins.[14] As part of the initial Spanish conquest of the Americas in the early 1500s, Las Casas served in brutal military campaigns against the natives of Hispaniola, and he was a slaveholder and priest.[15]

In reward for his participation in the military conquest of the Caribbean, he was granted special status as an *encomendero*—one of the economic elite of the island.[16] In the words of Las Casas himself (in the third person),

> Greed increased every day and every day Indians perished in greater numbers and the clergyman Bartolomé de Las Casas . . . went about his concerns like the others, sending his share of Indians to work fields and gold mines, taking advantage of them as much as he could.[17]

---

[12]This section is adapted from the essay "Toward a Perspective of 'Brown Theology'" by Robert Chao Romero, from *Evangelical Theologies of Liberation and Justice*, edited by Mae Elise Cannon and Andrea Smith. (Downers Grove, IL: IVP Academic, 2019), 75-95.

[13]See Kevin Terraciano, "The Struggle for Justification in the Conquest of America: Tolerance and Intolerance," in *Writings on Early Spanish America in Religious Toleration*, ed. John Christian Laursen (New York: St. Martin's Press, 1999).

[14]Bartolomé de Las Casas, *A Short Account of the Destruction of the Indies*, ed. Nigel Griffin (London: Penguin Books, 1992), xviii; Las Casas, *History of the Indies*, ed. Andrée Collard (New York: Harper Torchbooks, 1971), xxi.

[15]Las Casas, *A Short Account*, xix; Las Casas, *History of the Indies*, xi, xvi.

[16]As will be further discussed, an *encomendero* was a Spanish landowner who was "entrusted" with the labor of an indigenous community in exchange for the provision of religious instruction. Paul Vickery, *Bartolomé de las Casas: Great Prophet of the Americas* (Mahwah, NJ: Paulist Press, 2006), 37-38.

[17]Las Casas, *History of the Indies*, 208.

At first blush this seems paradoxical, or at least difficult to imagine. How could a missionary priest be given slaves and wealth, and be part of a racist and exploitive colonial project? And yet, if we bring it into today's context it is really not all that hard to imagine. How many pastors in the United States earn significant incomes, live in segregated suburbs, send their kids to segregated schools, and support laws and policies that embolden the racial status quo? How many pastors do this without even realizing that there is a problem?

On June 4, 1514, Las Casas experienced what scholars would call his "first conversion."[18] While preparing a sermon for Pentecost Sunday, his conscience was stricken after reading Sirach 34:18: "The sacrifice of an offering unjustly acquired is a mockery; the gifts of the impious are unacceptable" (NJB).

Las Casas reflected on this text from the Apocrypha in light of the suffering of the native peoples of the Indies and realized that he could not both follow Christ and participate in their exploitation. Las Casas speaks of this conversion experience (in the third person) in *History of the Indies*:

> As I said, he [Las Casas] began to consider the suffering and servitude of these people and he remembered having heard that the Dominican friars of Santo Domingo could not own Indians with a clear conscience and would neither confess nor absolve Indian owners, which the said clergyman disapproved. He remembered how one day on Hispaniola, where he had owned Indians with the same carelessness and blindness as in Cuba, a Dominican friar had refused him confession. . . .
>
> He spent a few days in meditation on the matter until by dint of applying his readings to this and that case he was convinced Indians were being treated unjustly and tyrannically all over the Indies. He read everything in this new light and found his opinion supported; as he used to say, from the day the darkness lifted from his eyes, he never read any book in Latin or a vulgar tongue—and he read an infinite number in forty-four

---

[18]Vickery, *Bartolomé de las Casas*, 2-3; Las Casas, *A Short Account*, xxi-xxii.

years—which did not in some way provide the proof of Indian rights and Spanish injustice.[19]

After "the darkness lifted from his eyes," Las Casas renounced his wealth and surrendered his Indian slaves to the governor of the island. He did this in order to "preach the subject of his sermons with a clear conscience," and that he might maintain a clear Christian witness.

Befuddled by the request of Las Casas to surrender his right to wealth and Indian labor, the governor replied, "By God, I would like to see you rich and prosperous! I do not accept the remission of Indians; instead, I will give you two weeks to think it over, at the end of which you may come and tell me your decision."[20] Unmoved by the governor's words, Las Casas held firm to his commitment and retorted forcefully:

> Sir, I thank you for your good wishes and signs of appreciation, but please pretend that the two weeks are already past. If I should regret my decision and in two weeks come to you with tears of blood for the restitution of my Indians, and for the love of God you should listen, I pray God to punish you rigorously for this and never to pardon your sin.[21]

Las Casas's conversion narrative represents one of the first recorded examples of concientización, or awakening of critical consciousness, in the Americas. As discussed by Paulo Freire, concientización is the experience of becoming awakened to the reality of injustice in the world.[22] In the experience of Las Casas, it was "the darkness lifting from his eyes" as he came to understand "the proof of Indian rights and Spanish injustice." In biblical language, and the language of El Plan Espiritual de Galilee, Las Casas experienced "repentance"—or a new consciousness. He started to think differently about his complicity with the injustice around him. He repented and changed the course of his life and ministry, for he realized that injustice towards the natives was inconsistent with the gospel of

---

[19]Las Casas, *History of the Indies*, 208, 209.
[20]Las Casas, *History of the Indies*, 210.
[21]Las Casas, *History of the Indies*, 210.
[22]Paulo Freire, *Pedagogy of the Oppressed* (New York: Continuum, 2005), 33, 67, 109.

Jesus Christ. In order to follow Jesus, he had to give up racial injustice. In the language of today, he got "woke."

Following his experience of concientización, Las Casas spent the next five decades condemning the conquest and challenging the enslavement of the native populations. In the process, he invented modern social justice advocacy as we have come to know it, as well as race-conscious social justice theology. In the spirit of the Old Testament prophets, of which Jesus was the climax, the message of Las Casas was simple and clear: the Spanish Conquest of the indigenous peoples of the Americas was unjust. God had given the Spaniards the opportunity to share the message of Jesus with love, and instead they exploited this divine opportunity for greed and selfish gain. The end result was genocide. If the Spaniards did not repent, they would face divine judgment.

Anticipating the methodology and approach of ethnic studies, Las Casas chronicled the racial violence of Spanish colonialism in several famous books, including *A Short Account of the Destruction of the Indies*, *In Defense of the Indians*, and *History of the Indies*.[23] As ethnic studies would come to do four centuries later, Las Casas utilized multidisciplinary intellectual tools—in his case history, theology, law, and philosophy—to condemn the violence of European conquest and to affirm the inherent human dignity of indigenous peoples. He also foreshadowed the intellectual model of ethnic studies insofar as his prophetic writings intentionally challenged the injustice of the status quo, sparking much political and religious dissent.

As a product of theological scholasticism, Las Casas based his arguments and advocacy on five major sources of authority: the Bible, theologians such as the church fathers, canon law, Roman civil law, and Aristotle.[24] I believe that his prophetic books may be considered the progenitors of Chicana/o and Latina/o studies. In *A Short Account of the Destruction of the Indies*, Las Casas chronicles the brutality of the Spanish military conquest of the Americas, including Hispaniola (Haiti and the

---

[23]Las Casas, *A Short Account*; Las Casas, *In Defense of the Indians* (DeKalb: Northern Illinois University Press, 1992); Las Casas, *History of the Indies*.
[24]Las Casas, *In Defense*, xxii.

Dominican Republic), Puerto Rico, Guatemala, Nicaragua, New Spain (Mexico), Cartagena, Florida, Peru, the River Plate, and New Granada (Colombia, Ecuador, Panama, and Venezuela). First sent as an advocacy piece to the king of Spain in 1542, and subsequently published for broader consumption in 1552, *A Short Account of the Destruction of the Indies* was the first book to challenge European imperialism in the Americas.[25] Spanish violence included the rape of children and women and the indiscriminate slaughter of entire indigenous communities. Of particular disgust was the way in which Europeans conducted their brutal atrocities in the explicit name of Jesus and the Christian faith.

The unbiblical conflation of European military conquest and Christianity is vividly described by Las Casas:

> As we have said, the island of Hispaniola was the first to witness the arrival of Europeans and the first to suffer the wholesale slaughter of its people and the devastation and depopulation of the land. It all began with the Europeans taking native women and children both as servants and to satisfy their own base appetites. . . . They forced their way into native settlements, slaughtering everyone they found there, including small children, old men, pregnant women, and even women who had just given birth. . . . They spared no one, erecting especially wide gibbets on which they could string their victims up with their feet just off the ground and then burn them alive thirteen at a time, in honour of our Saviour and the twelve Apostles.[26]

Perhaps owing to his possible Jewish background, Las Casas decried the use of force for purposes of sharing the good news of Jesus Christ.[27] According to Las Casas, the Christian faith should only be shared and preached through peaceful means.[28] He also argued that the most effective means of convincing the indigenous peoples of the love of God

---

[25]Las Casas, *A Short Account*, xiii.
[26]Las Casas, *A Short Account*, 14-15.
[27]Las Casas, *History of the Indies*, xxi.
[28]Hanke, *The Spanish Struggle*, 72.

was to model the examples and teachings of Christ.[29] The natives were children of God, sisters and brothers of the Spaniards, for whom Jesus also died in order to redeem. Las Casas passionately proclaimed,

> They are our brothers, redeemed by Christ's most precious blood, no less than the wisest and most learned men in the whole world. . . . Christ wanted love to be called his single commandment. This we owe to all men. Nobody is excepted. "There is no room for distinction between Greek and Jew, between the circumcised and the uncircumcised, or between barbarian and Scythian, slave and free man. There is only Christ: he is everything and he is in everything."[30]

And to those who continued to steal and pillage under the false pretext of spreading the gospel, Las Casas had sharp words:

> From the foregoing it is evident that war must not be waged against the Indians under the pretext that they should hear the preaching of Christ's teaching, even if they have killed preachers, since they do not kill the preachers or Christians as Christians, but as their most cruel public enemies, in order that they may not be oppressed or murdered by them. Therefore let those who, under the pretext of spreading the faith, invade, steal, and keep the possessions of others by force of arms—let them fear God, who punishes perverse endeavors.[31]

In addition to denouncing the conquest of the Americas, Las Casas also dedicated himself to the abolition of the forced labor system known as the *encomienda*.[32] As part of this system, entire indigenous communities were "entrusted" (from the Spanish, *encomendar*) to individual Spanish landowners (*encomenderos*) who were granted tribute in native labor in exchange for the provision of religious instruction.[33] Las Casas condemned this labor arrangement as a ruse for exploitation, and he protested it all the way to the crown of Spain. Owing in large measure to

---

[29]Las Casas, *In Defense*, 179.
[30]Las Casas, *In Defense*, 39.
[31]Las Casas, *In Defense*, 181.
[32]Las Casas, *In Defense*, xx; Las Casas, *History of the Indies*, xvii; Las Casas, *A Short Account*, 20.
[33]Hanke, *The Spanish Struggle*, 19.

the moral protests of Las Casas, the encomienda system was abolished through the passage of the New Laws in 1542.[34] Through his religious and political protests of the encomienda regime, Las Casas became the first labor organizer of the Americas.

At this point it is important to note that Las Casas has been rightly criticized for proposing in 1516 and again in 1518 that African slavery be a remedy to the enslavement of indigenous peoples. This led to the authorization of African slavery in the Indies by Charles V and the abhorrent evils of the transatlantic slave trade. Although Las Casas soon recanted this position, realizing "that black slavery was as unjust as Indian slavery and was no remedy at all,"[35] it is important to recognize this fundamental failure on his part.[36] Las Casas recognized his error and implored the forgiveness of God for his complicity in "all the sins committed by the Portuguese and the Africans, not to mention our own sin of buying the slaves."[37]

The moral outcry of Las Casas penetrated the royal courts of the Spanish crown and, in 1550, prompted what scholars call the Great Debate, or disputation of Valladolid.[38] As part of the Great Debate, Las Casas disputed theologian and royal historian Juan Ginés de Sepúlveda over the

---

[34]Juan Friede and Benjamin Keen, eds., *Bartolomé de Las Casas in History: Toward an Understanding of the Man and His Work* (DeKalb: Northern Illinois University Press, 1971), 528-529. The New Laws were so controversial that they prompted violent revolt on the part of Spanish landowners in Peru. In 1545, the New Laws were partially repealed. (Las Casas, *A Short Account*, xxvii.) In political terms, the New Laws were aimed at curbing the growing political and economic power of encomenderos in the Americas.

[35]Las Casas, *History of the Indies*, 257; Las Casas, *In Defense*, xvi.

[36]Las Casas is also criticized by some ethnic studies scholars because of his approval of the peaceful missionary endeavor, as well as for his belief that the Spanish Crown was the legitimate ruler of the Americas based on papal authority, or, "plenitude of power." (Las Casas, *A Short Account*, xxvi.) With respect to the former criticism, the Brown Christian believes that God is the loving Father of all ethnic groups of the world and that he desires for all to come to know the love and transformative grace of Jesus Christ. In response to the latter, the Brown Christian can rightly agree that this was another blind spot of Las Casas. Nothing in the Christian gospel of Jesus Christ condones the colonization of one ethnic group over another, no matter how peacefully executed. From the other direction, Las Casas has been criticized by some conservative Spanish authors for exaggerating the abuses of the conquest and perpetuating a "Black Legend" about Spaniards. (Las Casas, *In Defense*, xvi.)

[37]Las Casas, *History of the Indies*, xvi-xvii.

[38]Lewis Hanke, *All Mankind Is One: A Study of the Disputation Between Bartolomé de Las Casas and Juan Ginés de Sepúlveda on the Religious and Intellectual Capacity of the American Indians* (DeKalb: Northern Illinois University Press, 1974), 9.

biblical and theological validity of the Spanish conquest. Spanning two sessions held in August 1550 and spring 1551, the debate addressed the question, "Is it lawful for the King of Spain to wage war on the Indians, before preaching the faith to them, in order to subject them to his rule, so that afterward they may be more easily instructed in the faith?"[39] The Valladolid debate is the first known historical example of a nation stepping back to contemplate the morality of conquest and colonization.

Drawing from Aristotelian notions of "natural slavery," Sepúlveda and other supporters of the conquest asserted that the Indians should be subject to servitude because they were "natural slaves."[40] According to Aristotle in Book 1 of the Politics, some human beings are born "natural slaves."[41] Natural slaves lack reason and have an aptitude for manual labor. Moreover, Aristotle asserts, a slave may be properly regarded as part of his master's own body. Drawing from the writings of Aristotle, Sepúlveda argued that all natives were "natural slaves" who required the civilizing and Christianizing hand of the Spaniards to save their souls. Because Indians were "barbaric, uninstructed in letters and the art of government, and completely ignorant, unreasoning, and totally in-capable of learning anything but the mechanical arts," as well as "sunk in vice," they were required by natural law to submit to the Spaniards who were "outstanding in virtue and character, . . . wiser and superior in virtue and learning."[42]

Sepúlveda's arguments in support of colonization and conquest rep-resent one of the earliest examples of what critical race theory scholars call a cultural deficit approach.[43] According to cultural deficit thinking, people of color are culturally backwards insofar as they are unlike those of European descent. The path towards civilization therefore lies in

---

[39]Hanke, *All Mankind Is One*, 67, 68.
[40]Lewis Hanke, *The Spanish Struggle for Justice in the Conquest of America* (Dallas: Southern Meth-odist University Press, 2002), 23.
[41]Nicholas Smith, "Aristotle's Theory of Natural Slavery," *Phoenix* 37, no. 2 (1983): 110.
[42] Las Casas, *In Defense*, 11.
[43]See Tara J. Yosso, "Whose Culture Has Capital? A Critical Race Theory Discussion of Com-munity Cultural Wealth," *Race Ethnicity and Education* 8, no. 1 (March 2005): 75.

assimilation into European and Euro-American culture—to become "little Europeans" or, in our current context, white middle-class Americans. This line of racial essentialism begun in the sixteenth century undergirds the ugly racism against indigenous peoples in Latin America today. The belief in the fundamental inferiority of "Indians" that pervades Latina/o culture and society flows from these colonial perspectives, which painted natives as barbaric, ignorant, vice-ridden, and incapable of learning anything but manual labor. These perspectives are still reflected in twenty-first-century US perspectives of Mexicans as nothing but illegal aliens, criminals, drug dealers, and rapists.

The racist Aristotelian view of "Indians" was codified in the Laws of Burgos.[44] Promulgated on December 27, 1512, The Laws of Burgos gave birth to legal racism in the Americas. In the words of Critical Race theorist Ian Haney Lopez, "Race and racism are centrally about seeking, or contesting, power. They have their origins in efforts to rationalize the expropriation and exploitation of land and labor."[45] Moreover, according to Lopez, law has historically played an important role in such racism, "shaping the social meanings that define races, and rendering concrete the privileges and disadvantages justified by racial ideology."[46] The Laws of Burgos represent the first legislative effort by Europeans to rationalize the cultural-based expropriation and exploitation of indigenous land and labor in the Americas. These laws furthermore created the racial categories of Spanish and "Indian" and shaped their social meanings in such a way as to justify the privilege of Spaniards and the exploitation of the native populations. We've felt the effects for five hundred years.

Those lumped together in the Caribbean as "Indians" and excluded from the Spanish civil community were actually a diverse group of indigenous peoples known as Tainos, Guanahatabeys, and Island-Caribs.[47] Modern

---

[44]Hanke, *The Spanish Struggle*, 24; Las Casas, *A Short Account*, xxv.

[45]Ian Haney-Lopez, *White by Law: The Legal Construction of Race* (New York: New York University Press, 2006), xvi.

[46]Haney-Lopez, *White by Law*, 15.

[47]Irving Rouse, *The Tainos: Rise and Decline of the People Who Greeted Columbus* (New Haven: Yale University Press, 1993), 5.

scholars estimate that as many as 500,000 Tainos inhabited the island of Hispaniola at the time of Columbus's arrival; moreover, early chroniclers reported the existence of as many as 600,000 Tainos living on the islands of Puerto Rico and Jamaica. Cuba was also home to a large number of both Taino and Guanahatabeys. Island-Caribs resided in the Windward Islands and Guadeloupe.[48] This same racial designation of "Indian" would later be applied to tens of millions of diverse indigenous peoples throughout the Americas such as the Nahuas, Mexica, Maya, Inca, Tongva, Chumash, Hopi, Navajo, and so on.

Tragically, the entire native population of the Caribbean would disappear as a consequence of European colonization. On the Island of Hispaniola, 90 percent of the Taino died within twenty-five years of contact with the Spanish.[49] By 1509, only 60,000 Taino remained alive in the Caribbean. By 1524 the entire Taino population ceased to exist as a separate population group. Indigenous genocide resulted from forced labor, malnutrition, European diseases, rebellion, and outmarriage.[50] Indigenous genocide would also soon spread throughout the Americas, and in Mexico alone, as much as 95 percent of the native population—more than 20 million souls—would lose their lives by the early seventeenth century.[51]

The Spaniards invented race in the Americas by lumping these diverse indigenous ethnic groups together and calling them "Indians." It is significant to note that these various native communities did not possess an overarching social identity prior to the Spanish arrival. To the European conquerors, however, their Brown bodies made them all "Indian." As "Indians," they were perceived as sharing inherent cultural characteristics that made them inferior to Spaniards and that justified their conquest and exploitation. In the words of the Laws of Burgos, "By nature they

---

[48]Rouse, *The Tainos*, 7, 20-21.
[49]Samuel Wilson, *Hispaniola: Caribbean Chiefdoms in the Age of Columbus.* (Tuscaloosa: University Alabama Press, 1990), ix.
[50]Rouse, *The Tainos*, 169.
[51]Haines and Steckel, *A Population History of North America*, 253.

[Indians] are inclined to idleness and vice, and have no manner of virtue or doctrine."[52] To add insult to injury, these diverse native groups were incorrectly labeled "Indian" because Columbus believed he had arrived in the Indies of South Asia.

In addition to the creation of new racial categories, the Laws of Burgos also gave rise to the first race-based forced labor system in the Americas— the encomienda. The spiritual responsibilities of Spanish encomenderos were elaborated at great length in the Laws of Burgos. Encomenderos were expected to be benevolent task masters who paternalistically oversaw the religious instruction of the Indians charged to their care. They were to construct churches and accompany the natives at Mass and prayer. Spanish encomenderos were also responsible for teaching the Ten Commandments, the Seven Deadly Sins, and the Articles of Faith:

> Also, we order and command that the citizen to whom the said Indians are given in encomienda shall, upon the land that is assigned to him, be obliged to erect a structure to be used for a church . . . and he shall also teach them the Ten Commandments and the Seven Deadly Sins and the Articles of the Faith, that is, to those he thinks have the capacity and ability to learn them; but all this shall be done with great love and gentleness.[53]

The Laws of Burgos also gave birth to racist civil religion in the Americas. According to civil religion, religious clergy work in symbiotic relationship with a narrowly defined civil community and bring assurances of God's favor.[54] A civil community is defined by a set of religious understandings and practices, and also sometimes a racial or ethnic component.[55] Membership in the civil community is established by birth, and those of the civil community define themselves in relation

---

[52]"Laws of Burgos" text, Southern Methodist University, accessed September 20, 2018, http://faculty.smu.edu/bakewell/BAKEWELL/texts/burgoslaws.html.

[53]"Laws of Burgos."

[54]John Howard Yoder, *The Priestly Kingdom: Social Ethics as Gospel* (South Bend: University of Notre Dame Press, 1985), 173-92. For other definitions, and discussions, of civil religion, see, Robert N. Bellah and Phillip E. Hammond, *Varieties of Civil Religion* (San Francisco: Harper & Row, 1980).

[55]Yoder, *The Priestly Kingdom*, 173.

to "outsiders" and "enemies." In the case of Spanish colonialism, European colonists and conquistadors narrowly defined their own civil community as comprising those of Spanish Catholic descent. Natives were the outsiders and enemies. As chaplains of the empire, Gregorio, Sepúlveda, and others brought assurances of God's favor to Spanish colonists through the development of colonial theology that justified colonization and the seizure of native lands and communities.

Spanish legal justification for the conquest of indigenous communities was further encapsulated in a puzzling document known as "El Requerimiento," or, "The Requirement." The Requirement was based on a perverted line of theological reasoning developed by Spanish conquistador and lawyer Martín Fernández de Enciso.[56] According to Enciso, God entrusted the East Indies (the Americas) to Spain in the same manner that God had given the Palestinian Promised Land to the Israelites. Moreover, just as God had assigned Palestine to the Israelites because of the pagan idolatry of the Canaanites, so did God assign the land of the Indians to the Spaniards because of their idolatry. In other words, the Indians were the modern-day Canaanites and the Spaniards were God's chosen people. In the words of Enciso:

> And afterwards Joshua conquered all the land of Canaan by force of arms, and many were killed and those who were captured were given as slaves and served the people of Israel. And all this was done by the will of God because they were idolaters.[57]

Enciso further derived the Spanish right of conquest from papal authority:

> The king might very justly send men to require those idolatrous Indians to hand over their land to him, for it was given him by the pope. If the Indians would not do this, he might justly wage war against them, kill and enslave those captured in war, precisely as Joshua treated the inhabitants of the land of Canaan.[58]

---

[56]Hanke, *The Spanish Struggle*, 30, 31.
[57]Hanke, *The Spanish Struggle*, 32.
[58]Hanke, *The Spanish Struggle*, 32.

The Spanish lawyer Enciso holds the dubious distinction of sowing the theoretical seeds of what would become the Doctrine of Discovery and settler colonialism.[59] These theories express the idea that Europeans possess a God-given destiny to conquer and colonize the globe in the name of Christianity and European civilization. European monarchies possessed the right to colonize pagan lands that they had "discovered," and it was the destiny of white Christians to annihilate and supplant existing indigenous communities around the globe because they were God's new chosen people and the darker peoples they encountered were the new Canaanites. When historians and ethnic studies scholars claim that Christianity was used as a tool of colonization, this is what they mean. In a variation of the Doctrine of Discovery, Anglo Americans would later wrest control of North America from Mexico and its numerous indigenous populations based on the idea of Manifest Destiny.

The "we can conquer them in order to convert them" reasoning was legally codified in El Requerimiento in 1513.[60] This document was required to be read, through a translator, to indigenous populations prior to Spanish military conquest. El Requerimiento presented a brief biblical account of the story of creation and then asserted the global spiritual and temporal authority of the Pope based on the religious legacy of St. Peter. It goes on to describe the papal donation of the East Indies to the King and Queen of Spain. Finally, based on these claims of authority, El Requerimiento demanded submission of indigenous communities to European rule and religious instruction under penalty of military invasion, enslavement, and subjugation.

> If you do not do this [accept European rule and the Christian faith], however, or resort maliciously to delay, we warn you that, with the aid of God, we will enter your land against you with force and will make war in every place and

---

[59]See Lorenzo Veracini, *Settler Colonialism: A Theoretical Overview* (New York: Palgrave Macmillan, 2010); Mark Charles and Soong-Chan Rah, *Unsettling Truths: The Ongoing, Dehumanizing Legacy of the Doctrine of Discovery* (Downers Grove, IL: InterVarsity Press, 2019).
[60]Hanke, *The Spanish Struggle,* 31-36.

by every means we can and are able, and we will then subject you to the yoke and authority of the Church and Their Highnesses. We will take you and your wives and children and make them slaves, and as such we will sell them, and will dispose of you and them as Their Highnesses order. And we will take your property and will do to you all the harm and evil we can, as is done to vassals who will not obey their lord or who do not wish to accept him, or who resist and defy him. We avow that the deaths and harm which you will receive thereby will be your own blame, and not that of Their Highnesses, nor ours, nor of the gentlemen who come with us.[61]

El Requerimiento reveals the profound lengths to which European colonial nations would go to employ legalism in order to justify their naked pursuit of land, wealth, power, and privilege. A similar type of legalism occurs today in the United States when the Supreme Court strips Latinas/os, African Americans, and other people of color of long-standing civil rights protections in voting, education, and employment, based on narrow legal interpretations of the Constitution. Typically, such rights are stripped away because racially conservative courts assert that they infringe unconstitutionally upon white Americans. Critical race theory scholars call this principle "legal indeterminacy."[62] The historical roots of legal indeterminacy lay in El Requerimiento and the way in which Spanish colonial powers distorted the teachings of Scripture in a legalistic manner in order to justify the seizure of indigenous lands.

According to historian Lewis Hanke:

The Requirement was read to trees and empty huts when no Indians were to be found. Captains muttered its theological phrases into their beards on the edge of sleeping Indians settlements, or even a league away before starting the formal attack, and at times some leather-lunged Spanish notary hurled its sonorous phrases after the Indians as they fled into the mountains.

---

[61]"Requerimiento, 1514," NC State University, accessed September 20, 2018, https://faculty.chass .ncsu.edu/slatta/hi216/require.htm. The Requirement is also quoted by Las Casas in *History of the Indies*, 192-93.

[62]Legal indeterminacy means that judges can find legitimate legal grounds to justify any outcome in most civil rights cases. See George A. Martínez, "Legal Indeterminacy, Judicial Discretion, and the Mexican-American Litigation Experience, 1930-1980," *UC Davis Law Review* 27, no. 3 (1994).

Once it was read in camp before the soldiers to the beat of the drum. Ship captains would sometimes have the document read from the deck as they approached an island, and at night would send out enslaving expeditions, whose leaders would shout the traditional Castilian war cry, "Santiago"![63]

El Requerimiento made a mockery of the gospel of Jesus Christ and El Plan Espiritual de Galilee. In *History of the Indies*, Las Casas decried El Requerimiento as "unjust, impious, scandalous, irrational, and absurd" and stated, "I don't know whether to laugh or cry at the absurdity of the council" that authorized the document.[64] He declared that El Requerimiento defamed the witness of Christianity and that its methods were severe departures from "the Christian means of peace and love."[65] In a bold statement, Las Casas even asserted that indigenous peoples of the Americas had the right to wage war in self-defense against the Spaniards and their bold misrepresentation of Christ.

Rather than sharing Christ's freedom from oppression (Lk 4:18-19), the Spaniards invoked Christ's name to "make war in every place," "take . . . wives and children and make them slaves," and "take . . . property and . . . do . . . all the harm and evil we can." Rather than bringing good news and proclaiming the year of the Lord's favor, they perpetrated racial genocide and gave birth to systems of racial oppression that persist to the present moment. Brown Christians find solace knowing that many Brown Theologians, like Montesinos and Las Casas, soon rose up to challenge this unthinkable hypocrisy.

Las Casas countered the natural slavery arguments of Sepúlveda and the various racist legal, political, economic, and spiritual institutions that they engendered by asserting that the natives, just as the Europeans, were made in the image of God, and therefore equal to the Spaniards. "They are our brothers, redeemed by Christ's most precious blood, no less than the wisest and most learned men in the whole world."[66] In further refutation

---

[63]Hanke, *The Spanish Struggle, 34.*
[64]Las Casas, *History of the Indies,* 196.
[65]Las Casas, *History of the Indies,* 196.
[66]Las Casas, *In Defense of the Indians, 39.*

of Sepúlveda's claim that Indians were culturally backward, Las Casas took what may be called an approach of "community of cultural wealth."[67] To disprove Sepúlveda's argument that the natives were natural slaves, Las Casas also highlighted the advanced culture and civilization of the indigenous peoples, and praised the sophistication of their art and architecture:

> Rather, long before they had heard the word Spaniard, they had properly organized states, wisely ordered by excellent laws, religion, and custom.[68]
>
> Furthermore, they are so skilled in every mechanical art that with every right they should be set ahead of all the nations of the known world on this score, so very beautiful in their skill and artistry are the things these people produces in the grace of its architecture, its painting, and its needlework.[69]

Las Casas also argued in unequivocal terms that the gospel message should always be spread in the example of Christ—through peaceful means and the demonstration of Christian love. As previously discussed, this was perhaps owing to the historical experience of his possible Jewish forebears. For was that not how the Spaniards reportedly first received it from St. James?[70] Finally, Las Casas chided the theological reasoning of Sepúlveda as poison that would promote further injustice against native communities and forever sully the reputation of Christianity:

> Therefore, if Sepulveda's opinion (that the campaigns against the Indians are lawful) is approved, the most holy faith of Christ, to the reproach of the name Christian, will be hateful and detestable to all the peoples of that world to whom the word will come of the inhuman crimes that the Spaniards inflict

---

[67]As discussed in chapter one, critical race theory scholars Tara Yosso and Danny Solórzano developed the concept of community cultural wealth in the context of urban educational studies. In advancing a positive view of indigenous culture, Las Casas articulated an early, although admittedly clumsy, community cultural wealth approach. Las Casas has been criticized for articulating a perspective of natives as "noble savages." (Las Casas, *History of the Indies*, xi.) Given the fact that during the first half-century of Spanish imperialism natives were characterized in the extreme dichotomy of either "noble Indian" or "dirty dogs," this criticism is perhaps sometimes overstated.

[68]Las Casas, *In Defense*, 42-43.

[69]Las Casas, *In Defense*, 44.

[70]Las Casas, *In Defense*, 43, 44, 179.

on that unhappy race, so that neither in our lifetime nor in the future will they want to accept our faith under any condition, for they see that its first heralds are not pastors but plunderers, not fathers but tyrants, and that those who profess it are ungodly, cruel, and without pity in their merciless savagery.[71]

Five hundred years later, the warning of Las Casas still rings true. Millions of students, professors, and activists in Latin America and the United States continue to reject the Christian faith because they have learned that many of its first heralds were "not pastors but plunderers" and "without pity in their merciless savagery."

The prophetic ministry of Bartolomé de Las Casas laid the foundations of social justice in the Americas. Through his writings and social advocacy, Las Casas invented interdisciplinary social justice scholarship and theologizing, and became a central inspiration in the development of Liberation Theology in Latin America. His example of religious protest would go on to inspire many others throughout the colonial period and into the twenty-first century.[72]

LA VIRGEN DE GUADALUPE

As Las Casas was prophetically advocating on behalf of the natives and condemning the Spanish conquest, another spiritual advocate arose on their behalf. She was to become the "Mother" of the Brown Church. The story of La Virgen de Guadalupe is a matter of faith to some and a legend to others. She was designated the patron saint of Mexico in 1746, and shrines honoring La Virgen can be found not only in Mexico and Latin America but throughout Latina/o communities of the United States.[73]

---

[71]Las Casas, *In Defense*, 20.

[72]In the 17th century, Garcilaso de la Vega el Inca, Felipe Guaman Poma de Ayala, Catarina de San Juan, and Sor Juana Inés de la Cruz followed in the prophetic footsteps of Las Casas. This diverse group added indigenous, mestizo, female, and even Asian perspectives to Latin American religious discourse and laid the second layer of foundation for the Brown Church.

[73]Ondina E. González and Justo L. González, *Nuestra Fe: A Latin American Church History Sourcebook* (Nashville: Abingdon Press, 2014), 37; Edwin David Aponte, *¡Santo! Varieties of Latino/a Spirituality* (Maryknoll, NY: Orbis Books, 2012), 118-19.

In December 1531, in the midst of the protestations of Las Casas, and ten years after the Spanish conquest of Tenochtitlán (Mexico City), a mysterious event reportedly occurred that would change the course of Mexican and Latin American Christianity to the present day: the mysterious appearance of La Virgen de Guadalupe to the indigenous peasant Juan Diego.[74] It is believed that the story of La Virgen de Guadalupe was first recorded in written form in the Nahuatl language by Don Antonio Valeriano in 1545. The document was titled *Nican Mopohua*,[75] and Valeriano was a member of the royal house of Tacuba, which traced its lineage to the Emperor Moctezuma II.[76] For Catholic and Orthodox readers of this book, this story presents no theological conflict. For Protestants, and especially Latina/o Protestants, simply mentioning this topic can stir deep theological and emotional tension. Although controversial, no account of the Brown Church can ignore a weighty and honest discussion of "La Virgen."

Without compromising any of their theological convictions, I hope that my readers might consider a fresh perspective on the Virgen de Guadalupe: for the Brown Church throughout the ages, La Virgen points us to Christ, and she has been a powerful symbol of the fact that God loves the indigenous people of Mexico and is their protector.[77] Flowing from this understanding, many Latinas and Latinos in the United States look to La Virgen as a symbol of faith, identity, hope, female empowerment, and cultural liberation.[78] In the words of Chicana Catholic activist Lupe Anguiano, "To me she is a symbol of faith. She comes into our lives and shows us our importance as human beings and the love that God has for us. . . . To me she is the symbol of introducing me to Christ."[79]

---

[74]Ondina E. González and Justo L. González, *Christianity in Latin America: A History* (Cambridge: Cambridge University Press, 2008), 55-56, 58-59.

[75]"Thus It Is Said."

[76]Johann Roten, "Nican Mopohua: The Story of Our Lady of Guadalupe in Nahuatl," University of Dayton, accessed September 20, 2018, https://udayton.edu/imri/mary/n/nican-mopohua.php.

[77]González and González, *Christianity in Latin America*, 56, 58.

[78]Andrés Guerrero, *A Chicano Theology* (Maryknoll, NY: Orbis Books, 1987), 105, 107, 110, 113, 115.

[79]Guerrero, *A Chicano Theology*, 107.

In a similar vein, legendary Chicana labor organizer Dolores Huerta honors La Virgen as a critical symbol of faith-rooted justice and accomplishing the impossible in the power of Christ. For this reason, La Virgen was the central religious symbol for the United Farm Workers movement. According to Huerta, "She is a symbol of the impossible, of doing the impossible to win a victory, in humility, of being able to win with the faith. I mean that's the important thing that she symbolizes to the union: that with faith you can win. You know with faith you can overcome."[80]

Based on the account of Nican Mopohuyua, the Virgin Mary, clothed in the appearance of a humble, indigenous Mexican woman, appeared to Juan Diego in December 1531:

> At the beginning of December, a poor Indian named Juan Diego left his house one Saturday morning to attend divine service. On the way, as he passed the hill of Tepeyacac ("Hill of the Nose," in Nahuatl), he was startled by a song coming from the summit. . . .
>
> The singing ceased and a heavenly sweet voice called him from the hill-top, "Juan, my little one, Juan Diego." Filled with joy, Juan Diego was not at all frightened, but climbed the hill in search of the mysterious voice.
>
> When he reached the top, he saw a lady who bade him approach. It was a wonderful lady of superhuman beauty. Her raiment shone like the sun; the rock on which she set her foot seemed to be hewn from precious stones and the ground red like the rainbow. . . .
>
> Astonished by the appearance of La Virgen, Juan Diego listened as she gave him special instructions: I wish a shrine to be built here to show my love to you. I am your merciful mother, thine, and all the dwellers of this earth. To bring to pass what I bid thee, go thou and speak to the bishop of Mexico and say I sent thee to make manifest to him my will. . . .
>
> Juan Diego obeyed La Virgen de Guadalupe and went several times to speak with the bishop and request that a church be built. The Bishop each time refused and demanded a special sign from heaven. Juan Diego continued to experience apparitions of the Virgin Mary. On one of these occasions, it is reported that she helped him gather a bouquet of beautiful

---

[80]Guerrero, *A Chicano Theology*, 106.

flowers in his tilma, or cloak, as a sign for the bishop. Wielding the cloak and flowers, Juan went one last time to see the bishop. Juan Diego fell to the ground and declared:

"'Sir, I have done thy command. I went and told the Lady of Heaven thou wast asking for a sign that thou mightest believe me." Then he unfolded his white cloak and, as the lovely blooms were strewn on the floor, the miraculous image of Our Lady of Guadalupe suddenly appeared on the cloth just as it is to be seen today, painted by a divine hand on the cape of Juan Diego. [81]

In response to these reported miracles and apparitions, the church was built, and it is reported that millions of indigenous people subsequently came to faith in Christ. Mexicans of all ethnic backgrounds—indigenous, Spanish, African, mestizo, mulato, and Asian—have come to visit the church and honor La Virgen for the past five hundred years. The story of La Virgen de Guadalupe and Juan Diego is perhaps the most beautiful expression of the cultural and spiritual mestizaje of Mexico. In 1999, Pope John Paul II named La Virgen de Guadalupe the patroness of the Americas, and, in 2002, Juan Diego was canonized as the first indigenous Mexican saint.[82] You can still visit the church and see Juan Diego's white cloak with the miraculous image of Our Lady of Guadalupe "painted by a divine hand." And, miraculously, the image has not faded.

Through the story of Juan Diego and La Virgen de Guadalupe, we see that God "broke through" the misrepresentation of the conquest to the indigenous people of Mexico and revealed his concern for them. As an embodiment of God's love for Juan Diego and the Nahua people, La Virgen made herself an indigenous woman.[83] She spoke to Juan Diego in his native language of Nahuatl. She had brown skin, dark hair, and indigenous dress, and she addressed Juan Diego as her son.[84] In the words of Chicana labor organizer Dolores Huerta, "She came in the form of an

[81]Roten, "Nican Mopohua"; González and González, *Nuestra Fe*, 37.
[82]United States Conference of Catholic Bishops, "Saints Who Were Great Evangelizers," accessed September 20, 2018, www.usccb.org/prayer-and-worship/prayers-and-devotions/saints/evangelizing-saints.cfm.
[83]González and González, *Christianity in Latin America*, 59.
[84]González and González, *Christianity in Latin America*, 58-59.

Indian woman, and Indian maiden; that has an awful lot of meaning, especially in terms of machismo."[85]

La Virgen did what no violent male Spanish conquistador could do—she convinced Juan Diego and the Aztecs of the love of God. Why would an indigenous person listen to an olive-skinned, bearded man from Spain who raped their wives and daughters, pillaged their homes, and destroyed their millennia-old culture, all in the pursuit of gold, power, and riches? Through their violence and greed, the conquistadors tainted—almost irreparably—the representation of God the Father and his Son Jesus Christ to the tens of millions of natives who lived in Mexico and the Americas. If God was like the conquerors, why should they choose to believe in him? Through the loving and miraculous appearance of the indigenous Virgen de Guadalupe, God broke through. Through her, the indigenous peoples of Mexico would come to know her Son. And for the past five hundred years, the indigenous peoples of Mexico—together with millions of Mexicanas/os of mestizo descent—have viewed her as the protector of Mexico. La Virgen made spiritual peace. She indigenized Mexican Catholicism. She became the harbinger of the cultural and spiritual mestizaje that defines Christianity in Mexico and Latin America. Within the setting of sixteenth century Mexico, and up to the present moment, La Virgen de Guadalupe embodied, and embodies, the prophetic words spoken by Jesus' Mother more than two millennia ago:

> My soul magnifies the Lord,
>   and my spirit rejoices in God my Savior,
> for he has looked with favor on the lowliness of his servant.
>   Surely, from now on all generations will call me blessed;
> for the Mighty One has done great things for me,
>   and holy is his name.
> His mercy is for those who fear him
>   from generation to generation.
> He has shown strength with his arm;
>   he has scattered the proud in the thoughts of their hearts.

---

[85]Guerrero, *Chicano Theology*, 113.

He has brought down the powerful from their thrones,
    and lifted up the lowly;
he has filled the hungry with good things,
    and sent the rich away empty.
He has helped his servant Israel,
    in remembrance of his mercy,
according to the promise he made to our ancestors,
    to Abraham and to his descendants forever. (Lk 1:46-55)

CONCLUSION

Tragically, the prophetic words of Las Casas still ring true five hundred years later. Because of the prideful defense of conquest and profound misrepresentation of Christ by those like Sepúlveda, the "most holy faith of Christ" is still considered "hateful and detestable" by millions of people of color, professors, and activists throughout the globe. Like Rosa, Carlos, and Edwin from chapter one, thousands of Latina/o university students reject Christianity in the twenty-first century, because, in the fulfillment of Las Casas's words, they and their professors see that many of its first heralds in the Americas were "not pastors but plunderers, not fathers but tyrants," and that those who professed it were "ungodly, cruel, and without pity in their merciless savagery."

Thankfully, that is not the full picture. The blessed Virgen de Guadalupe symbolizes the fact that God did not overlook the grave injustices of the conquest. Jesus understood the profound misrepresentation it represented, and he sent his Mother and other prophets like Montesinos and Las Casas to make peace. Four centuries later, César Chávez would go on to challenge the injustice against farmworkers in the name of Jesus while wielding a banner of La Virgen as a symbol of the Mexican struggle in the United States. God would also send a multicultural cadre of male and female Christians to challenge the injustice of the Spanish conquest throughout the colonial period. Their protests, in addition to Las Casas, laid the foundations of the Brown Church. It is to them we now turn.

3

MULTICULTURAL VOICES OF COLONIAL RESISTANCE

Garcilaso de la Vega el Inca, Guaman Poma,
and Sor Juana Inés de la Cruz

As A CHILD I WAS TOLD, "The Romeros are from Chihuahua, from northern Mexico; we were 'hacendados' and 'Spanish,' and that's why my abuelito was six foot five and had green eyes. We lost our family fortune during the Mexican Revolution when my dad's abuelito cashed in his gold and silver to support Pancho Villa, and he died of a broken heart while rocking on a wooden chair and gazing upon a chest full of worthless revolutionary paper money." Even as a professor of Chicana/o studies and Latin American history, it has taken me many years to sift through the reality and folklore of my family's history. As far as I can tell, the Romeros did come from wealth and privilege, and indeed lost the family fortune during the Revolution. They also must have had something of a compassionate heart for supporting a revolutionary like Pancho Villa. At the same time, however, I always intuited arrogance and inaccuracy in my family's repeated claims that we were "Spanish." If we were Spanish, then why is my skin so dark? Why did some of my relatives look Middle Eastern? Why did some have almond eyes? Why did I suspect traces of African ancestry? And then my DNA test results came in.

I am *La Raza Cósmica*.[1] I am Chinese (43.5%); Native American (18.9%); Manchurian and Mongolian (2.1%); Siberian (.4%); broadly Chinese and Southeast Asian (5.8%); broadly Northern Asian and Native American (1.9%); broadly East Asian and Native American (.8%); Iberian (14%); broadly Southern European (6.1%); broadly European (.6%); Congolese (.5%); Senegambian & Guinean (2%); Nigerian (.1%); broadly West African (.3%); broadly Sub-Saharan African (.2%); South Asian (.3%); North African & Arabian (.1%); broadly Western Asian & North African (.3%); and unassigned (4%). I am blessed to have the blood of most of the cultural family groups of the world—Asian, Native American, European, African, and Middle Eastern—coursing through my veins.

I've been teaching about Africans and Asians in colonial Mexico for more than a decade, and I finally now know that their history runs through my own blood too! Africans in Mexico are known as the forgotten "third root" ("tercera raíz")[2] and it is estimated that 120,000 African slaves were forcibly settled in "New Spain" between 1519 and 1659.[3] During these years, Mexico received two-thirds of all African slaves sent to Spanish colonies in the Americas, and by 1650, the black and Afro-mestizo population of Mexico numbered more than 135,000. Black slaves were imported as chattel into New Spain following the decimation of the indigenous population as a result of the conquest—the native population of central Mexico plummeted from 25,000,000 in 1519 to 1,075,000 by 1605.[4] Black slaves labored in plantations, mines, and textile factories, or *obrajes*, and African slave migration outpaced Spanish immigration until

---

[1]The concept of La Raza Cósmica was developed by José Vasconcelos in his 1925 essay of the same title. According to Vasconcelos, Latin America possessed a divine destiny to serve as the cradle of a fifth, cosmic race that drew from all of the races of the earth. Though a progressive thesis for its time, a closer reading of the essay reveals strong bias in favor of the Spanish heritage of Mexico and racist attitudes towards Africans and Asians. See José Vasconcelos, *The Cosmic Race/ La Raza Cosmica* (Baltimore: Johns Hopkins University Press, 1997).

[2]*Afro America: La Tercera Raíz* (Veracruz: Instituto Veracruzano de la Cultura: CONACULTA: Gobierno Federal, 2010).

[3]David M. Davidson, "Negro Slave Control and Resistance in Colonial Mexico, 1519-1650," *Hispanic American Historical Review* 46, no. 3 (1966): 236. New Spain was the colonial name for Mexico.

[4]Davidson, "Negro Slave Control," 236-37.

1700.[5] Although some black freedmen from Seville arrived in Mexico, and some like Juan Gárrido even achieved a relatively high social status within colonial society, the vast majority of Africans occupied the lowest rungs of the racial and socioeconomic caste system of New Spain.[6] Black Mexicans did not take their oppression sitting down, and in 1537, African slaves of New Spain staged the second armed revolt in all of the Americas.[7] Between 1725 and 1768, five slave revolts shook the Veracruz area of eastern Mexico. Runaway slaves were known as *cimarrones*, and the autonomous communities which they established were called maroons. The most famous Mexican maroon community was founded by a Congolese rebel leader known as Gaspar Yanga, and his memorial can be visited in Veracruz today. African culture and identity continues to thrive in Mexico, and 1.4 million Mexicanos presently self-identify as Afro-Mexican.[8] Mixed race "Blaxicans" are also rising in the United States as important members of the US Latina/o community.[9] I am proud to be able to claim this heritage as part of my multilayered racial identity, *y estoy muy orgulloso de tener familia que son Blaxican, también.*[10]

Thousands of Asians also came to Mexico during the colonial period as slaves, servants, and sailors. They were a diverse group from China, the Philippines, Japan, and India, and they traveled to Mexico as part of the Manila Galleon trade of 1565–1815.[11] During this era, Manila galleons, or "China ships," transported thousands of Asian migrants and a wide variety of goods and luxury items to colonial Mexico. It is estimated

[5]Davidson, "Negro Slave Control," 236-37; Douglas Richmond, "The Legacy of African Slavery in Colonial Mexico, 1519-1810," *The Journal of Popular Culture* 35, no. 2 (2001): 5.

[6]Richmond, "The Legacy of African Slavery," 2-3; Patricia Seed, "Social Dimensions of Race: Mexico City, 1753," *The Hispanic American Historical Review* 62, no. 4 (1982): 569.

[7]Richmond. "Legacy of African Slavery," 9-10.

[8]NPR, "Now Counted by Their Country, Afro-Mexicans Grab Unprecedented Spotlight," *All Things Considered*, February 6, 2016, www.npr.org/2016/02/06/465710473/now-counted-by -their-country-afro-mexicans-grab-unprecedented-spotlight.

[9]Ebony Bailey, "'Blaxicans of L.A.': Capturing Two Cultures in One," *Los Angeles Times*, July 21, 2015, www.latimes.com/local/moments/la-me-scm-blaxicans-20150715-story.html.

[10]"and I am also very proud of having family members who are Blaxican."

[11]Edward R. Slack Jr., "The Chinos in New Spain: A Corrective Lens for a Distorted Image," *Journal of World History* 20, no. 1 (2009): 35.

that 40,000–100,000 Asian immigrants came to Mexico during the two and a half centuries of the Manila Galleon trade. My genes tell the story of the Manila Galleon trade because it was during this time period that Native American, Spanish, East and West African, South Asian, Middle Eastern, and East Asian all came together in my blood to form "Mexican."

Knowing this history, and how my genes corroborate this history, makes me feel betrayed. I feel like I have been lied to my whole life. I know now that my family's obsession with whiteness reflects the values of the three-hundred-year-old colonial caste system that idolized "Spanish" racial identity. As part of this racial hierarchy, those deemed "Spanish" reigned supreme and received special socioeconomic, political, and religious benefits and privileges; those racially categorized as "Indian" and "African" were at the bottom; and the *castas*, or mixed race individuals of Spanish and indigenous ancestry (*mestizos*) or Spanish and African heritage (*mulatos*) occupied an intermediary racial status and lived their lives on the edges of the Spanish world.[12] In fact, the Spanish created an insidious system of 14 to 20 official categories of racial mixture.[13] Other categories included *Castizo* (light-skinned mestizo); *Morisco* (light-skinned mulato); *Zambo* (Black-Indian); *ahí te estás* (there you are); and *tente en el aire* (hold yourself suspended in mid-air).[14] These categories were fluid, depending on phenotype and wealth, and some passed into the Spanish realm by gaining wealth, becoming a priest, or being appointed to a high governmental post.[15] In such cases, racial standing was raised to the level of "Spaniard"—sometimes through the issuance of certificates called *limpieza de sangre* (blood cleansing) or petitions of *gracias al sacar* (dispensation). In the words of Latin American historian Bruce Castleman,

---

[12]Seed, "Social Dimensions of Race," 572-73, 581, 583; Benjamin Keene, *A History of Latin America: Volume I* (Boston: Houghton Mifflin Company, 1992), 109-115.

[13]Magali M. Carrera, "Locating Race in Late Colonial Mexico," *Art Journal* 57, no. 3 (1998): 38.

[14]Seed, "Social Dimensions of Race," 572-73.

[15]Bruce A. Castleman, "Social Climbers in a Colonial Mexican City: Individual Mobility Within the Sistema de Castas in Orizaba, 1777-1791," *Colonial Latin American Review* 10, no. 2 (2001): 241.

Calidad [racial quality] was fundamentally a social construction, and so if a person claimed to be español, conformed to the norms of español society, and was accepted as español by that society, then that person was español no matter how many yndio [sic] ancestors he or she may have had.[16]

Idolatry lay at the center of the sistema de castas, and, as evidenced by the racial claims of many US Latinas/os, it still does today. Those from Spain, or those who imagined themselves from Spain, idolized themselves and their culture as the supreme manifestation of the image of God. According to their twisted, unbiblical logic, those from Spain possessed a monopoly on Jesus and cultural civility, and in order to become his follower, one had to first become a Spaniard. They confused and conflated Spanish culture with Christianity and thereby idolized themselves. This idolization of Spanish culture and identity is blasphemy, and continues to pervade Latin American and US Latina/o media, society, and even churches, to the present day.

Through their racial colonization project, the Spaniards missed the truth of the Bible and the gospel message. Instead of celebrating and honoring the "glory and honor" or community cultural wealth of the indigenous, African, and Asian peoples they encountered, and respecting them as children of God in their own right and uniqueness, the Spaniards idolized themselves and set themselves up as the cultural standard for the image of God.

Out of the ashes of Spanish racial imperialism and the sistema de castas, God raised up multicultural mestizo, indigenous, Spanish, and male and female voices to challenge the perverted racial and sexist logic of the Spanish colonial project. Following the important footsteps of Montesinos and Las Casas in the sixteenth century, Garcilaso de la Vega el Inca (mestizo), Guaman Poma de Ayala (indigenous), and Sor Juana Inés de la Cruz (Spanish/mestiza) struggled for racial and gender equality and laid the second layer of foundation of the Brown Church in the seventeenth century. Through their life stories we learn that there is great

---

[16]Castleman, "Social Climbers in a Colonial Mexican City," 236.

power when we, as people of color and members of marginalized communities, leverage our God-given community cultural wealth toward the promotion of social justice and biblical empowerment.

GARCILASO DE LA VEGA EL INCA

Garcilaso de la Vega was a mestizo born in Peru during the first generation of the Spanish conquest. His father, Captain Sebastián Garcilaso de la Vega Vargas, was a conquistador, and his mother, Chimpu Oclla, was of royal Inca lineage.[17] Though his parents never married, Garcilaso el Inca was raised in his father's house with most of the privilege afforded the offspring of the conquistador elite. In fact, Garcilaso was not alone among other mestizo offspring of Spanish conquistadors and members of the royal Inca nobility of the land. He received a private tutor, and was instructed in Latin, reading, writing, and mathematics. In the pattern of Spanish nobility, he was also taught swordsmanship, horsemanship, and how to use a lance.

As a child, Garcilaso often visited his Inca mother, who was the granddaughter of Tupa Inca Yupanqui, the last great emperor of the undivided Inca empire. At family gatherings he was taught the oral tradition and history of the Inca. In 1560, at the age of 20, Garcilaso immigrated to Spain and lived in the home of his uncle, Alonso Vargas y Figueroa, who lived in Córdoba.[18] For the next thirty years, he dedicated himself to an intellectual life, which was supported by a modest inheritance from his father and uncle. Garcilaso studied history, Latin, Italian, and the Greek and Roman classics, and modeled himself after a "knightly chronicler"—a historian, poet and soldier.[19] His two most important publications include *Royal Commentaries of the Incas* and *General History of Peru*. *Royal Commentaries* holds a unique place in the canon of Peruvian literature for its pioneering articulation of

---

[17]Garcilaso de la Vega El Inca, *Royal Commentaries of the Incas and General History of Peru*, abridged, trans. Harold V. Livermore and ed. Karen Spalding (Indianapolis: Hackett, 2006), xiv-xv.

[18]de la Vega, *Royal Commentaries*, xvi; Garcilaso de la Vega, *Comentarios Reales de los Incas* (Lima: Fondo Editorial Universidad Inca Garcilaso de la Vega, 2016), 16.

[19]de la Vega, *Royal Commentaries*, xviii.

Hispanic and Andean mestizaje, and for its early defense of the indigenous population. It has in fact been called the most important book of Peru.[20]

In *Royal Commentaries of the Incas* and *General History of Peru*, Garcilaso de la Vega makes three distinct contributions to the Brown Church. He is the first public figure to own and claim his mixed-race mestizo identity as a symbol of pride. Secondly, as a mestizo, his writings also elevate indigenous Inca culture. Lastly, in the tradition of Las Casas, his books detail the horrors of the Spanish conquest. In fact, his *Royal Commentaries of the Incas* was so controversial that it inspired the rebellion of fellow mestizo Tupac Amaru II in 1780, and, in 1782, the book was banned by King Charles III for its potential to inspire revolutionary foment.[21]

Although the term *mestizo* was considered an insult in the colonial Americas, Garcilaso claimed the term as a badge of honor. In *Royal Commentaries*, he writes:

> The children of Spaniards by Indians are called *mestizos*, meaning that we are a mixture of the two races. The word was applied by the first Spaniards who had children by Indian women, and because it was used by our fathers, as well as on account of its meaning, I call myself by it in public and am proud of it.[22]

Like Garcilaso, Latinas/os are culturally, and, in most cases, genetically, mixed race. Our mestizaje has only grown more beautiful and intense over the centuries since Garcilaso first penned these words. We are of diverse indigenous ancestries, as well as African, Spanish, Chinese, Japanese, Korean, Indian, Portuguese, Lebanese, Jewish, German, Armenian, and many other ethnicities. Both individually and collectively, we embody the "glory and honor of the nations" and uniquely reflect the image of God to the world. Rather than a badge of shame, we celebrate our cultural diversity as a gift from God—our gift to the world. We are the Brown Church.

---

[20]de la Vega, *Comentarios Reales*, 16-17.
[21]de la Vega, *Royal Commentaries*, xxv.
[22]de la Vega, *Royal Commentaries*, 88.

Like Las Casas before him, Garcilaso de la Vega elevated the history and culture of the indigenous peoples. Unlike Las Casas, however, Garcilaso did so as a mestizo and cultural insider. Drawing from the oral histories of his childhood and the traditions and "knot" recordings of the Inca,[23] he told the story of the Inca from their own perspective and sought to correct the earlier biased histories penned by the scribes of the Spanish conquerors.

The stakes were high, because if the Spanish historians were right, then the natives were Aristotelian "natural slaves," bereft of reason, natural law, and culture, and therefore the Spaniards were justified in brutalizing and colonizing them in the name of Christianity and Western civilization. If Garcilaso de la Vega was right, then the Incas ruled the pre-conquest Andes with justice, fairness, and a cultural sophistication rivaling that of any city in Europe.

De la Vega compared the Inca capital of Cusco to that of ancient Rome. Both were said to have ruled justly over diverse ethnic groups, created enlightened legal systems, and engendered famous historical figures.[24] According to de la Vega, the Inca kings of Peru ruled benignly over their subjects. Those defeated in conquest were welcomed with great banquets and were allowed to continue in their previous laws and rights, unless there was strong conflict with the laws of the Inca empire. In direct contrast to Spanish rule, tribute was light, and "soldiers were never allowed to rob or sack provinces or kingdoms that were reduced by force of arms to surrender."[25] De la Vega also goes to great lengths to highlight the benevolent treatment of the poor in Inca times. Kings were called *Huacchacúyac* or "lover and benefactor of the poor," and, according to royal law, indigenous communities were required to till the land of widows, the poor, and disabled, before attending to the agricultural needs of the able-bodied population.[26]

---

[23]de la Vega, *Royal Commentaries*, 2, 34. Knotted cord records were called "quipu."
[24]de la Vega, *Royal Commentaries*, 64.
[25]de la Vega, *Royal Commentaries*, 33, 34.
[26]de la Vega, *Royal Commentaries*, 9, 27, 28.

Finally, in an effort to further highlight the cultural splendor of his indigenous maternal line, de la Vega heaps high praise on Incan architectural achievements. He extolls the grand fortress of Cusco and other "marvelous buildings, fortresses, temples, royal palaces, gardens, storehouses, roads, and other constructions of great excellence."[27]

No doubt, de la Vega's historical account reflects some romantic bias passed on to him by his elite Inca family members. Moreover, his commentaries are also probably aimed at justifying the continued political power of his family under the Spanish colonial regime. Nonetheless, his writings are still immensely valuable, for they represent a native view of the Inca from the perspective of the Inca themselves.

In part two of the *Royal Commentaries*, de la Vega contrasts the enlightened rule of the Inca with the brutality of the Spanish conquest. In its day, part two was deemed so controversial by Spanish royal publishers that they required it to be published separately, under the distinct title, *General History of Peru*. In this text, de la Vega writes specifically to correct the account of the conquest put forth by Spanish historians. According to these chroniclers, Inca King Atahuallpa was himself to blame for the violence and wrath of the conquistadors because he refused to pay tribute to emperor Charles, dashed the Bible on the ground, and declared, "I worship the Sun and Moon, which are immortal. And who told you that your God was the maker of the Universe?"[28]

Garcilaso debunks these European reports and asserts, "The king did not say the words the historians ascribe to him. . . . All this is fabulous and may be set down to the false and flattering reports given to the historians."[29] In response to hearing the draconian demands of the Requerimiento, and threats of "war, fire, and the sword," de la Vega states that the Inca emperor "was filled with sadness, supposing that those whom he and his Indians called Viracochas . . . had turned into mortal

---

[27] de la Vega, *Royal Commentaries*, 71.
[28] de la Vega, *Royal Commentaries*, 105.
[29] de la Vega, *Royal Commentaries*, 105-6.

enemies since they made such harsh demands."[30] Atahuallpa then proceeded to ask reasonable questions: Doesn't God have pity and mercy,
too? Why must he pay tribute to the Emperor Charles and not to God or
the pope? The Incan king also presented further sensible questions about
Jesus: "I wish also to know about the good man called Jesus Christ who
never cast his sins on the other and who you say died—if he died of a
sickness or at the hands of his enemies; and if he was included among
the gods before his death or after it."[31]

Instead of responding to the honest questions of the Inca emperor
with good will and sincere discussion, the Spaniards pillaged the
native community. They "left their places and [fell] upon the Indians,
laying hands on them to seize the many gold and silver jewels and
precious stones with which the Indians had adorned their persons to
solemnize the occasion of hearing the embassy of the monarch of the
universe."[32] Subsequently, the Spanish imprisoned Atahuallpa and
killed 3,500 men of fighting age and 1,500 women, children, and el-
derly men. De la Vega continues his account by detailing the unjust
execution of Atahuallpa after his presentation of a ransom payment to
the Spaniards. De la Vega also offers a sympathetic account of the Inca
revolt that took place after the murder of Atahuallpa, and he describes
the unjust seizure and division of indigenous lands and the many
broken promises of the European colonizers.[33]

Much more could be said about the extensive chronicles of Garcilaso
de la Vega el Inca. He stands uniquely as the first mestizo historian and
intellectual of the Brown Church. It is significant to note that though he
condemned the cruelties of the Spanish conquest, he did not give up on
Jesus. Rather, he *saw through* the colonial misrepresentations of Christianity and still encountered Christ. Moreover, he was able to disassociate
the misrepresentations of colonialism from other Spaniards who "were

---

[30]de la Vega, *Royal Commentaries*, 102-3.
[31]de la Vega, *Royal Commentaries*, 104.
[32]de la Vega, *Royal Commentaries*, 104.
[33]de la Vega, *Royal Commentaries*, 106, 111, 122-23.

more moderate and regardful of the honor of God and the expansion of the holy Catholic faith."[34] This remains a difficult task for Brown Christians today in the twenty-first century who still wrestle with the detangling of faith in Jesus from the destructive legacy of colonial Christianity in Latin America and the United States.

As with us all, de la Vega also had blind spots. The most significant was his minimization of the many abuses of the Spanish encomenderos. Although he called out in clear terms the injustice of the initial conquest, he did not offer a systematic critique of the exploitive colonial regime that was established in the years following the conquest of Pizarro and Almagro. It seems de la Vega did not feel comfortable leveling a critique against his Spanish father who was himself an encomendero. In the decades following, indigenous Brown Christian Felipe Guaman Poma de Ayala would come to fill this gap in the analysis of Garcilaso de la Vega El Inca.

FELIPE GUAMAN POMA DE AYALA: *Y NO HAY REMEDIO*

Felipe Guaman Poma was born around 1550 to an elite indigenous family in the province of Huamanga in Southern Peru.[35] According to Guaman Poma himself, his father served as "second in command" of the Inca Empire, and his mother descended from the emperor, Topa Inca Yupanqui.[36] He also had a mestizo half-brother, Padre Martin de Ayala, who, ten to twenty years his senior, was born to his mother and a Spanish conquistador. Unlike Garcilaso de la Vega, Guaman Poma likely learned Spanish as a second language during his late childhood.

Guaman Poma is most famous for his prophetic bilingual publication *The First New Chronicle of the Indies of Peru, Profitable to Faithful Christians*, which was completed in 1615 and 1616.[37] Written in Spanish and

---

[34]de la Vega, *Royal Commentaries*, 111.

[35]Felipe Guaman Poma de Ayala, *The First New Chronicle and Good Government*, trans. David Frye (Indianapolis: Hackett, 2006), vii.

[36]Guaman Poma, *The First New Chronicle*, vii, 6-9.

[37]Guaman Poma, *The First New Chronicle*, vii, xxi-xxii, 6.

Quechua, *The First New Chronicle* is a blend of several written genres of the time, including history, Catholic moral teachings, policy recommendations, and personal prophetic (social justice) reflections. The book is a protest against the injustices suffered by the indigenous peoples of Peru as a consequence of poor colonial governance and clerical abuse.[38] A notable feature of *The First New Chronicle* is its use of hand-drawn illustrations to depict biblical, cultural, and historical themes. In contrast to Garcilaso de la Vega, Felipe Guaman Poma communicates using an explicitly theological and biblical lens. The message of Guaman Poma's 1,100-page tome is simple and direct: the Spanish conquistadors and encomenderos have exploited and ravished the indigenous peoples of Peru contrary to the Bible and Catholic Christian faith; as a result, the indigenous peoples of Peru should be entitled to Christian self-government.

As part of his argument for indigenous autonomy, Guaman Poma asserts that the Inca originally received the Christian message from St. Bartholomew more than 1,500 years before the arrival of the Spanish![39] According to Guaman Poma, Jesus Christ was born, crucified, and resurrected during the reign of the Inca ruler Cinche Roca, and it was St. Bartholomew who first brought the good news of Jesus to the Inca people. The apostle Bartholomew, moreover, convinced the Inca of the truth of the Christian message by performing the "miraculous deed of the Holy Cross" in the province of Collao:

> The first miracle performed by God in this kingdom, through his apostle
> St. Bartholomew, was as follows:
>
> - The pueblo of Cacha would burn with fire from heaven.
> - The saint would be attacked with slings and stones, to kill him, to chase him out of the pueblo.
> - The saint would bring a miracle from God to that province.

---

[38]Victoria Cox, *Guaman Poma de Ayala: Entre los Conceptos Andino y Europeo de Tiempo* (Cuzco: Centro de Estudios Regionales Andinos Bartolomé de Las Casas, 2002), 10.
[39]Guaman Poma, *The First New Chronicle*, 39-40.

■ Through a single miraculous deed of the Holy Cross, an Indian, a native of Carabuco named Anti, would be converted and later baptized with the name Anti Wiracho.[40]

As a reminder of the pre-Hispanic Christian roots of Peru, Guaman Poma claims that "St. Bartholomew left the Holy Cross of Carabuco, which stands to this day as a witness to this holy miracle and the arrival of the blessed apostle of Jesus Christ, St. Bartholomew."[41] Poma ostensibly presents this alternative Christian origins story as a way of countering the claim that Spanish encomenderos were needed in Peru in order to convert the natives from their pagan idolatry. According to Poma, this is not true, because Jesus already brought Christianity to Peru 1,500 years earlier through St. Bartholomew—long before the Spanish ever conquered and imposed their colonial rule upon Peru. In other words, the Inca did not need the Spaniards for their religious benefit and instruction.

In no uncertain terms, Guaman Poma proceeds in *The First New Chronicle* to prophetically denounce the greed, idolatry, and abuses of the Spanish colonizers. He contrasts European debauchery with the moral uprightness of the indigenous peoples, and calls out the hypocrisy of the former. Guaman Poma's opening prologue to Spanish Christian readers declares unabashedly,

> I have found no Indians who are greedy for gold nor silver, nor have I found any who owe a hundred pesos, nor liars, nor gamblers, nor slug-gards, nor whores, nor buggers, nor any who steal from one another. But you have all these ills among yourselves: you are disobedient to your fa-thers, mothers, prelates, and king; and when you blaspheme God, you blaspheme him wholeheartedly. You have all these ills, and you teach them to the poor Indians. . . . It seems to me, Christian, that you are all condemning yourselves to hell. . . . But you have your own idols—your treasuries and your silver—all over the world.[42]

---

[40]Guaman Poma, *The First New Chronicle*, 40.
[41]Guaman Poma, *The First New Chronicle*, 40.
[42]Guaman Poma, *The First New Chronicle*, 99.

According to Guaman Poma, Spaniards pillaged the natives in pursuit
of wealth. They also raped Inca women and girls. Even priests were
not exempt:

> After they had conquered and stolen, the Spaniards began taking the
> women and maidens and deflowering them by force. If they resisted, they
> killed them like dogs and punished them, without fear of God nor of
> justice; nor was there any justice.[43]
>
> Even priests took part in the rape: But the padres and doctrina priests
> pay no attention; they gather in the girls so that they can keep mistresses
> nearby, have dozens of children, multiply the numbers of little mestizos,
> and force unmarried women to work.[44]

Guaman Poma offers further specific critique of encomenderos, mine
owners, low ranking Spanish mule drivers, merchants, and shopkeepers.
He reserved some of his harshest criticism, however, for colonial administrators known as *corregidores*. Corregidores functioned as both judicial
and executive authorities over colonial provinces.[45] They had little over-
sight by higher level officials, and were known for abusing their authority
in the quest for wealth. Corregidores exploited indigenous nobles and
humble classes alike. According to Guaman Poma:

> [Corregidores] live as absolute rulers with little fear of justice or of God,
> throughout the kingdom. One of them will extract thirty thousand pesos
> from a corregimiento and become rich before he leaves, harming the poor
> Indians and the nobles, scorning them, and taking away their offices and
> duties, in this kingdom.[46]
>
> And there is no remedy (y no hay remedio).[47]

For those corregidores who were willing to listen, Guaman Poma prof-
fered pastoral counseling and professional advice. He advised them to
fear God and show a preferential option of concern for the marginalized

---

[43]Guaman Poma, *The First New Chronicle*, 124.
[44]Guaman Poma, *The First New Chronicle*, 150.
[45]Guaman Poma, *The First New Chronicle*, 167.
[46]Guaman Poma, *The First New Chronicle*, 167.
[47]Guaman Poma, *The First New Chronicle*, 173.

indigenous peoples. Guaman Poma also admonished them to stand up to corrupt Spaniards of whatever rank or religious standing:

> First of all, you should do your work as God ordained. Be a good Christian, fear God, and favor the poor of Jesus Christ.
>
> Second, you should be a brave judge, and display justice and a lion's eyes and teeth to the Spaniards, encomenderos, padres, and doctrina priests.[48]

According to Guaman Poma, corregidores should also resist the temptation to punish anyone without sufficient evidence and protect against favoritism by avoiding friendships with other high-ranking Spaniards.[49] Effective corregidores, moreover, should honor all subjects, whether high ranking, or humble Indians, and avoid conflicts of interest through business dealings while in office. In the daring spirit of an Old Testament prophet, Guaman Poma concludes, "Read everything that has been set down and written in these chapters, the right and the wrong, in this *Chronicle*, so that you might punish the wrong in your own spirit and flesh first, and might honor what is right."[50]

For all of his prophetic fire and spiritual insight, Felipe Guaman Poma possessed two analytical blind spots. The first was sexism. Although Andean peoples structured gender relations before the conquest based on notions of male and female complementarity, it appears that Poma came to embrace the machísmo that prevailed in Spanish colonial culture.[51] His adoption of paternalistic European values is reflected in the following quotation from *The First New Chronicle*, which blames women unilaterally for the fall of humankind:

> Do not be shocked, women! Women committed the first sin: Eve sinned with the apple, breaking God's commandment. Thus you began the first idolatry, woman, and you served the demons. All of that is a matter of mockery and lies. Leave it all behind, and devote yourself to the Most Holy Trinity.[52]

---

[48]Guaman Poma, *The First New Chronicle*, 177.
[49]Guaman Poma, *The First New Chronicle*, 178.
[50]Guaman Poma, *The First New Chronicle*, 177-78.
[51]Guaman Poma, *The First New Chronicle*, 26, 50.
[52]Guaman Poma, *The First New Chronicle*, 50.

Thankfully, Sor Juana Inés de la Cruz would come along less than a century later to offer a necessary corrective.

Guaman Poma's second glaring blind spot was his paternalism toward Indian commoners.[53] Throughout *The First New Chronicle,* Poma depicts himself as a noble descendant of the Inca elite whose job it is to decry injustice on behalf of the poor. He does not give them voice, nor does he assign them agency.

Despite these shortcomings, Felipe Guaman Poma de Ayala was a monumental indigenous prophet of the Brown Church. He decried, in no uncertain Christian terms, the horrendous abuses of the Spanish colonial regime and, in the process, invented a new interdisciplinary and multilingual prophetic genre that combined history, law, politics, theology, and art. In its humble way, this book follows in this tradition. Along with Las Casas, Guaman Poma was one of the earliest and foremost Brown theologians. As an indigenous Christian, however, he rightfully extended the protestations of Las Casas to include the demand for Andean political autonomy.

SOR JUANA INÉS DE LA CRUZ

Juana Ramírez de Asbaje—better known as Sor Juana Inés de la Cruz— stepped into the prophetic role of challenging patriarchy and machísmo in colonial New Spain and became the first mujerista theologian of the Brown Church and "first feminist of the Americas."[54] Through her writings, theological treatises, poems, plays, and even social justice– themed worship hymns, or, *villancicos,* Sor Juana critiqued the patriarchal theology of the Catholic Church, which reserved the powers of

---

[53]Guaman Poma, *The First New Chronicle,* 26.

[54]Theresa A. Yugar, *Sor Juana Inés de la Cruz: Feminist Reconstruction of Biography and Text* (Wipf & Stock, 2014), xii, 39. Chicana and white feminists alike have claimed Sor Juana as representative of their respective movements. Alicia Gaspar de Alba has written influential works on Sor Juana from a Chicana feminist and lesbian perspective. See, for example, Gaspar de Alba, *Sor Juana's Second Dream: A Novel* (Albuquerque: University of New Mexico Press, 1999) and *[Un] framing the "Bad Woman": Sor Juana, Malinche, Coyolxauhqui, and Other Rebels with a Cause* (Austin: University of Texas Press, 2014). For a white feminist perspective, see Pamela Kirk, *Sor Juana Inés de la Cruz: Religion, Art, and Feminism* (New York: Continuum, 1998).

rational thought for men and limited women to a subservient status as "pure, modest, silent, and virtuous" wives and nuns.[55] She also strove to reconcile the clashing cultural world views of Spanish and indigenous in the Americas. In the powerful words of Latina theologian Theresa Yugar:

> Sor Juana Inés de la Cruz challenged the Church to be more authentic to Jesus' mission of inclusivity of all people, Christian, non-Christian, pagan, non-pagan, indigenous, *mestizo* and black. For her, each had a place in Christian salvation history. In her lifetime, she bridged different cultures and worldviews.[56]

Juana Inés de Asbaje y Ramírez de Santillana was born in Mexico in 1651 as the illegitimate daughter of middle class Criolla mother and a Spanish captain.[57] As one of six full and half siblings, she was raised by her mother, Doña Isabel Ramírez, in a single-parent Criollo household of relative wealth. Notably, her mother never married and was the head administrator of two haciendas owned by the Ramírez de Santillana family.[58] As is the case for many Latinas/os today, Sor Juana's force of character was no doubt inspired by her mother's example.

Juana displayed passion for learning at a very young age, and at the age of three she was sent to an *Amigas* school with her older sister.[59] Amigas were informal schools organized by wealthy women where girls could get a basic education.

Young Juana loved learning so much that her desire to acquire knowledge was stronger than her desire to eat. After learning that there was a university in Mexico City that only men could attend, at the age of six or seven Juana tried to convince her mother to dress her in boys' clothes and send her to live with family members in Mexico City so that

---

[55]Yugar, *Sor Juana*, 7.

[56]Yugar, *Sor Juana*, 23.

[57]Nina M. Scott, "Sor Juana Inés de la Cruz: 'Let Your Women Keep Silence in the Churches . . . ,'" *Women's Studies International Forum* 8, no. 5 (1985): 512.

[58]Scott, "Sor Juana Inés de la Cruz," 41, 43, 44.

[59]Sor Juana Inés de la Cruz, "Answer by the Poet to the Most Illustrious Sister Filotea de la Cruz," trans. William Little, accessed September 27, 2018, http://dept.sfcollege.edu/hfl/hum2461/pdfs/SJICAnswer.pdf.

she could eventually attend the university. Because formal education was not available, Juana dedicated herself to self-study. She read the books from her grandfather's library and taught herself Latin. To discipline herself to learn, she would cut off her hair. Juana's self-imposed penalty for not meeting her learning goals was to cut her hair even shorter!

At the age of thirteen, Juana moved to live with family members in Mexico City, where she continued her informal studies and gained mastery of the Latin language. In 1663, she was invited to live in the viceregal court and become a "lady in waiting." As a member of the royal court, Juana wrote poetry and plays that challenged patriarchal values and defended the right of women to study and pursue education.[60] In a poem titled "Hombres Necios" ("Foolish Men"), she wrote, "Thus I prove with all my forces the ways your arrogance does battle: for in your offers and your demands we have devil, flesh, and world: a man."[61] Her literary prowess garnered her acclaim even at a young age.

Arriving in adulthood in colonial Spanish society, Juana had two options: marry a man of her same social standing, or become a nun. She chose the latter so that she could devote her life to study and writing:

> I entered a religious order because, although I was aware that that lifestyle had certain things (I'm talking about incidental not official ones), or rather many things that were abhorrent to my character—given my total rejection of marriage—it was the least objectionable and the most respectable one I could choose with regard to my desire to safeguard my salvation.[62]

After a short stint in the ascetic convent of San José, Juana found her place as a sister of the convent of San Jerónimo and Santa Paula.[63] It is altogether fitting that Santa Paula was a pioneering female leader of the early Christian church who founded the monastic movement and helped translate the earliest version of the Latin Bible. With formal university study forbidden to her as a young woman, Sor Juana continued her

---

[60]Yugar, *Sor Juana*, 49-51.
[61]Yugar, *Sor Juana*, 51.
[62]Sor Juana, "Answer by the Poet," 6.
[63]Yugar, *Sor Juana*, 54.

pursuit of self-study and famously remarked, "Instead, I only had a mute book for a teacher and an oblivious inkwell for a fellow student."[64]

Sor Juana's great intellect was recognized by both the religious establishment and broader Mexican and Spanish society. Her intellectual reputation and literary giftings garnered her the titles "The Tenth Muse," "The Phoenix of America," and the "Mexican Phoenix." Sor Juana wrote famous plays, poetry, and theological essays, including "First Dream," "Love in More a Labyrinth," "Letter Worthy of Athena," and "Answer by the Poet to the Most Illustrious Sister Filotea de la Cruz." She even wrote sixteen sets of villancicos, or church carols/hymns, some of which honored the feminist legacy of St. Catherine of Alexandria. Sor Juana had great affinity for St. Catherine of Alexandria, who is said to have convinced Egypt's pagan philosophers of the truth of the Christian faith in the fourth century.[65]

Sor Juana's writings drew protest and criticism from many in the religious establishment. Male religious authorities condemned her poetry, plays, and writings as profane "secular literature," inappropriate for a nun called to the religious life. Instead, she was admonished to focus her study on the sacred texts of Scripture as opposed to "secular" topics such as literature, science, mathematics and the humanities. Sor Juana was rebuked by Catholic officials for rejecting her subordinate role below that of men and God. In their view, she faced divine judgment for continuing her secular studies.[66]

A firestorm of controversy rained down upon Sor Juana for her "Letter Worthy of Athena." In this letter Sor Juana challenged the Christology of a sermon by Antonio de Viera, a renowned Portuguese Jesuit theologian. Viera asserted that Christ's greatest expression of love was that "He absented Himself from us" following the resurrection.[67] In contradiction of Viera, Sor Juana argued a different Christological perspective by claiming

---

[64]Sor Juana, "Answer by the Poet," 10.
[65]Sor Juana, "Answer by the Poet," 20.
[66]Yugar, *Sor Juana,* 66.
[67]Yugar, *Sor Juana,* 64.

that the greatest gift of Jesus was his continued presence with humanity through the celebration of Mass and the *Santa Cena* (the Lord's Supper). Sor Juana's public disagreement drew the ire of Fernández de Santa Cruz, Bishop of Puebla, who chastised her in two written publications. These publications included *Carta Atenagorica* ("Letter Worthy of Athena") and a second theological treatise, which disputed Sor Juana's Christology. This persecution also brought Sor Juana close to the dangerous fires of the Spanish Inquisition: "But all this has pushed me closer to the fire of persecution, to the crucible of torment; and to such an extent that people have gone so far as to request that I be forbidden to study."[68]

"Answer by the Poet to the Most Illustrious Sister Filotea de la Cruz" ("La Respuesta a Sor Filotea de la Cruz") (1691) was Sor Juana's response to the maelstrom of public ridicule and critique. In *La Respuesta*, she defends her right as a woman to study secular and theological topics, based on Scripture, established Christian authority, and church doctrine. Early in her essay, Sor Juana asserts that her love of learning came from God:

> What is really true—and I will not deny it . . . is that since the first light of reason dawned on me my inclination toward letters was so intense and powerful that neither reprimands by others, of which I have had many, nor self-reflection, of which I have done not a little, have been sufficient for me to stop pursuing this natural impulse that God put in me.[69]

In justification of her investigation of so-called secular subjects, Sor Juana argues that an understanding of the sciences and humanities better prepared her for the study of theology. In making this claim, Sor Juana was several centuries ahead of her time, because it is just now that theologians in many esteemed seminaries of the United States are beginning to argue for a similar interdisciplinarity. Even so, it is far from the norm, and most theologians find themselves cordoned off from serious training in the hard sciences, social sciences, and humanities. In perhaps one of the earliest arguments for theological interdisciplinarity, Sor Juana asserts,

---

[68]Sor Juana, "Answer by the Poet," 16.
[69]Sor Juana, "Answer by the Poet," 5.

I proceeded in this way, as I've said, always directing the path of my studies toward the summit of holy Theology. In order to reach it, it seemed to me necessary to ascend the ladder of the humanities, for how can one who does not first know the ancillary fields possibly understand the queen of sciences? Without logic, how could I possibly know the general and specific methods by which the Holy Scriptures are written? . . . Without arithmetic could one possibly comprehend the computation of so many years, days, months, hours, and the mysterious seventy weeks like those found in Daniel. . . . Without a firm command of both branches of the law, how can one comprehend the books of the Law? . . . In sum, this Book encompasses all books, and this science includes all sciences (all of which are used to fathom the one Book).[70]

Sor Juana further lays out a direct sexist critique of the prohibitions against her intellectual pursuits. Her argument is based on personal experience, Scripture, and historical examples of women leaders. If academic study is a quality celebrated in men, Sor Juana muses, then why is she being condemned for it? "If they are blameworthy, for the same reason I believe that I am faultless."[71] She proceeds to cite examples of strong female leaders from the Bible, such as Deborah, the Queen of Sheba, Esther, Rahab, and Abigail.[72] To buttress her argument, Sor Juana also presents examples of well-respected female saints and spiritual leaders who were also writers:

Then how is it that the Church has allowed women like Gertrude or Teresa or Birgitta or the nun of Ágreda or many others to write? So now we see that the Church permits women who are saints and those who are not saints to write, for the woman from Ágreda and Maria de la Antigua are not canonized, yet their writings circulate widely.[73]

Finally, in support of her right to study, Sor Juana also appeals to the spiritual authority of well-respected Mexican theologian Juan Díaz de

---

[70]Sor Juana, "Answer by the Poet," 7, 8.
[71]Sor Juana, "Answer by the Poet," 18.
[72]Sor Juana, "Answer by the Poet," 19-20.
[73]Sor Juana, "Answer by the Poet," 28.

Arce. Although not supportive of female writing and teaching in the public sphere, Arce believed that nuns should be allowed to engage privately in such activities. According to Arce, "It is not only licit for them to study, write, and teach privately, but it is very beneficial and useful for them to do so."[74] As unprogressive as this may sound to twenty-first century ears, it did afford Sor Juana support for her position and helped lay the groundwork for theological egalitarianism.

In response to the critics who chastised her for disagreeing with the Jesuit theologian Viera, Sor Juana claims that it was entirely within her right to do so. Though differing with the perspective of Viera, her theological ruminations did not violate any church rule or policy: "If my crime lies in the Letter Worthy of Athena, was that piece anything more than simply relating my views with all of the sanctions for which I am grateful to our Holy Mother Church? For if she, with her most holy authority, does not forbid me so, why must others so forbid me?"[75] The implication, according to Sor Juana, is that she was being criticized simply for disagreeing with a male theologian. What crime or offense against God is that? It is simply because she is a woman.

Sor Juana also defends her right to compose poetry. Poetry is her natural gifting, and is found throughout the Bible in books such as Psalms, Job, and Jeremiah. Such verse is also used in Catholic hymns and worship, and other Christian women have been lauded for their use of poetry. The explanation once again must be that she is a woman. "Other women have been commended by the church who have used poetry. Therefore, if the evil lies in verses being used by a woman, we have already seen how many women have used them commendably. Then, what is the problem with me being one?"[76] Like Jesus, Sor Juana felt scorned and persecuted without cause.[77]

The weightiness of Sor Juana's challenges to Mexican patriarchal authority cannot be overstated. In a day and age when the Catholic Church

---

[74]Sor Juana, "Answer by the Poet," 22.
[75]Sor Juana, "Answer by the Poet," 29.
[76]Sor Juana, "Answer by the Poet," 31.
[77]Yugar, *Sor Juana*, 77.

ruled with an iron male hand and all the authority and tools of the Spanish Inquisition, Sor Juana fought mightily with her pen, with little to no political or spiritual support. She also took on the Bishop of Puebla, the man who would become chief representative of the Spanish Inquisition in New Spain.

In the end, the weight of persecution grew too heavy for Sor Juana Inés de la Cruz, and she experienced a spiritual, emotional, and, some would say—physical—martyrdom. In 1691, under pressure of the Bishop of Puebla, Sor Juana sold off her library, which was renowned as the largest in all of Latin America. Then, on February 8, 1694, she signed a public statement of repentance "using blood from her veins as ink."[78] Her signature read, "I, Sister Juana Inés de la Cruz, the worst in the world" ("Yo, Sor Juana Inés de la Cruz, la peor de todas.")[79] For the last year of her life, Sor Juana returned to her religious order to live a life of penance and quiet reflection. On April 17, 1695, at the still young age of 45, she died.[80] Like Mirrha-Catarina de San Juan, upon her death, the religious authorities sought to erase her memory by burning her papers. Sor Juana's works were suppressed for three hundred years and did not surface again publicly until 1952. Though the Latin American church of the status quo tried to stamp her out, in the words of Jesus, "nothing is hidden that will not be disclosed, nor is anything secret that will not become known and come to light" (Lk 8:17). The Brown Church honors Sor Juana Inés de la Cruz as the first Latina feminist intellectual and theologian of the Americas.

CONCLUSION

The Brown Church in the twenty-first century is surrounded by a great multiethnic "cloud of witnesses" (Heb 12:1) from the Latin American colonial period. Antonio de Montesinos, Bartolomé de Las Casas, Garcilaso de la Vega el Inca, Guaman Poma de Ayala, and Sor Juana Inés de

---

[78]Yugar, *Sor Juana*, 15.
[79]Yugar, *Sor Juana*, 15.
[80]Yugar, *Sor Juana*, 15, 56, 58-59.

la Cruz—Spanish, indigenous, mestizo—male and female—each in their own way challenged the racial, patriarchal, and socioeconomic status quo of the colonial church. Far ahead of their time, hundreds of years before the creation of ethnic studies, they declared in a unified voice: *Christianity that is faithful to Jesus, La Virgen, and Holy Scripture can never be a racist, classist, and sexist religion.*

The historical picture painted in the previous chapters is only a brief introduction. Indeed, it has only scratched the surface of the history of prophetic Christianity during the Latin American colonial period. If space and time permitted, many other leaders of the Brown Church could have been included, such as the mestiza Santa Rosa de Lima; Mirrha-Catarina de San Juan—"La China Poblana"; the black saint, St. Martin de Porres; and Friar Martín de Rada, the "Las Casas of the Philippines." Despite its limited scope, this chapter hopefully presents an inspiring impressionistic picture of the multicultural mothers and fathers of the Brown Church.

Less than two centuries after the protestations of Sor Juana, the border would cross the Brown Church. Fueled by the false theology of Manifest Destiny, Anglo Americans would conquer and colonize the Southwest and seize half of Mexican territories as part of the unjust US-Mexico War of 1846–1848. In response to the spiritual and military conquest of the Southwest, the Brown Church of the United States was born.

4

PADRE ANTONIO JOSÉ MARTÍNEZ, THE U.S.-MEXICO WAR, AND THE BIRTH OF "BROWN"

MEXICANS and other US Latinas/os became *Brown* on February 2, 1848.

On that day, Mexico signed the Treaty of Guadalupe-Hidalgo, bringing the unjust US-Mexico War to its inequitable conclusion. Although the supposed cause of the war was a disputed 150-mile sliver of territory between the Río Grande and the Nueces River in Texas, the lopsided treaty gave the United States almost half of Mexican territory in exchange for 15 million dollars.[1] As an outcome of the war, the United States swallowed up California, New Mexico, Nevada and parts of Colorado, Arizona, Utah, and even Oklahoma. In all, the United States stole over half a million square miles from Mexico. The Treaty of Guadalupe-Hidalgo also relegated former Mexicans residing in US territories to a murky legal status somewhere in between that of white and black—what might metaphorically be called "brown." The Mexican-American War set in motion a pattern of structural injustice against Mexicans and other Latina/o groups that continues to the present day.

---

[1]Rodolfo F. Acuña, *Occupied America: A History of Chicanos* (New York: Pearson Longman, 2007), 42, 43, 48; Zaragosa Vargas, *Crucible of Struggle: A History of Mexican Americans from Colonial Times to the Present Era* (Oxford: Oxford University Press, 2011), 79, 101.

Nicholas Trist was sent by the United States to Mexico to act as peace commissioner and negotiate the treaty. In no uncertain terms, he publicly lamented the injustice of the treaty:

> If those Mexicans . . . had been able to look into my heart at that moment, they would have found that the sincere shame I felt as a North American was stronger than theirs as Mexicans. Although I was unable to say it at the time, it was something that any North American should be ashamed of. [2]

Trist was not alone in his lament. Abraham Lincoln and Ulysses S. Grant were also among those who famously decried the US-Mexico War.[3] As a young congressman, Lincoln staked his entire political future on the claim that the war was unjust.[4] Together with other members of Congress, he famously declared that the US-Mexico War "was unnecessarily and unconstitutionally commenced by the President."[5] In prophetic condemnation of President James Polk, Lincoln thundered:

> [Unless Polk could] show that the soil was ours where the first blood of the war was shed . . . then I shall be fully convinced, of what I more than suspect already, that he is deeply conscious of being in the wrong; that he feels the blood of this war, like the blood of Abel, is crying to Heaven against him; that he ordered General Taylor into the midst of a peaceful Mexican settlement, purposely to bring on a war.[6]

It would take Grant many years to publicly confess his opposition to the war. A young solider at the time of the war, Grant did not reveal his true feelings until later in life. In 1877, he confessed to journalist John Russell Young: "I do not think there was ever a more wicked war than that waged by the United States on Mexico. . . . Only I had not moral courage enough to resign. . . . I considered my supreme duty was to my

---

[2]Acuña, *Occupied America*, 48, 50.
[3]Acuña, *Occupied America*, 43.
[4]Abraham Lincoln, "Spot Resolutions," December 22, 1847, accessed September 28, 2018, www .digitalhistory.uh.edu/disp_textbook.cfm?smtid=3&psid=3672.
[5]Abraham Lincoln, "The War with Mexico: Speech in the United States House of Representatives," January 12, 1848, accessed September 28, 2018, teachingamericanhistory.org/library/document /the-war-with-mexico-speech-in-the-united-states-house-of-representatives.
[6]Lincoln, "The War with Mexico."

flag."[7] Grant went so far as to say that he felt the Civil War was God's punishment of the United States for the Mexican-American War:

> To us it [Mexico] was an empire and of incalculable value. . . . The Southern rebellion was largely the outgrowth of the Mexican war. Nations, like individuals, are punished for their transgressions. We got our punishment in the most sanguinary and expensive war of modern times.[8]

As Latinas/os, we do not need Lincoln and Grant to convince us that the US-Mexico War was unjust. From our longstanding viewpoint, the Mexican-American war was a war of aggression. In Mexico it is known as "the US Invasion." We know that the war was provoked and that the US government was greedy for our land. In the words of one Spanish language newspaper of the time: "The American government acted like a bandit who came upon a traveler."[9]

The US-Mexico war was not only an avaricious land grab, but sinful in its theological justification. According to the theology of Manifest Destiny, which undergirded the war as well as westward expansion through Native American territories, Anglo-Saxons had been given a "manifest destiny" by God to conquer and control North America.[10] They possessed a divine calling to kill and plunder Native Americans and Mexicans in order to claim the land for God and to spread democracy and their version of Christianity:

> The old Saxon blood must stride the continent, must command all its northern shores, must here press the grape and the olive, here eat the orange and the fig, and in their own unaided might, erect the altar of civil and religious freedom on the plains of the Californias.[11]

---

[7] John Russell Young, *Around the World with General Grant* (Baltimore: John Hopkins University Press, 2002), 376.

[8] Ulysses S. Grant, "Personal Memoirs. 1885–86. Chapter III. Army Life—Causes of the Mexican War—Camp Salubrity," accessed September 28, 2018, www.bartleby.com/1011/3.html.

[9] Jesús Velasco-Márquez, "A Mexican Viewpoint on the War with the United States," accessed September 28, 2018, www.pbs.org/kera/usmexicanwar/prelude/md_a_mexican_viewpoint.html.

[10] Richard Griswold del Castillo, *The Treaty of Guadalupe Hidalgo: A Legacy of Conflict* (Norman: University of Oklahoma Press, 1990), 4; Acuña, *Occupied America*, 43-44.

[11] Robert F. Heizer and Alan J. Almquist, *The Other Californians: Prejudice and Discrimination Under Spain, Mexico, and the United States to 1920* (Berkeley: University of California Press, 1977), 140.

John O'Sullivan, editor of the *Democratic Review,* coined the term
"Manifest Destiny." He claimed that it was American "destiny to over-
spread the whole North American continent with an immense democratic population."[12] According to Chicano historian Richard Griswold
del Castillo, "The North Americans [believed they] were the pioneers of
the continent, who inevitably would spread the benefits of democracy
and freedom to the lesser peoples [First Nations and Mexicans] inhab-
iting the region."[13] Manifest Destiny was not a fringe ideological
movement. It enjoyed a broad swath of social support ranging from rural
communities, New England poets, northern abolitionists, southern slave
holders, and famous public figures such as Walt Whitman, John Quincy
Adams, and Andrew Jackson.

The diaries of US soldiers at the time reflect the theological conviction
of Manifest Destiny. The following excerpt from the diary of one vol-
unteer officer to his Protestant minister cousin extolls the virtues of
Manifest Destiny and expressed outright cultural and racial disdain for
Mexican clergy:

> I wish I had the power to stop their churches, . . . to bring off this treasure
> hoard of gold and jewels, and to put the greasy priests, monks, friars and
> other officials at work on the public highways as a preliminary step to
> mending their ways. . . . It is perfectly certain that this war is a divine
> dispensation intended to purify and punish this misguided nation. [14]

Unfortunately, some American Catholics were also not immune to the
cultural tribalism and twisted racial logic of Manifest Destiny. One
Catholic soldier wrote: "I cannot help but think, that God has fought
upon our side, to chastize them for their sins."[15]

American soldiers acted on their belief in Manifest Destiny through
brutal violence on the battlefield. Accounts of such military misconduct

---

[12]Griswold del Castillo, *Treaty of Guadalupe Hidalgo,* 4.
[13]Griswold del Castillo, *Treaty of Guadalupe Hidalgo,* 4.
[14]Paul Foos, *A Short, Offhand Killing Affair: Soldiers and Social Conflict During the Mexican-American War* (Chapel Hill: University of North Carolina Press, 2002), 128.
[15]Foos, *A Short, Offhand Killing Affair,* 129.

during the Mexican-American War were often squelched. Highlighting the military abuses committed by American soldiers, and the silencing of voices of opposition, one military private wrote the following to his father:

> The majority of the Volunteers sent here, are a disgrace to the nation; think of one of them shooting a woman while washing in the bank of the river— merely to test his rifle; another tore forcibly from a Mexican woman the rings from her ears. Their officers take no notice of these outrages, and the offenders escape.[16]

One officer commented on the destruction left in the wake of U.S. military incursion in northern Mexico:

> The smiling villages which welcomed our troops on their upward march are now black and smouldering ruins, the gardens and orange groves destroyed, and the inhabitants, who administered to their necessities, have sought refuge in the mountains.[17]

Manifest Destiny formed the theological backbone of American civil religion. As discussed in chapter two, in civil religion, religious clergy work in symbiotic relationship with a narrowly defined civil community and bless their wars and social engineering by bringing assurances of God's favor. A civil community is defined by a set of religious understandings and practices, and, as in the case of the United States, often includes a racial or ethnic component. Membership for most of its members is not voluntary, and children become part of the civil community by birth. Those of the civil community define themselves in relation to "outsiders" and "enemies." In the case of Spanish colonialism, European colonists and conquistadors narrowly defined their own civil community as comprising those of "Spanish," Catholic descent. Natives were the outsiders and quasi-enemies. In the case of the United States, Protestant pastors and theologians brought assurances of God's favor to Anglo colonists through the creation of Manifest Destiny theology, which

---

[16]Foos, *A Short, Offhand Killing Affair*, 116.
[17]Foos, *A Short, Offhand Killing Affair*, 119, 120.

justified settler colonialism and the seizure of native and Mexican lands. For Anglos, Native Americans and Mexicans were racially inferior heathen, and as such should be subjected to the enlightened conquest and rule of the United States. In the present moment, many in the evangelical church of the United States have appropriated civil religion to justify the racist regime of Donald Trump. For them, the American civil community excludes asylees from Central America and undocumented immigrants from Latin America. They limit Christianity to a narrow definition of religious and political beliefs, and exclude from full membership all who do not subscribe to their theological and political bright lines.

As evidenced by the advocacy efforts of Abraham Lincoln, some Anglo allies did rise up to challenge the US-Mexico war in both political and theological terms. As we will see, the war also gave birth to the Brown Church in the United States.

White Quakers and Congregationalists opposed the war on grounds of Christian pacifism and opposition to imperialism and slavery. In *The War with Mexico Reviewed* (1850), Abiel Abbott Livermore challenged the war and its underlying moral, theological, and political justifications.[18] According to Livermore, the war with Mexico was really about expanding the reach of slavery in the United States and lust for land. To these ends, Fourth of July celebrations in the mid-nineteenth century had become co-opted as a form of indoctrination for youth in the ways of war and the poisonous ideology of Manifest Destiny:

> Our fourth-of-July oratory has inserted in youthful veins the deadly virus of warlike passion. . . . The passion for land, also, is a leading characteristic of the American people. . . . The god Terminus is an unknown deity in America. Like the hunger of the pauper boy of fiction, the cry has been, "More, more, give us more."[19]

In no uncertain terms, Livermore also condemned the faulty religious logic of Manifest Destiny. He completely rejected US and European

---

[18]Abiel Abbott Livermore, *The War with Mexico Reviewed* (Boston: American Peace Society, 1850).
[19]Livermore, *The War with Mexico Reviewed*, 12-14.

religious nationalism as unbiblical, and anathema. According to these beliefs, Anglo people were the contemporary "chosen" people of God who were destined to seize the American territories from Native American and Mexican inhabitants of the land. Such darker-skinned peoples were the modern-day Canaanites, and, as the living instantiation of biblical Israel, Anglos held a sacred responsibility to uproot them from their lands and colonize them. Livermore called the United States to repentance for its immoral acts of conquest and colonization:

> Again; the pride of race has swollen to still greater insolence the pride of country, always quite active enough for the due observance of the claims of universal brotherhood. The Anglo-Saxons have been apparently persuaded to think themselves the chosen people, the anointed race of the Lord, commissioned to drive out the heathen, and plant their religion and institutions in every Canaan they could subjugate. The idea of a "destiny," connected with this race, has gone far to justify, if not to sanctify, many an act on either side of the Atlantic; for which both England and the United States, if nations can be personified, ought to hang their heads in shame, and weep scalding tears of repentance.[20]

In recognition for his prophetic pacifistic efforts, Livermore received the American Peace Society prize for "the best review of the Mexican War and the principles of Christianity, and an enlightened statesmanship."[21]

TREATY OF GUADALUPE-HIDALGO

As previously discussed, Mexicans became "brown" through the treaty that ended the unjust war with the United States. According to Article VIII of the Treaty of Guadalupe-Hidalgo, Mexicans could "elect," or choose, to become United States citizens after the war.[22] This might not seem very significant today, but in the nineteenth century, this was substantial insofar

---

[20]Livermore, *The War with Mexico Reviewed*, 8.
[21]Acuña, *Occupied America*, 46.
[22]"Treaty with the Republic of Mexico," February 2, 1848, A Century of Lawmaking for a New Nation: U.S. Congressional Documents and Debates, 1774–1875, The Library of Congress, 929, accessed October 1, 2018, https://lccn.loc.gov/18014905.

as citizenship was a privilege only afforded to those deemed legally "white." In fact, from 1790 until 1952, naturalization was restricted by Congress to "white persons."[23] Therefore, with citizenship and legal whiteness, the former Mexican citizens would theoretically inherit equal socioeconomic and political rights to that of their Anglo counterparts. There was one catch, however: just because they chose to become US citizens did not mean that they automatically became US citizens. Instead, according to Article IX, the right of citizenship would take effect "at the proper time"— an undelineated future point in time that would be determined by Congress at some unspecified future date.

> Mexicans who, in the territories aforesaid, shall not preserve the character of citizens of the Mexican Republic, conformably with what is stipulated in the preceding article, shall be incorporated into the Union of the United States and be admitted *at the proper time* (*to be judged of by the Congress of the United States*) to the enjoyment of all the rights of citizens of the United States.[24]

The Treaty of Guadalupe-Hidalgo granted Mexicans "halfway" citizenship. Mexicans could choose to become US citizens, but they would not actually become citizens until "the proper time (to be judged of by the Congress of the United States)." Congress reluctantly granted us Mexicans the right to become citizens because they wanted our land, and, as part of treaty negotiations with Mexico were required to at least grant citizenship at a future date. They in no way, however, viewed us as their legal or racial equals. Mexicans were deemed mixed-blood Catholic "mongrels" who would pollute the Anglo nation. They did not want to grant citizenship to the estimated 100,000 erstwhile Mexicans, but they were forced to do so out of political expediency in order to receive the payoff of half of the territories of Mexico. In the words of Connecticut congressman Truman Smith,

---

[23]Ian Haney-López, *White By Law: The Legal Construction of Race* (New York: New York University Press, 2006), 1.
[24]Haney-López, *White By Law*, 930.

The standard of morals [of Mexico] is exceedingly low. . . . The country is little better than Sodom. . . . I am free to say that if all the vices which can corrupt the human heart, and all the qualities which reduce man to the level of brute, are to be "annexed" to the virtue and intelligence of the American people, I DO NOT DESIRE TO BELONG TO ANY SUCH UNION.[25]

The political compromise was this: sign the treaty, take the land, and kick the can of full citizenship rights for Mexicans down the road into an unforeseeable future. In other words, as neither legally white nor black, and excluded from full inclusion in the American polity, we Mexicans, and by extension other Latinas/os, became Brown. We were assigned to legal, racial, and political liminality. We've been Brown ever since.[26]

By 1849, the citizenship rights of former Mexicans became a major political issue in California. Delegates to the California state constitutional convention wrestled with the question of which Mexicans would be granted the full rights of citizenship.[27] Six of the delegates to the constitutional convention were Californios, or former upper class Mexican citizens of the landholding class. They had a big decision to make. Would they look after their own privileged interests and seek state citizenship only for themselves and those of their own "Spanish" social class, or would they seek to advocate for the broader interests of all former Mexicans regardless of racial and socioeconomic status? Would they side with the new empire or would they look after the interests of the poor and marginalized of "Galilee" as well? In the end, they decided to protect only their own privilege and, according to the California Constitution of 1849 granted the right to vote only to "every white, male citizen of Mexico who shall have elected to become a citizen of the U.S."[28]

---

[25]Ray John de Aragon, *Padre Martinez and Bishop Lamy* (Las Vegas, NM: The Pan-American Publishing Company, 1978), 47.

[26]Or, to use another metaphor used by renowned Chicana legal scholar Laura Gómez, the Treaty made us "off white." See Laura E. Gómez, *Manifest Destinies: The Making of the Mexican American Race* (New York: New York University Press, 2007), 2.

[27]Griswold del Castillo, *The Treaty of Guadalupe*, 66; Juan F. Perea, et al., *Race and Races: Cases and Resources for a Diverse America* (St. Paul: West Group, 2000), 265-67.

[28]Griswold del Castillo, *The Treaty of Guadalupe*, 66-67.

Because they could pass as white, the Californios gave the vote only to "white" Mexicans. They kicked the majority of Mexicans—mestizo, mulato, indigenous, and black—to the curb.

This has been the curious predicament of Latinas/os in the United States ever since. As "Brown"—somewhere between white and black—a select minority among us has always had the option to slip into whiteness and forget about the rest.[29] The vast majority of Latinas/os, however, have never had this option of assimilating into whiteness because of their skin color and their poor economic standing. Like the Sadducees of Jesus' day, the Californios colluded with Empire. In this historical example it was the upper class Californios; in the twenty-first century it is the Ted Cruzes of our community—those who leverage their education, money, and light pigmentation to gain honorary membership in the white social club of privilege.

As Latinas/os and followers of Jesus, will we opt for whiteness and advantage, or will we stand with the vast majority of our hermanas and hermanos who have no choice but to live in the Goshens of the United States for the rest of their lives? Like Moses, will we choose to share ill-treatment with the people of God rather than the fleeting pleasures of sin, and consider abuse suffered for Christ to be greater wealth than the treasures of the United States (Heb 11:25-26)? This is a serious question for many of the readers of this book, who, by virtue of even having access to this academic material probably enjoy some modicum of educational and economic privilege. Will we opt to assimilate into whiteness and privilege, and turn our backs to the vast majority of Latinas/os who labor under a weight of oppression in the United States? Will we forsake our sisters and brothers of Goshen for the sake of the luxuries of Egypt?

By 1869, Congress had still not explicitly granted citizenship to the erstwhile Mexicans who had elected to become US citizens. Twenty-one

---

[29]According to Laura Gomez, those of Mexican descent could slip into whiteness in the nineteenth century based on a "reverse one-drop rule." Socioeconomic standing plus "one drop" of Spanish blood could make one white in New Mexico, and by extension, the rest of the Southwest. See Gómez, *Manifest Destinies*, 5, 11-12, 142-43.

years later, the "proper time" still had not come, and the issue came to significantly affect even the privileged Californios who had attempted to pass into whiteness. This is clearly demonstrated by the story of Pablo de la Guerra.[30] De la Guerra came from an elite Californio family and had even been a delegate to the convention that crafted the California state constitution.[31] In 1869, he ran for the elected office of district judge, but his Anglo opponents challenged his right to hold office based upon the argument that he, along with thousands of other Californios, were not yet US citizens. Though they had opted for US citizenship two decades before, Congress had not yet formally granted them citizenship. This legal dispute traveled all the way up to the California Supreme Court, which eventually sided with Pablo de la Guerra. According to the court, the admission of California as a state of the union constituted the positive act that conferred citizenship on former Mexican nationals such as de la Guerra.[32] Although deemed the legal equals of their Anglo counterparts in terms of federal citizenship, de la Guerra and other Mexican Americans would continue to experience social discrimination in practice.

LAND

The "brown" liminal legal status of Mexicans also played itself out with respect to land ownership. According to Article VIII of the Treaty of Guadalupe Hidalgo, the rights of Mexican landowners would be "inviolably respected" and "the present owners, the heirs of these, and all Mexicans who may hereafter acquire said property by contract, shall enjoy with respect to it guarantees *equally ample as if the same belonged to citizens of the United States*."[33] At first blush, these provisions would appear to guarantee overarching legal protections for Mexican landowners. In reality,

---

[30]F. Michael Higginbotham, *Race Law: Cases, Commentary, and Questions* (Durham: Carolina Academic Press, 2010), 307, 308; Griswold del Castillo, *The Treaty of Guadalupe*, 69; People v. De La Guerra, 40 Cal. 311 (1870).

[31]Louise Pubols, *The Father of All: The de la Guerra Family, Power, and Patriarchy in Mexican California* (San Marino: Huntington-USC Institute on California and the West, 2009), 285-86.

[32]Griswold del Castillo, *The Treaty of Guadalupe*, 69.

[33]"Treaty with the Republic of Mexico," 929-30; emphasis added.

the ambiguity of this legal language would result in most Mexicans losing their land by the turn of the twentieth century.

In its original form, the Treaty contained an additional Article X, which provided comprehensive guarantees protecting "all prior and pending titles to property of every description" and which stated, "All grants of land made by the Mexican government . . . shall be respected as valid, *to the same extent that the same grants would be valid, if the said territories had remained within the limits of Mexico*."[34] Upon the presentation of the treaty to Congress, however, this sweeping provision was removed. In short, the deletion of Article X allowed the US government to deny the explicit legitimacy of all Mexican land grants, and thereby made it easier to create legal loopholes resulting in the seizure of Mexican lands.[35] As a result, most Mexican landowners, large and small, lost their lands.[36] Territorial dispossession took place in California and in New Mexico through the manipulation of similar legal procedures.

In 1851, Congress created the California Board of Land Commissioners. As part of this land commission, every Mexican landowner was required to appear before the board within two years to prove that their Mexican land grants were valid. This legislation was passed in Congress based on the pressures of Anglo gold rush squatters who demanded that something be done to "liberate" the land.[37] As a foreseeable consequence, most Mexicans lost their lands for two reasons: First, because Mexican property law was based on Roman law, it had different standards than Anglo-American property law. As a result, many land grants that were perfectly valid under Mexican law were not deemed contractually binding under American law. Second, even if they could prove their claim, many Mexicans eventually lost their property because of high lawyer fees.[38] In order to raise the funds for expensive Anglo lawyers,

---

[34]Griswold del Castillo, *The Treaty of Guadalupe*, 95; emphasis added.
[35]Griswold del Castillo, *The Treaty of Guadalupe*, 44-45, 48.
[36]Vargas, *Crucible of Struggle*, 102.
[37]Griswold del Castillo, *The Treaty of Guadalupe*, 73.
[38]Griswold del Castillo, *The Treaty of Guadalupe*, 73-74, 78.

many went into debt and mortgaged their ranchos. With the plummeting of cattle prices, many could not keep up with their debt and lost their lands. Pablo de la Guerra testified to the California state legislature about this common occurrence:

> Sir, if he gained his suit—if his title was confirmed, the expenses of the suit would confiscate his property, and millions have already been spent in carrying up cases that have been confirmed by the (Land Commission), and land owners in CA have been obligated to dispose of their property at half its value, in order to pay for the expenses of the suit.[39]

A similar legal process resulted in the dispossession of Mexican landholdings in New Mexico. Unlike California, which became a state soon after the US-Mexico War, New Mexico was accorded the status of federal territory under the Compromise of 1850.[40] Under this unique legal status, federally appointed officials were charged with determining the validity of Mexican land grants, and the Office of Surveyor General (1854) and Court of Private Land Claims (1891) were both established for this purpose.[41] The legal process was expensive and often politicized,[42] and, as in California, many New Mexicans lost their lands. Lands were lost through intimidation, bribery, and fraud, and American territorial politics that controlled the appointment of government officials such as governors, judges, and surveyor.[43] Elite Hispanics known as *ricos* sadly worked with the broader Anglo political machine to maintain their own economic interests at the expense of the New Mexican rural poor. Ultimate control of territorial politics lay in the hands of the Santa Fe Ring, a group of Anglo ranchers and government officials who systematically dispossessed Hispanos of their lands from 1848 until 1904.[44]

---

[39]Griswold del Castillo, *The Treaty of Guadalupe*, 74, 154.
[40]Gómez, *Manifest Destinies*, 45.
[41]Griswold del Castillo, *The Treaty of Guadalupe,* 77-81.
[42]Griswold del Castillo, *The Treaty of Guadalupe,* 77-78; Acuña, *Occupied America*, 79.
[43]Acuña, *Occupied America*, 78-81.
[44]Acuña, *Occupied America*, 78-81; Griswold del Castillo, *The Treaty of Guadalupe*, 78.

THE SPIRITUAL CONQUEST:
Padre Antonio José Martínez of Taos and the Birth of the Brown Church in the United States

Beyond property and citizenship rights, Anglo racial colonialism extended to the spiritual realm and institutions of Christian religion. As previously discussed, many Protestant Anglo Americans believed that they possessed a "manifest destiny" to conquer and convert the heathen Mexicans and Native Americans who occupied the lands of the West and Southwest. Some Anglo Catholics also followed suit. Following the US-Mexico War, the American Catholic Church conducted a spiritual conquest of the Mexican Catholic Church of the Southwest. New Mexico was the site of a stirring example of Anglo religious colonialism that can be viewed as emblematic of the larger spiritual conquest of the Latina/o community of the nineteenth century. Out of this cauldron of socioeconomic, political, and religious upheaval, the Brown Church of the United States was born.

Prior to the US conquest, New Mexico was part of the governmental jurisdiction of Mexico. As such, it fell under the ecclesiastical authority of the bishop of Durango, Mexico. After New Mexico came under the territorial sovereignty of the United States, Anglo bishops clamored for the cultural and spiritual conquest of the Mexican Catholic Church of New Mexico. While meeting in Baltimore in May of 1849, American bishops gathered to discuss the integration of New Mexico, and the other former Mexican territories, into Anglo religious life. They came to the conclusion that New Mexico should be seized from the spiritual authority of the bishop of Durango, and that a new vicariate should be created for New Mexico under the jurisdiction of American bishops.[45] To justify this seizure of ecclesiastical authority, the American bishops drew straight from the playbook of Manifest Destiny. In fact, they borrowed from the racist accounts of US army officers who took part in the US-Mexico War. They painted a picture of New Mexicans, both lay and

---

[45]Aragon, *Padre Martínez and Bishop Lamy*, 50-51.

clergy alike, as immoral people engaged in excessive drinking, gambling, prostitution, and all manner of vice. The Mexican Bishop of Durango was deemed responsible for the spiritual depravity of New Mexico, and because of its alleged degradation, New Mexico was viewed as fertile ground for Anglo missionary efforts and spiritual revival—even though Mexican Catholicism was the first expression of Christianity in the Americas, and had been continuously present in New Mexico and the Southwest for 350 years.

On July 19, 1850, New Mexico was ripped from the diocesan authority of the bishop of Durango, and the vicariate apostolic of New Mexico was established in its place. French priest John Baptiste Lamy of Covington, Kentucky, was soon declared bishop of Agathonica with spiritual authority over New Mexico. Lamy did not speak Spanish and had no personal knowledge of Mexican culture. To prepare himself for the task ahead, Lamy read soldier accounts that painted New Mexicans as barbarous and backwards Indians and Mexicans who were in need of American missionaries to save and civilize them:

> They pertinaciously cling to the customs of their forefathers, and are becoming every year more and more impoverished. . . . In short, they are morally, physically, and intellectually distanced in the great race of improvement which is run in almost every quarter of the earth. Give them but tortillas, frijoles, and chile Colorado to supply their animal wants for the day, and seven tenths of the Mexicans are satisfied.[46]

As part of the American project of spiritual conquest, Lamy removed Mexican clergy who did not agree with him or who refused to pledge to him their allegiance.[47] Such racial defrocking stemmed from a fear that some New Mexican priests might remain loyal to the Mexican Catholic Church and the spiritual authority of the bishop of Durango, as well as from a low view of Mexican clergy and the Hispanic church of the

---

[46] Aragon, *Padre Martinez and Bishop Lamy*, 51.
[47] E.A. Mares et al., *Padre Martinez: New Perspectives from Taos* (Taos: Millicent Rogers Museum, 1988), 140.

Southwest.[48] Of the native priests of Santa Fe, he wrote, "There were fifteen, six of whom are now old. . . . Even now they are either incapable or unworthy."[49] Mexican Christianity of the Southwest, Lamy believed, was characterized by superficial spirituality, and their churches reminded him of the stables of Bethlehem. In his view, the priests were "more in the way than help," and this led to the recruitment of French missionaries to reform the fallen Mexican church of New Mexico.[50]

In addition to the ouster of native clergy, Lamy also uprooted native cultural traditions.[51] In an expression of cultural manifest destiny, he condemned New Mexican *fandango* dances as causes of sin and fornication.[52] He also denounced the *santero* folk art[53] that adorned the churches and chapels of the area, and that represented the prize cultural production of local families. Such folk art consisted of wood paintings and religious statues, as well as cathedral vestments and costumes. Lamy mocked the santero art as grotesque and comical. Reflective of his actions and words of cultural and spiritual violence, he wrote, concerning a santero portrayal of St. Michael:

> A more comical figure than this same San Miguel it would be difficult either to imagine or discover. I cannot say that his saintship had ever been tarred, but he had certainly been feathered from head to foot. From his shoulders hung listlessly a pair of huge, ill-constructed wings, while his head to complete ludicrous tout ensemble, was covered with a lace cap of the fashion of our grandmothers. . . . Nothing could be more grotesque and laughable than this comical head of St. Michael."[54]

In an unspeakable act of cultural genocide, Lamy ordered that all santero folk art be removed from every church and chapel of New

---

[48]Mares et al., *Padre Martinez: New Perspectives*, 140; Aragon, *Padre Martinez and Bishop Lamy*, 56, 58, 61.
[49]Aragon, *Padre Martinez and Bishop Lamy*, 58.
[50]Aragon, *Padre Martinez and Bishop Lamy*, 56, 58-59.
[51]Mares et al., *Padre Martinez: New Perspectives*, 143.
[52]Aragon, *Padre Martinez and Bishop Lamy*, 65, 77-79.
[53]Artwork of the saints.
[54]Aragon, *Padre Martinez and Bishop Lamy*, 77-78.

Mexico, and that they be replaced with standard European religious images and art as used in the United States. One Hispanic priest recalled the spiritual violence: "Many of the cathedral vestments had been burned, along with forty different costumes once used to dress the statue of Our Lady of the Rosary."[55]

Beyond this cultural massacre of the New Mexican church, one of Lamy's greatest controversies involved the imposition of exorbitant mandatory tithes upon the rural Hispanic poor. For Lamy, these mandatory tithes would provide funding for the creation of new schools, churches, and hospitals; for most New Mexicans, however, the tithes were an oppressive obligation that perpetuated poverty and oppression.[56] Excessive fees were charged for the basic rites of the church, such as marriage, baptism, and burial.[57] Because these religious fees were so expensive, they forced many to avoid marriage and to have children out of wedlock. Others were discouraged from baptizing their children.

Lamy's tithing fees were so controversial that they triggered the intervention of William Watts Hart Davis, United States Attorney of the territory of New Mexico. Davis decried the exorbitant prices charged by the Anglo Catholic Church for marriage, baptism, and burial services, and characterized them publicly as "abuse." With respect to marriage, the actions of Catholic authorities were especially egregious because couples could turn to no other civil institution to perform nuptial ceremonies:

> Another abuse that should be remedied is the high price of marriage, baptismal, and burial fees that the Church exacts from the people. In the case of marriage the high rates have heretofore prevented lawful wedlock, and driven a large portion of the population into licentiousness. They were not able to pay the fees demanded by the priest, and no civil officer had power to unite people in matrimony."[58]

[55] Aragon, *Padre Martinez and Bishop Lamy*, 78-79.
[56] Mares et al., *Padre Martínez: New Perspectives*, 141.
[57] Aragon, *Padre Martinez and Bishop Lamy*, 80-81.
[58] Aragon, *Padre Martinez and Bishop Lamy*, 80-81.

To put these excessive tithes in perspective, it was recorded that in one instance, the funeral of one, Getrudis Barcelo, cost $1,600. In today's terms, accounting for inflation, that translates to $48,331.11.[59]

Out of this cultural and religious conquest and abuse, the Brown Church of the United States was born. Native New Mexican priests and laity, such as Padre Antonio José Martínez of Taos, rose up to challenge Anglo religious colonialism and claimed a unique Mexican Catholic Christian identity. In so doing, they gave rise to a new expression of the Brown Church in North America.[60]

Antonio José Martínez was born in 1793 in the town of Abiquiu, New Mexico.[61] As a member of the elite landowning class, his family possessed extensive financial interests in cattle, and he was raised and educated to take over the family business. After only a year of marriage, Martínez was widowed and became a single father. In 1816 he left to attend seminary in Durango, Mexico, and in 1822 was ordained a priest. The following year, Martínez began his longstanding tenure as the resident priest of Taos, New Mexico. He holds the distinction of being the first native-born secular priest of New Mexico (not affiliated with a specific order such as the Franciscans). As part of his ministry endeavors, Martínez opened up a coed school for boys and girls, as well as an orphanage. He also established a seminary to train New Mexicans for the priesthood, and purchased the first major printing press in all of New Mexico. A strong believer in the value of education, Padre Martínez published various religious and educational materials for the general public.[62]

In his role as priest of Taos and major religious leader in New Mexico, Padre Martínez worked closely with the lay Catholic confraternity called Los Hermanos de Nuestro Padre Jesús Nazareno, or the "Penitentes," as they were better known. The Penitentes devoted themselves to deep

---

[59]This number was calculated utilizing the CPI Inflation Calculator, which assumes that prices in 2019 are 2,920.69% higher than average prices in 1856. CPI Inflation Calculator, www.official data.org/us/inflation/1856?amount=1600.

[60]Mares et al., *Padre Martinez: New Perspectives*, 9.

[61]Mares et al., *Padre Martinez: New Perspectives*, 10, 127.

[62]Mares et al., *Padre Martinez: New Perspectives*, 10, 128, 140.

Christian spirituality, mutual aid, and communal charity, and since there was a shortage of priests in New Mexico, they performed many religious functions and served as unofficial lay religious leaders for many communities and families.[63] Their female counterparts were known as the Carmelitas. Both the Penitentes and Carmelitas found their inspiration and spiritual model in the Franciscan order. Padre Martínez played an important pastoral role for the Penitentes and was given the honorific title of el Supremo.

As previously discussed, upon his arrival as bishop, Lamy systematically dismantled the cultural and religious structures established by the Penitentes and the Mexican Catholic church during the previous 350 years. Through appeal to canon law, scholarly treatises, and public letters, Padre Martínez rebuffed the abuses of Bishop Lamy and his French compatriot, Vicar Machebeuf.[64] In particular, Martínez publicly criticized the bishop's implementation of mandatory tithes that brought financial ruin to native New Mexicans and distanced them from the Catholic Church. In a letter dated January 14, 1854, Bishop Lamy commanded priests to "exclude from the sacraments all household heads who refused to pay the tithes, and to demand triple fees for Baptisms from other members of such families."[65] In response to this draconian order, in May of 1856, Padre Martínez published a letter to the editor of the *Santa Fe Weekly Gazette* objecting to the policy of mandatory tithes and offering to resign as priest of Taos as soon as a native priest could be found to replace him. Martinez's public censure incurred the wrath of Lamy, who tried to replace him with another priest, Damaso Taladrid, who maintained loyalty to Lamy. In the short-term, the attempted ouster of Martínez was unsuccessful, but led to persecution and public defamation at the hands of Taladrid.[66] In reaction, Martínez published a second letter in the *Gazette* that denounced the ecclesial administration of the Catholic

---

[63]Mares et al., *Padre Martinez: New Perspectives*, 22, 127, 128.
[64]Mares et al., *Padre Martinez: New Perspectives*, 141, 143.
[65]Aragon, *Padre Martinez and Bishop Lamy*, 85.
[66]Aragon, *Padre Martinez and Bishop Lamy*, 85-86, 88-91.

Church in New Mexico. Lamy subsequently suspended Padre Martínez from his priestly duties in September 1856. One month later, Martínez published yet another article in the newspaper challenging the oppressive tithing policies of Lamy.

Notwithstanding the suspension of his priestly powers, Martínez continued to lead Mass and administer the sacraments in chapels of Ranchos de Taos, Río Chiquito, and Llano de Talpa. Padre Martínez was excommunicated from the Catholic Church sometime between 1858 and 1860. Believing the excommunication to be unjust, Martínez continued as a rogue priest until his death in 1867 at the age of 74. Though ostracized by official church leadership, he continued to be held in high esteem by native New Mexicans, and, upon his death, was given the "funeral services of a hero" by the Hermandad de Nuestro Padre Jesús Nazareno.[67] Based on his fierce challenge to the spiritual conquest of the Southwest, Martínez may be called the father of the Brown Church in the United States.

CONCLUSION

The US-Mexico War, and the resultant Treaty of Guadalupe Hidalgo, made Mexicans, and by extension, other US Latinas/os, *Brown*. Though we were not wanted because of our color and mestizo culture, we were reluctantly granted future citizenship in exchange for the millions of acres of land that were ours by legal and historic right. "At the proper time" we were to become US citizens, and in the meantime we were trapped in legal and racial liminality, somewhere between and betwixt that of black and white. We were *Brown*. We've been Brown ever since.

The seizure of our lands, and our exile to liminality, was justified by the theology of Manifest Destiny. Anglo Americans felt they had been given a divine right to conquer us because they believed that they were culturally and religiously superior. They possessed a Christian monopoly on God, so they thought, and were divinely sanctioned to spread their superior version of Christianity, culture, and democracy to the darker

---

[67]Mares et al., *Padre Martinez: New Perspectives*, 10-12.

Mexican and Native American peoples of North America. As embodied by the stories and struggles of Padre Antonio José Martínez, los Penitentes, and las Carmelitas, the Brown Church in the United States was born in resistance to this spiritual conquest.

As we will see in the next chapter, the theology of Manifest Destiny naturally gave birth to racial segregation and the socioeconomic and political marginalization of Latinas/os in the twentieth century. If God had given Anglo Americans the right to conquer the lands of Native Americans and Mexicans because of our racial inferiority, then it only made sense that we should be forced to live apart and be consigned to exploitive labor conditions in the fields and urban centers of the United States. Building on the spiritual legacy of Las Casas, Guaman Poma de Ayala, Garcilaso de la Vega, Sor Juana Inés de la Cruz, Padre Martínez, and los Penitentes and las Carmelitas, the Brown Church of the civil rights era would once again rise up to challenge the racism and moral logic of Jim Crow segregation. César Chávez shines as the most illustrative example during the Chicana/o movement of the 1960s.

5

THE SPIRITUAL PRAXIS
OF CÉSAR CHÁVEZ

CÉSAR CHÁVEZ WAS the pre-
eminent leader, voice, and public face of the Mexican American Civil
Rights Movement of the 1960s.[1] Chávez is to Latinas/os what Rev. Dr.
Martin Luther King Jr. is to the African American community.
Moreover, as the posthumous recipient of the Presidential Medal of
Freedom, the Aztec Eagle,[2] and a US postage stamp in his honor,
Chávez has been called the world's most famous Latino.[3] Together
with Dolores Huerta and Filipino organizers Larry Itliong and Philip
Vera Cruz, Chávez founded the United Farmworkers of America
(UFW).[4] The UFW fought for increased wages and better working
conditions for exploited California farmworkers and rose to national
attention through the famous Delano grape strike and international
boycotts of 1965–1970.

---

[1]This chapter first appeared in article form and is reprinted here with permission. Robert Chao
Romero, "The Spiritual Praxis of César Chávez," *Perspectivas* 14 (2017): 24-39.

[2]The Aztec Eagle is the highest recognition awarded by the Mexican government to a non-
Mexican citizen.

[3]Luis D. León, *The Political Spirituality of César Chávez* (Berkeley: University of California Press,
2015), 6.

[4]Although popularly known as the UFW, Chávez's organization went through several name
changes before finally landing on this name. The UFW was originally known as the Farm Workers Association (April 1962) and the National Farmworkers Association (September 1962). Richard Griswold Del Castillo and Richard A. García, *César Chávez: A Triumph of Spirit* (Norman:
University of Oklahoma Press, 1997), 35, 37.

Although César Chávez is revered as the most highly regarded Latina/o civil rights icon of the 1960s, his critical role as faith-rooted activist of the Brown Church has been largely overlooked. Most scholars of Chicana/o studies, as well as activists, have ignored the centrality of Christian spirituality in his personal life and the broader farm workers movement. In the words of Chávez, "Today I don't think I could base my will to struggle on cold economics or on some political doctrine. I don't think there would be enough to sustain me. For me, the base must be faith."[5]

This chapter explores the spiritual formation and praxis of famed Chicano civil rights leader César Chávez during the famous grape strike of 1965–1970, and highlights his role as the most famous twentieth century community organizer and activist of the Brown Church. Methodologically, it draws from the broad—and disparate—secondary literature on the life of Chávez. Some of this literature explicitly highlights the Christian spirituality of Chávez;[6] most of it hints at the profound role of faith in his upbringing and praxis, but does not offer explicit analysis of religion in the farmworkers movement.[7] In addition to synthesizing the existing secondary literature, this essay is also based on a systematic review of Chávez's own words about faith as expressed in his autobiography.[8]

This chapter follows a chronological analysis of the life of Chávez. It begins with a discussion of his early familial upbringing in popular Mexican Catholicism and his later mentorship in Catholic social teachings by white clergyman Father Donald McDonnell. Building on this Christian foundation and the practical skills gained as community

[5] Jacques E. Levy, *César Chávez: Autobiography of La Causa* (Minneapolis: University of Minnesota Press, 2007), 27.
[6] For example, see: Mario T. García, *The Gospel of César Chávez: My Faith in Action* (Lanham: Sheed & Ward, 2007); Frederick John Dalton, *The Moral Vision of César Chávez* (Maryknoll, NY: Orbis Books, 2003); and, Luis D. León, *The Political Spirituality of César Chávez*.
[7] See Del Castillo and García, *César Chávez*; Dan La Botz, *César Chávez and la Causa* (New York: Pearson, 2006); and Levy, *César Chávez*.
[8] Levy, *César Chávez*.

organizer for the Alinksy-based Community Service Organization, Chávez led the UFW to historic victories over powerful agricultural interests in the Central Valley of California. Chávez fused popular Mexican religious symbols and practices—such as La Virgen de Gua- dalupe, *peregrinación* (pilgrimage), and fasting—with Catholic social teaching, leading to the first successful unionization of farm workers in United States history. Despite his many successes, like many civil rights icons before and after, Chávez had moral failures. This chapter also examines the decline and fall of Chávez following the movement's crescendo in 1975.

"ABUELITA THEOLOGY" AND THE EARLY YEARS

César Chávez was born in 1927 to a moderately successful immigrant family in Yuma Valley, Arizona.[9] The earliest members of the Chávez family immigrated to the United States in the 1880s from Chihuahua, Mexico. In Arizona, they established a freight business and ran a family farm on 160 acres of land acquired through the Homestead Act. At the age of 38, César's father, Librado, left the family farm to marry Juana Estrada and become a businessman, owning a grocery store, an auto repair shop, and a poolroom. Following the onset of the Great De- pression, however, the Chávez family lost their grocery store and moved back onto their grandmother's farm in Yuma. Eventually the farm was also lost, and, at the age of twelve, César Chávez, together with his parents and siblings, was launched into a lifetime of migrant labor in the fields of California.

The years spent on the farm with his grandmother, "Mama Tella," were deeply formidable for the young César. During these years he first felt the sting of racism in the public schools. He was called "dirty Mexican" by classmates and was swatted with a ruler for speaking Spanish. Chávez recalled, "When we spoke Spanish, the teacher swooped down on us. I remember the ruler whistling through the air as its edge came down

---

[9]Del Castillo and García, *César Chávez*, 4-6.

sharply across my knuckles."[10] Racial preference for white students was blatant, and when fights broke out between Mexican and Anglo students, teachers and administrators sided with the latter.

Unfortunately, such racist experiences were typical for Mexican Americans living in the Southwest during the first half of the twentieth century. Similar to African Americans, Latinas/os were segregated within poor neighborhoods through racially restrictive housing covenants.[11] Segregated Latina/o communities were known as *colonias*, or *barrios*, and they proliferated throughout California, Arizona, Colorado, Texas, and New Mexico as part of the Great Mexican Migration of 1910–1930. During these years, 750,000 Mexican immigrants came to the United States in search of work and respite from the violence and disruption of the Mexican Revolution.[12] They were recruited by the US government and big business interests in order to fill labor shortages caused by WWI and the racist ban on immigration from Asia and Southern and Eastern Europe. The Chinese Exclusion Act of 1882 and the Asiatic Barred Zone Act of 1917 closed off labor migration from most of Asia, with the exception of Japan and the Philippines; the Immigration Act of 1924 limited migration from Southern and Eastern Europe to a trickle and extended earlier restrictions to exclude immigration from all of Asia.[13] As a consequence, the United States encountered vast labor shortages and turned to Mexico for its labor needs. Mexicans filled vital low-wage roles in agriculture, railroad, construction, mines, and factory work. Though they were desired for their cheap labor, they were not welcomed as neighbors by their white counterparts. This gave rise to legalized Latina/o apartheid and the creation of hundreds of segregated

---

[10]Del Castillo and García, *César Chávez*, 6.

[11]Robert Chao Romero, "*Doss v. Bernal*: Ending Apartheid in Orange County," *UCLA Chicano Studies Research Center Research Report* no. 14 (February 2012).

[12]Romero, "*Doss v. Bernal*," 1, 2.

[13]Roger Daniels, *Coming to America: A History of Immigration and Ethnicity in American Life* (New York: Perennial, 2002), 245-46; Office of the Historian, Milestones: 1921-1936, "The Immigration Act of 1924 (The Johnson-Reed Act)," history.state.gov/milestones/1921-1936 /immigration-act.

Latina/o communities throughout the United States. Segregated housing, in turn, gave rise to segregated parks, pools, schools, restaurants, movie theaters, and even hiking trails and mortuaries! For Latinos like César Chávez and his family, segregation was comprehensive and followed them from the cradle to the grave.

César's early years of living on the family farm were also important because of their impact on his spiritual formation. His spirituality was shaped by his family and grounded in what Latina/o theologians have termed "Abuelita Theology."[14] Because formal religious instruction is often lacking among Latinas/os, the best theologians of the Mexican American community are often grandmothers, or, abuelitas: "Our *abuelitas* [grandmothers], *viejitas* [older women], and *madrecitas* [mothers] have been the functional priestesses and theologians of our *iglesia del pueblo* [church of the people]."[15] In consonance with this common pattern, Chávez acquired Mexican popular Catholicism from his abuelita, "Mama Tella." As an orphan, Mama Tella was raised in a convent, and it was there that she developed literacy in Latin and Spanish, as well as acquired a deep understanding of Christian doctrine.[16] As the theologian of the family, it was she who taught César about prayer, the Catholic catechism, and devotion to the Virgin Mary. As Chávez later recalled:

> "Mama Tella [grandmother] gave us our formal religious training. . . . She was always praying, just praying. Every evening she would sit in bed, and we would gather in front of her. . . . After the Rosary she would tell us about a particular saint and drill us on our Catechism."[17]

From his mother Juana, César learned the biblical value of loving the poor. As a faithful Catholic, Juana was deeply inspired by the life and ministry of Santa Eduviges, (Saint Hedvig), who, in the thirteenth

---

[14]García, *Gospel of César Chávez*, 25; Del Castillo and García, *César Chávez*, 5-6. Moises Sandoval, *The Mexican American in the Church: Reflection on Identity and Mission* (New York: Sadlier Books, 1983), 125.

[15]Dalton, *Moral Vision*, 33-34.

[16]Levy, *Autobiography of La Causa*, 26.

[17]García, *Gospel of César Chávez*, 26-27.

century was renowned for her generosity to the poor, the imprisoned, and the outcast.[18] Following the example of Santa Eduviges, Juana taught César, "You always have to help the needy, and God will help you."[19] In a way reminiscent of the early church, Juana searched the streets for people in need and invited them to her home for food and assistance. As later recounted by the adult César,

> On the saint's birthday, October 16, my mom would find some needy person to help, and, until recently, she would always invite people to the house, usually hobos. She would go out purposely to look for someone in need, give him something, and never take anything in return.[20]

The power of "Abuelita theology" is vividly exemplified in the story of César Chávez's first Communion. Because the family lived many miles outside of Yuma where official catechism classes were held, the task of preparing César and his sister Rita for first Communion fell on their abuela, Mama Tella.[21] One day, following the completion of Mama Tella's religious instruction, the Chávez family traveled to the Catholic Church in Yuma to request first Communion. Initially the Anglo priest refused because they had not received formal religious instruction: "They haven't had any religious training. They can't take Communion. . . . They must attend class here in Yuma first." To this, Juana retorted, "They can't because we live out in the valley twenty miles away. We can't travel that far every week." After a second stubborn refusal from the priest, she firmly insisted, "Well, ask them something." The priest proceeded to drill the Chávez children with questions from the Catholic catechism, and, because of their thorough training in "abuelita theology," César and Rita passed with flying colors. The children received their first Communion the following day.

In a similar way to the biblical account of the Exodus, it can be said that the farm worker movement has its origins with women. The Israelite

---

[18]Levy, *Autobiography of La Causa*, 25-26.
[19]García, *Gospel of César Chávez*, 26.
[20]Levy, *Autobiography of La Causa*, 26.
[21]Levy, *Autobiography of La Causa*, 26-27.

exodus from slavery in Egypt originated in the daring acts of faithful civil rebellion on the part of Moses' mother and sister Miriam; in a similar way, the farmworker movement began with the faithfulness of Chávez's mother Juana, and grandmother, Mama Tella, who first taught him to love God and care for the marginalized of society.

Following his family's flight from Arizona in the midst of the Great Depression, César spent his teenage years as a migrant farm worker in California.[22] The entire family picked fruits and vegetables in Brawley and Oxnard, and cotton in the San Joaquin Valley. Quite notably, it is during these years that César experienced firsthand the deplorable working conditions and exploitation of the farmworker community. As a teenager, he also continued to feel the sting of racism in the forms of segregated schools, housing, restaurants, stores, and movie theaters.[23] The adult Chávez recalled the extreme prejudice of the public schools:

> They would make you run laps around the track if they caught you speaking Spanish, or a teacher in a classroom would make you write "I won't speak Spanish" on the board 300 times, or I remember once a teacher hung a sign on me that said "I am a clown, I speak Spanish."

At the age of 17, César enlisted in the Navy to fight in World War II. After two years of service in the South Pacific, he returned to labor in the fields once more. In 1948, he married Helen Fabela and began a family. In 1952, they moved to San José where César acquired employment in a lumber mill.[24]

THE CSO AND CATHOLIC SOCIAL TEACHING

It was in that same city of Saint Joseph that Chávez was introduced to the formal theology of social justice under the mentorship of a white Roman Catholic clergyman, Father Donald McDonnell.[25] The two met in a parish church in the barrio of Sal Si Puedes, and McDonnell was one of four priests

---

[22]Del Castillo and Garcia, *César Chávez*, 11.
[23]Del Castillo and Garcia, *César Chávez*, 13.
[24]Del Castillo and Garcia, *César Chávez*, 18-19, 21.
[25]León, *Political Spirituality*, 46-47.

composing the "Spanish Mission Band," which was assigned to minister among Mexican rural communities such as San José and Stockton.[26]

Seeing his leadership potential, McDonnell took Chávez under his wing and introduced him to labor history, community organizing, and the social teachings of the Catholic church.[27] In the words of Chávez,

> I began to spend a lot of time with Father McDonnell. We had long talks about farm workers. I knew a lot about the work, but I didn't know anything about the economics. . . . And then we did a lot of reading. That's when I started reading the Encyclicals, St. Francis, and Gandhi and having the case for attaining social justice explained.[28]

Chávez was especially influenced by Pope Leo XIII's encyclical *Rerum novarum* (1891) and Pope Pius XI's encyclical *Quadragesimo anno* (1931), which discussed the moral duties owed by capital to labor.[29] According to papal teaching in *Rerum novarum*, employers possess a moral obligation to pay their workers wages that are sufficient to sustain the livelihood of their families.[30] Moreover, this encyclical upholds the right of workers to form trade union associations and to go on strike.[31] In a powerful assertion of God's love and concern for the poor and marginalized, Pope Leo XIII writes in *Rerum novarum*,

> God Himself seems to incline rather to those who suffer misfortune; for Jesus Christ calls the poor "blessed"; He lovingly invites those in labor and

---

[26]Del Castillo and Garcia, *César Chávez*,; Dalton, *Moral Vision*, 48-49. As an interesting aside, Chávez met Dolores Huerta, another key figure in the farmworkers' struggle, through the work of the Mission Band in Stockton.

[27]Dalton, *Moral Vision*, 48.

[28]Dalton, *Moral Vision*, 48. A further influence upon the Catholic spirituality of Chávez in his adult years was the Cursillo Movement or, Cursillos de Cristiandad. Frank Bardacke explores the ways in which Chavez's participation in the Cursillo movement altered his social practice. See Frank Bardacke, *Trampling Out the Vintage: César Chávez and the Two Souls of the United Farm Workers* (Brooklyn: Verso Books, 2012).

[29]Dalton, *Moral Vision*.

[30]"Rerum Novarum: On Capital and Labor," Encyclical of Pope Leo XIII, May 15, 1891, *Papal Encyclicals Online*, accessed September 29, 2016, www.papalencyclicals.net/Leo13/l13rerum.htm; "Quadragesimo Anno: On Reconstruction of the Social Order," Encyclical of Pope Pius XI, May 15, 1931, *Papal Encyclicals Online*, accessed February 11, 2017, www.papalencyclicals.net/Pius11/P11QUADR.HTM.

[31]Dalton, *Moral Vision*, 49.

grief to come to Him for solace; and He displays the tenderest charity toward the lowly and the oppressed.[32]

Following his formative spiritual training with Father McDonnell, Chávez went to work as a community organizer with the Community Service Organization (CSO).[33] The CSO was founded in Boyle Heights in 1948 by Edward Roybal (the first Latino elected to the Los Angeles City Council in the twentieth century), Fred Ross, and Mexican American veterans. The CSO created a movement against discrimination in housing, employment, and education, and sought to build a political power base for the Mexican American community in California. Through his work with the CSO, Chávez became immersed in the world of politics and community organizing, and also received mentorship by veteran labor organizers Fred Ross and Saul Alinsky. Chávez organized CSO chapters in small towns and barrios throughout California, led citizenship classes and voter registration campaigns, and served as a lobbyist for Mexican American issues in Sacramento. He served ten years as a community organizer among Mexican American urban populations in California,[34] and he eventually rose to the rank of national director of the CSO.[35]

FAITH, STRUGGLE, AND NONVIOLENCE IN THE FARMWORKERS MOVEMENT

In 1962, Chávez quit his post with the CSO to pursue his dream of organizing Mexican farm workers.[36] With little funding and few supporters, Chávez, together with Dolores Huerta, Fred Ross, and cousin Manuel Chávez, launched the National Farm Workers Association (NFWA) in the San Joaquin Valley.[37] The NFWA functioned largely as a mutual aid association, as opposed to a traditional union, sponsoring

---

[32]Leo XIII (pope), "Rerum novarum."
[33]García, *Gospel of César Chávez*, 9.
[34]García, *Gospel of César Chávez*, 9.
[35]García, *Gospel of César Chávez*, 9; Dalton, *The Moral Vision*, 7.
[36]Dalton, *Moral Vision*, 8.
[37]Dalton, *Moral Vision*, 8; García, *Gospel of César Chávez*, 11; La Botz, *César Chávez*, 47.

burial insurance, a credit union, a gas station, and a grocery store.[38] Chávez recruited new members for the NFWA on a grassroots level by going house to house and speaking to small groups of workers.[39] The house-meeting strategy eased the fears of farmworkers because it allowed them to plan and organize outside of the purview of growers who might otherwise retaliate against them. In order to join, members were required to pay dues of $3.50 each month.[40] This fostered a sense of commitment and ownership, as well as allowed the NFWA to remain independent and unbeholden to outside interests.

In 1965, the fledgling organization was asked by Larry Itliong and other Filipino leaders of the Agricultural Workers Organizing Committee (AWOC) to participate in a strike against the major grape growers of the Central Valley.[41] On Mexican Independence Day, September 16, 1965, Chávez and the NFWA voted unanimously to join the grape strike. As a natural outflow of their collaboration in the grape strike, the NFWA and the AWOC merged to form the United Farm Workers Organizing Committee on August 22, 1966.[42] The strike was to last five years and resulted in the first successful organizing of agricultural workers in US history.[43] It also catapulted Chávez into international acclaim. In a strange twist of irony, Chávez did not even start the very strike that made him famous.

The central role played by Christian faith in the life of Chávez and the farmworkers' struggle is often overlooked. The radical uniqueness of the United Farmworkers movement was in fact its creative fusion of popular Mexican Catholicism, traditional Catholic social teachings,

---

[38]García, *Gospel of César Chávez*, 11.

[39]Levy, *Autobiography of La Causa*, 162; La Botz, *César Chávez*, 46, 49-50.

[40]La Botz, *César Chávez*, 47.

[41]La Botz, *César Chávez*, 53. To learn more about the important role of Filipino farmworkers in the UFW, see the recent documentary, "Delano Manongs: Forgotten Heroes of the United Farmworkers," accessed October 3, 2016, www.delanomanongs.com/about.

[42]"La Huelga Continues," UFW History, United Farm Workers, accessed September 29, 2016, https://ufw.org/research/history/ufw-history. In 1972 the union became part of the AFL-CIO and changed its name to the United Farmworkers Union. Roger Bruns, *César Chávez: A Biography* (Westport: Greenwood Press, 2005), xiv.

[43]García, *Gospel of César Chávez*, 1, 12.

and Alinsky-based community organizing methods. In the words of noted Chicano historian Mario García, "It was César's faith more than anything else that provided the strength for his long and arduous struggles. His movement of farm workers was first and foremost a faith-based movement because César understood the power of faith."[44] Chávez was open and direct about the critical role of faith in his union organizing efforts: "While most people drawn toward liberalism or radicalism leave the church, I went the other way. I drew closer to the church the more I learned and understood."[45] As previously discussed, the uniqueness of the UFW lay in its joining of popular practices from Mexican Catholicism with the formal social teachings of the Roman Catholic Church. This religious praxis is most clearly embodied in the famous march to Sacramento, as well as in Chávez's twenty-five-day fast of 1968.

In March 1966, the farmworker movement garnered national attention as part of a famous 250-mile, twenty-five-day march from Delano to Sacramento.[46] Unknown to many, however, Chávez fashioned this famous march from the Central Valley to Sacramento as a penitential pilgrimage, or "peregrinación." Drawing from popular Mexican religious tradition, he called the march, "Penitence, Pilgrimage, and Revolution."[47] According to Catholic tradition, penitence is a spiritual practice by which participants atone for their post-baptismal sins. Pilgrimage, moreover, is a spiritual practice through which pilgrims acquire merit before God. Chávez viewed the Sacramento march in terms of this Mexican, Catholic spiritual tradition:

> The penitential procession is also in the blood of the Mexican American, and the Delano march [1966] will therefore be one of penance—public penance for the sins of the strikers, their own personal sins as well as their yielding perhaps to feelings of hatred and revenge in the strike itself. They

---

[44]García, *Gospel of César Chávez*, 31.
[45]Levy, *Autobiography of La Causa*, 27.
[46]Del Castillo and García, *César Chávez*, 51.
[47]García, *Gospel of César Chávez*, 12, 16.

hope by the march to set themselves at peace with the Lord, so that the justice of their cause will be purified of all lesser motivation.[48]

In further religious significance, the penitential pilgrimage was led by a priest in full clerical garb and a banner of La Virgen de Guadalupe.[49] Chávez and his followers arrived in Sacramento on Easter and concluded their pilgrimage with the celebration of Mass.[50]

By 1968, some union members had turned to violence in response to physical attacks on the part of the growers and a perceived lack of progress.[51] Demoralized workers threw nails on roads to flatten the tires of growers and the police, blew up irrigation pumps, and even burned down packing sheds full of grapes. In response, on February 15, 1968, Chávez embarked upon a twenty-five-day fast in order to "bring the Movement to a halt, do something that would force them and me to deal with the whole question of violence and ourselves."[52] The fast was aimed at reinforcing the UFW commitment to nonviolence, and it marked the second special turning point in the farm workers' struggle.

For Chávez, fasting was a spiritual exercise and a form of penance for his own sins as well as those of his supporters.[53] It was not a "hunger strike" aimed at accomplishing a political goal or forcing his adversaries to submit to his demands. Through fasting, he sought God's divine intervention in "la causa" (the cause) and sought to purify himself and the farmworkers movement from sin and the temptation to appropriate violence. In fact, during each day of the strike, Chávez celebrated Mass and received Communion.[54] Such celebrations of Mass were common throughout the strike and have been called "liturgies of protest."[55] Speaking of the Christian underpinnings of his 1968 fast, Chávez stated:

---

[48]García, Gospel of César Chávez, 96-97.
[49]León, The Political Spirituality, 24.
[50]García, Gospel of César Chávez, 95.
[51]La Botz, César Chávez, 92-93.
[52]Levy, Autobiography of La Causa, 272, 277.
[53]García, Gospel of César Chávez, 103.
[54]Levy, Autobiography of La Causa, 275.
[55]León, The Political Spirituality, 129.

My fast is informed by my religious faith and by my deep roots in the Church. It is not intended as pressure on anyone but only is an expression of my own deep feelings and my own need to do penance and to be in prayer.[56]

I pray to God that this fast will be a preparation for a multiple of simple deeds of justice, carried out by men and women whose hearts are focused on the suffering of the poor and who yearn, with us, for a better world.[57]

Chávez was misunderstood by many in the movement who viewed his fasting as heavenly "pie in the sky." He received vehement critique from Tony Orendain, secretary treasurer of the Union, as well as by supporters of Saul Alinsky's Industrial Areas Foundation and other union progressives.[58] UFW attorney Jerry Cohen reflected honestly upon the liberal conundrum of purporting to support religious freedom, while at the same time denouncing religious expression as part of the farmworkers struggle: "It's strange how some people react who profess to believe in freedom of speech and freedom of religion. They tolerate anything except religion. A lot of liberals and radicals were pissed."[59]

According to Dolores Huerta, Chávez viewed prayer and fasting as the keys to the success of the grape strike and the larger farm worker struggle:

I know it's hard for people who are not Mexican to understand, but this is part of the Mexican culture—the penance, the whole idea of suffering for something, of self-inflicted punishment. It's a tradition of very long standing. In fact, César has often mentioned in speeches that we will not win through violence, we will win through fasting and prayer.[60]

In the end, Chávez was vindicated. His fast engendered a critical turning point in the movement and, in the words of one observer: "The irony of the fast was that it turned out to be the greatest organizing tool in the history of the labor movement."[61] According to Chávez, the results were

---

[56]García, *Gospel of César Chávez*, 110.
[57]García, *Gospel of César Chávez*, 103-4.
[58]Levy, *Autobiography of La Causa*, 277.
[59]Levy, *Autobiography of La Causa*, 282.
[60]Levy, *Autobiography of La Causa*, 277.
[61]Levy, *Autobiography of La Causa*, 95.

"like a miracle" because "the work schedule began to pick up, dedication increased, and the whole question of using violence ended immediately."[62] The grape boycott expanded internationally, and the union even received a fifty thousand dollar donation for the purchase of a new building. Bringing crucifixes and altars to La Virgen de Guadalupe, thousands of farmworkers visited Chávez at the Forty Acres headquarters in Delano, and even established a tent city.[63] In religious solidarity, moreover, Chávez and his many supporters celebrated Mass together daily. The services were led by priests donning vestments made of union flags, and Holy Eucharist was celebrated with union wine and tortillas.

This fast garnered wide attention in the national media. Rev. Dr. Martin Luther King Jr. sent a telegram of support just one month before his assassination, and Chávez was also famously visited by Senator Robert Kennedy, who was then a presidential candidate. On March 11, 1968, with Kennedy by his side, Chávez broke his fast with the celebration of Mass on the back of a flatbed truck.[64]

Chávez's firm belief in nonviolence flowed centrally from his Christian convictions. These convictions were shaped most directly by the "abuelita theology" of his youth, Catholic social teachings, and the historical examples of St. Francis of Assisi, Gandhi, and Martin Luther King, Jr.[65] For Chávez, nonviolence was not the same as passivity, but involved the employment of peaceful, strategic methods such as boycotts, strikes, pilgrimages, prayer, and fasting: "People equate nonviolence with inaction—with not doing anything—and it's not that at all. It's exactly the opposite."[66] Chávez referred to this approach as "militant nonviolence" and Gandhian "moral jujitsu."[67] According to Chávez, moreover, the utilization of violence was ineffective because

---

[62]Levy, *Autobiography of La Causa*, 275.
[63]Roger Bruns, *César Chávez*, xiii; La Botz, *César Chávez*, 94.
[64]Del Castillo and García, *César Chávez*, 86; La Botz, *César Chávez*, 95.
[65]García, *Gospel of César Chávez*, 63-64; José-Antonio Orosco, *César Chávez and the Common Sense of Nonviolence* (Albuquerque: University of New Mexico Press, 2008), 24.
[66]García, *Gospel of César Chávez*, 65.
[67]García, *Gospel of César Chávez*, 63-64.

the growers wielded greater physical power through local police forces. Simply put, the growers would always win a violent standoff because they had the police on their side. To draw a biblical analogy, challenging the growers to a battle of physical force would be akin to the fledgling early Christian church waging direct war with Rome and Caesar's mighty army.

Chávez's mother communicated to him the wisdom of nonviolence through *dichos*, or Mexican folk sayings. These dichos challenged the logic of machísmo and echoed Jesus' admonitions to love your enemy and "turn the other cheek." According to Chávez,

> She taught her children to reject that part of a culture which too often tells its young men that you're not a man if you don't fight back. She would say, "No, it's best to turn the other cheek. God gave you senses like eyes and mind and tongue and you can get out of anything. It takes two to fight and one can't do it alone."[68]

Chávez also looked to history in search of successful role models of nonviolent activism. Drawing from his Catholic background, he found inspiration in the story of Moses and the Israelite exodus from slavery in Egypt, as well as in the life of Christ and the Roman persecution of the early church. Gandhi was also a central inspiration:

> Some great nonviolent successes have been achieved in history. Moses is about the best example, and the first one. Christ is also a beautiful example, as is the way Christians overcame tyranny. They needed over three hundred years, but they did it. The most recent example is Gandhi. To me that's the most beautiful one. We can examine it more closely because it happened during our lifetime.[69]

Echoing the teachings of Jesus and the dichos of his early upbringing, Chávez viewed suffering, sacrifice, and love of enemy as the path to farmworker liberation. Although Chávez claimed that love of enemies was a

[68]Orosco, *César Chávez*, 24.
[69]Levy, *Autobiography of La Causa*, 270, 271.

key principal of nonviolent resistance, he was honest in his assessment that this was difficult to embody:

> Love is the most important ingredient in nonviolent work—love the opponent—but we really haven't learned yet how to love the growers. I think we've learned how not to hate them, and maybe love comes in stages.[70]

Central to Chávez's practice of nonviolence were the beliefs that God was on the side of the farmworkers and that Jesus was the source of justice. The idea of God's special concern for agricultural workers is supported poignantly in the book of James:

> Listen! The wages of the laborers who mowed your fields, which you kept back by fraud, cry out, and the cries of the harvesters have reached the ears of the Lord of hosts. You have lived on the earth in luxury and in pleasure; you have fattened your hearts in a day of slaughter. You have condemned and murdered the righteous one, who does not resist you. (Jas 5:4-6)

Because God had heard the cries of the farmworkers, moreover, victory in the grape boycott would come ultimately by the hand of God. It would not be the result of human efforts, no matter how strategic. In the words of César:

> The only justice is Christ—God's justice. We're the victims of a lot of shenanigans by the courts but ultimately, down the line, real justice comes. It does not come from the courts, but it comes from a set of circumstances and I think God's hand is in it. God tends to write very straight with crooked lines.[71]

Although Chávez is often cited as an icon of cultural nationalism in Chicana/o studies, like King, he subscribed to a notion of community that transcended racial and denominational boundaries.[72] Using the language of King, his vision was the "beloved community" of people of all

---

[70]García, *Gospel of César Chávez*, 116.
[71]García, *Gospel of César Chávez*, 31, 32.
[72]García, *Gospel of César Chávez*, 16.

nations, languages, and tongues (Rev 7:9-10; Gal 3:28-29).[73] In simple, poignant words, Chávez asserted that the goal of his movement was to help all of humanity, regardless of racial affiliation. Chávez opposed the extreme cultural nationalism that characterized some of the Chicana/o movement, and rejected narrow nationalism as racist and divisive:

> La Raza? Why be racist? Our belief is to help everyone, not just one race. Humanity is our belief.[74]
>
> We oppose some of this La Raza business so much. We know what it does. When La Raza means or implies racism, we don't support it. But if it means our struggle, our dignity, our cultural roots then we're for it.[75]

It is also worth noting that Chávez, like King, embraced Christian ecumenism. Although a devout Roman Catholic, Chávez partnered with both the Pentecostal community and the Protestant California Migrant Ministry.[76] Under the auspices of the National Council of Churches, and the leadership of Presbyterian pastor Chris Hartmire, the CMM worked closely with the UFW and served as a catalyst for the recruitment of Protestant church support.[77] Chávez met Chris Hartmire and the CMM through organizers Fred Ross and Saul Alinsky.[78] The CMM underwrote many actions of the UFW and even developed a persuasive "huelga theology" to counter the protests of conservative critics.[79] In fact, many Protestants supported La Causa not only financially and theologically, but also by serving in picket lines and boycotts, writing letters to politicians and newspapers, and by documenting the violence of growers against the UFW.[80] CMM support of

---

[73]For more on King's notion of the "beloved community," see Hak Joon Lee, *We Will Get to the Promised Land: Martin Luther King, Jr.'s Communal-Political Spirituality* (Cleveland: The Pilgrim Press, 2006).

[74]García, *Gospel of César Chávez*, 131.

[75]García, *Gospel of César Chávez*, 131.

[76]García, *Gospel of César Chávez*, 135-36.

[77]Ronald A. Wells, "César Chávez's Protestant Allies: The California Migrant Ministry and the Farmworkers," *Journal of Presbyterian History* (Spring/Summer 2009): 5-16, libraries.ucsd.edu/farmworkermovement/essays/essays/cec.pdf; León, *The Political Spirituality*, 127-28. For further discussion of Protestant-farmworker coalitions, see, Alan Watt, *Farmworkers and the Churches: The Movement in California and Texas* (College Station: Texas A&M University Press, 2010).

[78]Levy, *Autobiography of La Causa*, 162.

[79]León, *The Political Spirituality*, 128.

[80]Wells, "César Chávez's Protestant Allies," 11-13.

the UFW was not without a political cost, however, and the CMM faced strong opposition by Protestant growers, as well as by conservative forces within the Presbyterian denomination. Drawing upon his interdenominational Christian experiences, Chávez redefined the Christian church in broad, ecumenical terms. He also strongly asserted that the Church should play a vital role in all justice movements:

> When we refer to the Church we should define the word a little. We mean the whole Church, the Church as an ecumenical body spread around the world, and not just its particular form in a parish in a local community. . . . That Church is one form of the Presence of God on earth, and so naturally it is powerful. It is a powerful moral and spiritual force which cannot be ignored by any movement.[81]

THE DECLINE OF CHÁVEZ AND THE UFW

Thus far, I have focused on the spiritual praxis of César Chávez and the UFW during the "glory years" of the first grape strike from 1965 to 1970. By the close of the 1960s, nearly all grape growers had signed union contracts, and by 1970, the wages of farmworkers had increased by 40 percent.[82] For the next five years, the UFW continued in a series of victories against the growers, culminating in passage of the California Agricultural Labor Relations Act (ALRA) in May of 1975.[83] This legislation granted many concessions to the UFW, including the right to boycott, secret ballot elections, voting rights for migrant seasonal workers, and control over the timing of union elections.

According to historian Matthew García and others, Chávez and the UFW began a precipitous decline in November 1976 with the failure of Proposition 14.[84] Spearheaded by Chávez, Proposition 14 sought to guarantee funding for the ALRA, as well as to require unfettered access by union

---

[81]García, *Gospel of César Chávez*, 46.

[82]La Botz, *César Chávez*, 199.

[83]Del Castillo and Garcia, *César Chávez*, 128.

[84]Matthew García, *From the Jaws of Victory: The Triumph and Tragedy of César Chávez and the Farm Worker Movement* (Berkeley: University of California Press, 2014), 287, 289, 224, 239, 272; La Botz, *César Chávez*, 148.

organizers to farm workers in the fields. Proposition 14 was solidly rejected by California voters by a 2 to 1 margin.[85] Following this major political loss, Chávez became increasingly autocratic and dismissive of dissent. He also launched a purge of union staff and volunteers at union headquarters and throughout the country. According to Filipino farmworker leader Philip Vera Cruz, "in the UFW power was held by César alone, and he handed out some power to individuals at his direction."[86]

As a further means of establishing control, Chávez even tried to create a religious order centered on his own personality and the New Age religion of Synanon.[87] One defining feature of Synanon was "the game." As part of the game, one person sat in the middle of a circle while others hurled insults and accusations at them for one hour. The goal was to "yield truth, communication, a catharsis."[88] Chávez became so strongly influenced by the teachings of Synanon that he even came to declare, "I use my aura to run the Union."[89] According to religious studies scholar Luis León, Chávez "came to believe his own myth, exhibiting signs of megalomania and paranoia."[90] By the late 1970s, Chávez and the UFW seemed to be more closely associated with Synanon than with Catholicism.[91]

In the wake of Synanon and Chávez's autocratic purges and practices, many left the UFW.[92] Though the UFW would continue with some modicum of success for a number of years to come, by the time of Chávez's death in 1993, the UFW plummeted in membership from a high of 80,000, to 5,000.[93]

---

[85]Del Castillo and Garcia, *César Chávez*, 130.
[86]La Botz, *César Chávez*, 151.
[87]León, *The Political Spirituality*, 146, 152.
[88]León, *The Political Spirituality*, 154.
[89]León, *The Political Spirituality*, 147.
[90]León, *The Political Spirituality*, 16.
[91]García, *Gospel of César Chávez*, 285.
[92]La Botz, *César Chávez*, 148-49.
[93]León, *The Political Spirituality*, 16.

CONCLUSION

The creative genius of Chávez as an organizer shone most brightly during the first grape strike. And it was during this time period that he cemented his important role as the most acclaimed faith-rooted organizer of the Brown Church in the twentieth century. Drawing from the "abuelita theology" of his youth, Chávez uniquely fused popular Mexican Catholicism, Catholic social teachings, and Alinsky-based community organizing methods, leading to the formation of the first successful agricultural union in United States history. The famous Easter pilgrimage to Sacramento and twenty-five-day spiritual fast of 1968 represent sterling examples of this innovative fusion. Chávez's deep commitment to nonviolence also flowed from his Christian faith and was inspired by the examples of Moses, Jesus Christ, the early church, Gandhi, and Rev. Dr. Martin Luther King Jr.

From the perspective of church history, however, the movement began a steady decline after 1975 when Chávez took his focus away from Christ and became increasingly self-focused. Though he continued in his commitment to nonviolence, he ignored two central principles of biblical teaching—servant leadership and abiding in Christ.

The Christian call to servant leadership was clearly articulated by Jesus in his rebuke of the disciples on the road to Jerusalem. Following the egoistic request of James and John to sit in positions of honor and authority next to Jesus in the coming Kingdom, Jesus explained to them the nature of "upside down" leadership in the Kingdom of God. Unlike Roman authorities who ruled by force and fiat, Jesus' followers were to lead based on the model of humility and service:

> You know that the rulers of the Gentiles lord it over them, and their great ones are tyrants over them. It will not be so among you; but whoever wishes to be great among you must be your servant, and whoever wishes to be first among you must be your slave; just as the Son of Man came not to be served but to serve, and to give his life a ransom for many. (Mt 20:25-28)

Sadly, Chávez did not take this important aspect of Jesus' teaching to heart, and instead became increasingly authoritarian following the failure of Proposition 14 in 1975. In so doing, he mimicked the leadership model of the very growers which he opposed, and consequently fomented widescale rebellion among the leadership and rank and file membership of the UFW.

From the perspective of pastoral theology, Chávez's self-centeredness, by its very nature, caused him to take his eyes off Christ, who he claimed was the source of his earlier success. This spiritual decentering was demonstrated most clearly in his failed attempt to establish a religious group based on his own personality. As a result, he ceased to "abide in Christ," and the decline of the UFW was the natural consequence. As Jesus teaches—ironically using the metaphor of grapes—"I am the vine; you are the branches. If you remain in me and I in you, you will bear much fruit; apart from me you can do nothing" (Jn 15:5-6). The example of Chávez offers a clear warning to all Christians who aspire to a life of social justice and activism: success in Christian social justice endeavors is not the product of human cleverness or carefully conceived strategies and tactics—it is first and foremost the fruit of God experienced in the lives of all those who would cling to Christ.

Unfortunately, the centrality of faith in the praxis of César Chávez, as well as in the lives of other civil rights leaders such as Martin Luther King Jr., is often overlooked in both academic and activist circles. Almost without exception, academic and popular discussions of Chávez and King claim them as role models while at the same time scrubbing them of their Christian faith. They take the "Rev." away from King and the "abuelita theology" away from Chávez. They also ignore the important role played by the Christian church in the major civil rights successes of the 1960s.

Remembering the spiritual roots and praxis of César Chávez is more important than ever. In the wake of the recent presidential election and the tsunami of anti-immigrant sentiment and violence that has ensued, thousands of Latinas/os have been stirred to action. They look to Chávez as an icon of Latina/o social justice, but are often unaware of the critical role which Christianity played in his organizing and praxis. Moreover, many wish to integrate their Christian spirituality with their activism but have few role models, either in the world of secular activism or the church. As an inspiring example for the rising generation of Latina/o activists, Chávez can provide a roadmap of basic spiritual principles and methods that empowered him and the United Farm Workers movement.

Although Chávez possessed keen spiritual insight, he was not formally trained as a theologian or pastor. As a result, his theological reflections were largely ad hoc. The monumental task of systematizing a theology of social justice would fall to activist priests and nuns of Latin America, who, in 1968, launched the Liberation Theology Movement.

6

SOCIAL JUSTICE THEOLOGIES OF LATIN AMERICA

Liberation Theology and Misión Integral

As **THE BROWN CHURCH** was forcefully awakening in the United States during the United Farm Workers boycott, a watershed moment occurred for their sisters and brothers in Latin America. Confronted with the ravages of poverty, oppression, and a decade of failed programs of economic modernization, Latin American clergy convened the Second Latin American Episcopal Conference (CELAM) in 1968 and launched the Liberation Theology Movement.[1] In the spirit of Bartolomé de Las Casas, they declared:

> The Latin American bishops cannot remain indifferent in the face of the tremendous social injustices existent in Latin America, which keep the majority of our peoples in dismal poverty, which in many cases becomes inhuman wretchedness.
>
> A deafening cry pours from the throats of millions of men, asking their pastors for a liberation that reaches them from nowhere else.[2]

---

[1]Leonardo Boff and Clodovis Boff, *Introducing Liberation Theology* (Maryknoll, NY: Orbis Books, 2005), 9.

[2]Conference of Latin American Bishops, "Medellín 1968 (excerpts)," Poverty of the Church. I. Latin American Scene, www.geraldschlabach.net/medellin-1968-excerpts.

The Liberation Theology movement was launched as a pastoral response to the socioeconomic injustice and violent political repression that characterized Latin America in the 1960s through the 1980s.

According to the bishops gathered in Medellín, Colombia, this injustice was characterized by extreme inequality between the masses of Latin Americans and the few privileged elite. This inequity, moreover, expressed itself in lack of educational opportunity, sexism, extreme poverty among agricultural and urban laborers, and even diminished options for the Latin American middle class:

> Often families do not find concrete possibilities for the education of their children. The young demand their right to enter universities or centers of higher learning for both intellectual and technical training; women demand their right to a legitimate equality with men; peasants demand better conditions of life; or if they are workers, they demand better prices and security in buying and selling; the growing middle class feels frustrated by the lack of expectations.[3]

The bishops based their socioeconomic and political analysis on social scientific data and approaches. In their view, although Latin America was rich in natural resources, its economy had become dependent on Western nations such as the United States. In the industrializing global economy of the twentieth century, Latin America was exploited by Western nations as a source of natural resources and a market for industrialized goods. Often, specific Latin American nations sold only one or two crops for export and were forced to import both food and manufactured products from the West. In this arrangement, an elite class of Latin Americans monopolized land and natural resources and controlled the economy; the masses of Latin Americans on the other hand, lost their land and earned poverty wages as unskilled labor. Although this approach allowed for economic growth and modernization at a national level for countries such as Brazil and Argentina, it did not translate into economic development and prosperity for most people. This economic

---

[3]Latin American Bishops, "Medellin 1968," Justice, I. Pertinent Facts.

analysis is known as Dependency Theory.[4] The priests of Medellín decried the oppressive outcomes of such economic dependency.[5]

In response to this increasingly untenable situation "where a few have much (culture, wealth, power, prestige) while the majority has very little," the Latin American bishops believed that they possessed a profound pastoral responsibility to effect change and alleviate the suffering of the poor who were their congregants.

In their assembly at Medellín, Roman Catholic clergy also spoke out in support of employee unions. According to long-established Catholic social teachings, workers were entitled to organize themselves in effective coalition. Such unions would allow workers to express their legitimate complaints against the abuses of the capitalist system and promote the common good.[6] The bishops also denounced the use of violence by Latin American elites against the peasant and working classes. Some from the upper classes rejected any attempt at social reform as communism, or unjustified attacks upon the rule of law.[7]

The priests of Medellín rejected the extreme poles of both liberal capitalism and Marxism as the only two viable economic solutions for Latin America. They argued that both systems, each in its own way, militated against the "dignity of the human person."[8] In their view, "one takes for granted the primacy of capital, its power and its discriminatory utilization in the function of profit-making. The other, although it ideologically supports a kind of humanism, is more concerned with collective humanity and in practice becomes a totalitarian concentration of state power."[9] Instead, the bishops appealed to the business owners

---

[4]For more on dependency theory and its historical origins, see E. Bradford Burns, *The Poverty of Progress: Latin America in the Nineteenth Century* (Berkeley: University of California Press, 1983).

[5]Latin American Bishops, "Medellin 1968," International Tensions and External Neo Colonialism, 9(a).

[6]Latin American Bishops, "Medellin 1968," Direction of Social Change, d(12).

[7]Latin American Bishops, "Medellin 1968," Tensions Between Classes and Internal Colonialism, 6.

[8]Latin American Bishops, "Medellin 1968," Direction of Social Change, (c) Business Enterprises and the Economy.

[9]Latin American Bishops, "Medellin 1968," Direction of Social Change, (c) Business Enterprises and the Economy.

of Latin America and political authorities to support reform that would create "a truly human economy"[10] and dignify the lives and labor of the poor and their families.

Latin American clergy also called the Christian church to account, and to a deep level of spiritual and social solidarity with the poor. They insisted that the church must be

> the evangelizer of the poor and one with them, a witness to the value of the riches of the Kingdom, and the humble servant of all our people. Its pastors and the other members of the People of God have to correlate their life and words, their attitudes and actions to the demands of the Gospel and the necessities of the [people] of Latin America.[11]

With the conference of Medellín as a springboard, the Liberation Theology movement launched forward as a pastoral response to the socioeconomic injustice and violent political repression it witnessed.

The central tenet of Liberation Theology that emerged from Medellin and the subsequent gathering of the bishops in Puebla, Mexico, in 1978 was that of the "preferential option for the poor." According to this concept, God "opts for," or takes the side of, the poor whenever they are oppressed. This expression is translated from the Spanish, *opción preferencial*, and in its original language connotes that God gives priority to the poor and marginalized in their suffering.[12]

In the words of Gustavo Gutiérrez, a central founder of Liberation Theology:

> The entire Bible, beginning with the story of Cain and Abel, mirrors God's predilection for the weak and abused of human history. This preference brings out the gratuitous or unmerited character of God's love. The same revelation is given in the evangelical Beatitudes, for they tell us with the

---

[10]Latin American Bishops, "Medellin 1968," Direction of Social Change, (c) Business Enterprises and the Economy.

[11]Ondina E. González and Justo L. González, *Nuestra Fe: A Latin American Church History Sourcebook* (Nashville: Abingdon Press, 2014), 174.

[12]Gustavo Gutiérrez, *Gustavo Gutiérrez: Essential Writings*, ed. James B. Nickoloff (Minneapolis: Fortress Press, 1996), 13.

utmost simplicity that God's predilection for the poor, the hungry, and the suffering is based on God's unmerited goodness to us.[13]

God's preferential option for the poor . . . cannot be understood apart from the absolute freedom and gratuitousness of God's love. . . . Universality and preference mark the proclamation of the kingdom. God addresses a message of life to every human being without exception, while at the same time God shows preference for the poor and the oppressed.[14]

Although God loves all people equally, God expresses a unique love and concern for the poor because of their distinct suffering. Poverty is a scandal to God because God desires all his children to flourish and live with dignity.[15] Like a loving father, God cannot stand idly by when one of his children is mistreated or oppressed—especially when they are being taken advantage of by another sibling. He must intervene on their behalf in the face of their suffering. To remain neutral would be to condone their abuse and the structures and circumstances that give rise to their suffering.[16]

Liberation theologians parallel the suffering of the poor of Latin America to that of the enslaved Israelites in Egypt. They feel close attachment to the book of Exodus "because it recounts the epic of the politico-religious liberation of a mass of slaves who, through the power of the covenant with God, became the people of God."[17] Just as Yahweh heard the cries of the Israelites in their slavery and oppression in Egypt, so does God hear the cries of all who are oppressed. According to Leonardo Boff, God is compelled to rush to the aid of the poor:

The biblical God is fundamentally a living God, the author and sustainer of all life. Whenever persons see their lives threatened, they can count on

---

[13]Gustavo Gutiérrez, *A Theology of Liberation* (Maryknoll, NY: Orbis Books, 1988), xxvii, in Roberto S. Goizueta, *Caminemos Con Jesús: Toward a Hispanic/Latino Theology of Accompaniment* (Maryknoll, NY: Orbis Books, 1995), 175.
[14]Gustavo Gutierrez, *The God of Life* (Maryknoll, NY: Orbis Books, 1991), 116.
[15]Michelle A. Gonzalez, *A Critical Introduction to Religion in the Americas: Bridging the Liberation Theology and Religious Studies Divide* (New York: New York University Press, 2014), 48.
[16]Goizueta, *Caminemos Con Jesús*, 177.
[17]Boff and Boff, *Introducing Liberation Theology*, 35.

the presence and power of God who comes to their aid. . . . God feels impelled to come to the help of the oppressed poor: "I have seen the miserable state of my people in Egypt. I have heard their appeal to be free of their slave-drivers. Yes, I am well aware of their sufferings. . . . And now the cry of the sons of Israel has come to me, and I have witnessed the way in which the Egyptians oppress them." (Ex 3:7, 9)[18]

Because God is he who liberates, he is also the God of life.[19] God is the "go'el," the liberator and protector of Israel and the one who enacts justice for his people.[20] His liberation brings life. This theme of liberation is consistently sounded throughout sacred Scripture:

> The messianic proclamation of Jesus Christ is likewise focused on liberation. The theme runs through the entire Bible and reveals to us a God who loves life; life is God's will for all beings. To believe in Yahweh, the God who liberates, and to maintain that Jesus, "the author of life" (Acts 3:15), is the Son of God, is to be a friend of life.[21]

In declaring a "preferential option for the poor," liberation theologians draw from a corpus of more than two thousand Bible verses that speak of God's heart for the poor, immigrants, and all who are marginalized.[22] Because of its central focus on God's deep compassion for those on the margins of society, "the Bible is . . . the expression of the faith and hope of the poor . . . because it reveals to us a God who has a preferential love for those whom the world passes over."[23] The topic of poverty and God's concern for the poor is the second-most common topic in the Old Testament, second only to that of idolatry. The two themes are in fact, related, because taking one's eyes off God and God's commandments leads to the oppression of immigrants and the poor. In the New Testament, the topic of the poor and money is found in one out of every ten verses of

---

[18]Boff and Boff, *Introducing Liberation Theology*, 44.

[19]Gutiérrez, *God of Life*, 3.

[20]Gutiérrez, *God of Life*, 20, 21.

[21]Gutiérrez, *God of Life*, 3.

[22]Robert Chao Romero, *Jesus for Revolutionaries: An Introduction to Race, Social Justice, and Christianity* (Los Angeles, CA: Christian Ethnic Studies Press, 2013), 29.

[23]Gutiérrez, *God of Life*, xv.

the Gospels.[24] In Luke, this ratio is increased to one in seven verses. Jesus speaks much more about his love and concern for the poor and the devastating consequences of greed than he even does about the important topics of heaven and hell.

Perhaps the clearest articulation of the preferential option for the poor are Jesus' own words found in Matthew 25:

> When the Son of Man comes in his glory, and all the angels with him, then he will sit on the throne of his glory. All the nations will be gathered before him, and he will separate people one from another as a shepherd separates the sheep from the goats, and he will put the sheep at his right hand and the goats at the left. Then the king will say to those at his right hand, "Come, you that are blessed by my Father, inherit the kingdom prepared for you from the foundation of the world; for I was hungry and you gave me food, I was thirsty and you gave me something to drink, I was a stranger [*xenos*/foreigner/immigrant; from where we get our English word *xenophobia*] and you welcomed me, I was naked and you gave me clothing, I was sick and you took care of me, I was in prison and you visited me." Then the righteous will answer him, "Lord, when was it that we saw you hungry and gave you food, or thirsty and gave you something to drink? And when was it that we saw you a stranger [foreigner/immigrant] and welcomed you, or naked and gave you clothing? And when was it that we saw you sick or in prison and visited you?" And the king will answer them, "Truly I tell you, just as you did it to one of the least of these who are members of my family, you did it to me." Then he will say to those at his left hand, "You that are accursed, depart from me into the eternal fire prepared for the devil and his angels. . . . Truly I tell you, just as you did not do it to one of the least of these, you did not do it to me." (Mt 25:31-41, 45).

In this passage depicting the final judgment, Jesus clearly articulates a preferential option for immigrants, the poor, and all who are disregarded by society. Jesus takes their side. Not only that, but he identifies so closely with the struggles of the poor that he sees himself in them. If we love him,

---

[24]Romero, *Jesus for Revolutionaries*, 31.

then we will love the poor. When we love the poor, we are loving him. According to Jesus, our compassion towards the most vulnerable of society is a barometer of the sincerity of our relationship with him.[25]

Referring to Matthew 25:40—"Whatever you did for one of the least of these brothers and sisters of mine, you did for me"—Augustine stated, "I confess that in God's scripture this has moved me the most."[26] In fact, Augustine cites Matthew 25:31-46 275 times in his various sermons and writings, and one scholar has called this passage one of Augustine's hermeneutical rules for interpreting, even when it comes to reading the Psalms.[27] According to Augustine, Christ is continually present with us on earth in the poor, and "Christ is needy when a poor person is in need" and "is hungry when the poor are hungry."[28] "To come to the aid of the poor people, members of Christ, is to come to the aid of Christ the head who is present and in need within poor people."[29] In her Nobel speech, Mother Teresa stated simply, "Jesus makes Himself the hungry one, the naked one, the homeless one, the unwanted one, and He says, 'You did it to me.'"[30]

Inspired by the biblical principles of Matthew 25, Latin American liberation theologians sought to implement the preferential option for the poor on three structural levels: the popular, the pastoral, and the academic.[31] At the grassroots level, liberation theology worked itself out through "Base Church Communities" or "Base Christian Communities" (BCCs).[32] BCCs were small groups that came together for Bible study, liturgical worship, and community activism, and their aim was to fuse

---

[25]Romero, *Jesus for Revolutionaries*, 42.

[26]Andrew Hofer Op, "Matthew 25:31-46 as an Hermeneutical Rule in Augustine's *Enarrationes in Psalmos*," *The Downside Review* 126, no. 445 (2008): 285.

[27]Op, "Matthew 25:31-46," 293; Raymond Canning, "Christ's Self-identification with 'The Least of Mine' (Matthew 25:40, 45) According to Augustine: 'Is This the Humility of God?'" *Australian eJournal of Theology* 15 (2010).

[28]St. Augustine, Sermon 38, 8, quoted in Augnet, "The Poor," accessed October 4, 2018, www.augnet .org/en/works-of-augustine/his-ideas/2325-the-poor.

[29]St. Augustine, Sermon 53 A, 6; Sermon 236, 3.

[30]Veronica Carrasco Juarez, "Give Until It Hurts: The Speeches and Letters of Mother Teresa," (Master's thesis, Texas Tech University, 2007), 62, 63.

[31]González, *A Critical Introduction*, 25.

[32]Boff and Boff, *Introducing Liberation Theology*, 10-11.

the spiritual and the political. They were communities of *concientización* in which the oppressed came together to understand structural injustice through biblical reflection.[33] Applying a "liberative hermeneutics" that approached the Bible "as a book of life, not as a book of strange stories," the members of BCCs read the Bible in light of their personal and social circumstances of oppression, and were stirred to action.[34] Liberative hermeneutics sought "to discover and activate the transforming energy of biblical texts" leading to "individual change (conversion) and change in history (revolution)." Utilizing this tool of biblical reflection and study, BCCs were to be the basis for community organizing and social change. According to Leonardo Boff,

> In liberation, the oppressed come together, come to understand their situation through the process of conscientization, discover the causes of their oppression, organize themselves into movements, and act in a coordinated fashion.[35]

Base Christian Communities were typically led by trained lay leaders and, as a further distinction, were characterized by communitarianism and minimal institutionalization.[36] BCCs were to be the operational base of liberation theology on the popular level and represented the "true Church of the poor," "a Church of and with the poor."[37] Although largely a lay movement, BCCs maintained close ties to the institutional church and were sanctioned and supported by formal church leadership. The lay leadership of BCCs, moreover, was appointed by local priests and bishops.[38] Following Medellín, tens of thousands of base communities sprung up throughout Latin America. The Medellín conference defined the concept of base communities for a larger audience and inspired their spread.[39]

---

[33]*Concientización* refers to the development of social consciousness related to issues of injustice.
[34]Boff and Boff, *Introducing Liberation Theology*, 34; William T. Cavanaugh, "The Ecclesiologies of Medellín and the Lessons of the Base Communities," *CrossCurrents* 44, no. 1 (1994): 75.
[35]Boff and Boff, *Introducing Liberation Theology*, 5.
[36]González, *A Critical Introduction*, 28, 29.
[37]González, *A Critical Introduction*, 29; Boff and Boff, *Introducing Liberation Theology*, 10.
[38]Cavanaugh, "The Ecclesiologies of Medellín," 75.
[39]Cavanaugh, "The Ecclesiologies of Medellín," 74.

As a complement to Base Christian Communities, liberation theology also operated on the "professional" and the "pastoral" levels. The professional level involved theologians, professors, and teachers who worked in theological institutes and seminaries, and who supported the movement through the production of books, articles, lectures, and conference presentations.[40] Between BCCs and professors were clergy and lay religious leaders whose role was to provide pastoral support as well as to lead in the practical application of the theology developed by movement intellectuals. This shepherding work took place in institutes, study centers, and congresses, and was embodied in sermons and pastoral writings. Quite notably, Pope Francis hails from this theological and pastoral tradition.

In addition to the preferential option for the poor, Liberation Theology expounds on several other key concepts, including orthopraxis and the kingdom of God. Unlike secular notions of social justice, liberation theology insists that faith in God is the starting point for both personal liberation and social action. Faith allows the Christian believer to see God's presence and action in all aspects of history and the world and empowers them to join God in God's work of liberation. Faith in the abstract is not enough. As Leonardo Boff states, "Living and true faith includes the practice of liberation" and must be enfleshed in concrete works of justice and mercy for the poor.[41] Otherwise, as James tells us, it is dead faith:

> What good is it, my brothers and sisters, if you say you have faith but do not have works? Can faith save you? If a brother or sister is naked and lacks daily food, and one of you says to them, "Go in peace; keep warm and eat your fill," and yet you do not supply their bodily needs, what is the good of that? So faith by itself, if it has no works, is dead. (Jas 2:14-17)

In the language of Liberation Theology, faith, embodied by good works, is labeled "orthopraxis."[42] Orthopraxis emphasizes embodied justice and the creation of a just social order, over abstract theory and belief.

---

[40]Boff and Boff, *Introducing Liberation Theology*, 13.
[41]Boff and Boff, *Introducing Liberation Theology*, 49.
[42]Boff and Boff, *Introducing Liberation Theology*, 50.

A third core theme of Liberation Theology is that of the kingdom of God. The "kingdom is God's project in history and eternity," and Jesus Christ, God incarnate, the second person of the Blessed Trinity, came as King and Lord to liberate all of creation from sin, death, and suffering.[43] According to Boff, Christ's liberation is holistic: "The kingdom or reign of God means the full and total liberation of all of creation, in the end, purified of all that oppresses it, transfigured by the full presence of God."[44] This liberation is all encompassing, and it includes freedom from both personal and social sin. "Because the kingdom is absolute, it embraces all things: sacred and profane history, the church and the world, human beings and the cosmos."[45] The reign of God is also both here now, and not yet. God establishes his kingdom now, "on earth as it is in heaven," through the church, the body of Christ. And yet it is also a future eschatological reality—something much more than historical political revolutions— which will only find its full realization upon the return of Christ and the coming of the new heaven and the new earth (Rev 21:1).

As king and liberator, Jesus is much more than a "Santa Claus Christ," "passport Christ," or "Ché Guevara Christ."[46] According to the former, Jesus gives blessings and good things to those who believe. He is a "'Father Christmas Christ,' one who comes to give only because he's so rich. He has lots of capital. Christ becomes a commodity, and the highest bidder gets him."[47] Closely related to the Santa Claus portrayal of Jesus is the "middle class Christ" who was brought to Latin America through the Spanish and Portuguese conquests and American missionaries. The middle-class Jesus colludes with materialism and consumer society, and is satisfied with a superficial faith that tithes, attends church on a regular basis, and does not drink or smoke. This misrepresentation of Jesus condones the status quo, even when it results in human suffering, and offers "a sweet, soft Christ

---

[43]Boff and Boff, *Introducing Liberation Theology*, 52.
[44]Boff and Boff, *Introducing Liberation Theology*, 52.
[45]Boff and Boff, *Introducing Liberation Theology*, 53.
[46]Saúl Trinidad and Juan Stam, "Christ in Latin American Protestant Preaching," in *Faces of Jesus: Latin American Christologies*, ed. José Míguez Bonino (Maryknoll, NY: Orbis Books, 1985), 40-42.
[47]Trinidad and Stam, "Christ in Latin American Protestant Preaching," 40, 43.

who always goes the second mile, always turns the other cheek, and who soothes souls—but who never denounced injustice or led a demonstration or grabbed a whip to spill everything over in the temple."[48] For those who subscribe to a passport Christology, Jesus is important only insofar as he is our personal savior who allows us to enter heaven when we die. This limited Christology can produce escapism and justify apathy in the face of social inequality and injustice.

At the same time, Jesus is not simply a "guerrilla Christ," or a Che Guevara messiah who slaps superficial Christian theology on a Marxist revolution.[49] This too, falls short of the biblical Jesus. In claiming to be Son of God, Lord, and king over and against Caesar and the Roman Empire, and in challenging the political and religious elites of his day, Jesus was certainly subversive. And yet, his message was distinct from the Zealots of his day whose method was to "pray and sharpen their swords."[50] Jesus was a Messiah who challenged injustice and the oppressive status quo, but also one who gave his life on a Roman cross, rose again, and called his followers to personal and social transformation through repentance, discipleship, and life in the kingdom of God.

In the end, each of these limited Christologies—whether the Santa Claus, passport, or Che Guevara Christ—are insufficient, for they ignore the all-encompassing nature of Christ's salvation and the kingdom of God, which has arrived to make us and the whole world new. Each portrayal, in its own way, ignores the fullness of "Jesus, the Son of God, who took on oppression in order to set us free," the central role of his "church as a sign and instrument of liberation," and the "Holy Spirit, 'Father of the poor,'" who is "present in the struggles of the oppressed."[51] Christ's salvation leaves nothing out, whether personal salvation, individual and social transformation, or the joy of heaven. In the words of the Protestant

---

[48]Boff and Boff, *Introducing Liberation Theology*, 43.
[49]Trinidad and Stam, "Christ in Latin American Protestant Preaching," 43.
[50]N.T. Wright, *The Challenge of Jesus: Rediscovering Who Jesus Was and Is* (Downers Grove, IL: InterVarsity Press, 2015), 37.
[51]Boff and Boff, *Introducing Liberation Theology*, 53, 55, 59.

evangélico theologians to whom we shall now turn, the salvation and mission of Jesus is *integral* and holistic.

"MISIÓN INTEGRAL": A HOLISTIC GOSPEL

Stirred by the same milieu of poverty, militarism, and oppression as their Roman Catholic counterparts, Latin American evangélicos of the 1960s and '70s wrestled with creating a movement and a theology that was faithful to their contextualized experience and distinct theological commitments.[52] As Protestant evangelicals, they held firmly to the centrality of Christ as Savior of the world, the Bible as the authoritative Word of God, and the Holy Spirit as transformative and active agent in the lives of believers. According to theologian Emilio Antonio Nuñez of El Salvador, Latin American evangelical theology is characterized as Theocentric, Bibliocentric, Christocentric, and Pneumatological.[53] As "radical evangelicals," they "sought to remain faithful to the Scriptures and, at the same time, incarnated in the Latin American socio-political reality."[54] Although theologically conservative, they remained steadfastly committed to the outworking of the Gospel through works of transformative justice. While welcoming dialogue with liberation theology, radical evangelicals labored in polemical tension with liberation theologians—both Catholic and Protestant.[55] Moreover, despite being sympathetic to many of the concerns of Liberation Theology, radical evangelicals opposed the explicit adoption of Marxist ideology, the sacralization of revolution, disregard

---

[52]This section adapted from the essay "Toward a Perspective of 'Brown Theology'" by Robert Chao Romero, from *Evangelical Theologies of Liberation and Justice*, edited by Mae Elise Cannon and Andrea Smith (Downers Grove, IL: IVP Academic, 2019), 75-95.

[53]Ruth Irene Padilla DeBorst, "Integral Mission Formation in Abya Yala (Latin America): A Study of the Centro de Studios Teológicos Interdisciplinarios (1982–2002) and Radical Evangélicos" (PhD diss., Boston University, 2016), 28.

[54]Padilla DeBorst, "Integral Mission Formation," 29-30.

[55]For a detailed discussion of the negotiation of theological tensions between Latin American evangélicos and liberation theology, see Sharon E. Heaney, *Contextual Theology for Latin America: Liberation Themes in Evangelical Perspective* (Colorado Springs: Paternoster, 2008). Heaney's important work also explores the conflicts between Latin American evangelicalism and Protestant fundamentalism.

for the authority of the Bible, and any simplistic reduction of the gospel to political, sociological or economic terms.[56]

The radical evangelical movement of Latin America was birthed, in part, out of the ministry endeavors of the Comunidad Internacional de Estudiantes Evangélicos (CIEE), and closely associated with Carlos René Padilla, J. Samuel Escobar Aguirre, and Pedro Arana Quiroz.[57] Mortimer Arias, Orlando Enrique Costas, Emilio Antonio Nuñez, and Peter Savage were theologians and pastors who also played central roles in the development of Latin American evangelical theology in the 1970's. The CIEE was formally established in Cochabamba, Bolivia, in 1958 and was the Latin American expression of the International Fellowship of Evangelical Students (IFES). The IFES was formed in 1947 in Boston by the leaders of ten evangelical student movements from throughout the world. The IFES is the worldwide representative body that emerged from InterVarsity Fellowship and the InterVarsity Christian Fellowship-USA.[58]

CIEE leaders René Padilla and Samuel Escobar created innovative campus ministry programs that helped produce the radical evangelical movement, and served as a petri dish for the theology of misión integral.[59] Padilla was born in Quito, Ecuador, in 1932, and spent much of his childhood in Colombia.[60] Following graduation from Wheaton College with a BA in philosophy and an MA in theology, Padilla was appointed IFES traveling secretary for Venezuela, Colombia, Peru, and his native Ecuador.[61] His Western, Protestant evangelical theological training had not adequately prepared him, however, for the social questions and revolutionary milieu he would encounter on the Latin American university campus. In his words, "In this [university] context

---

[56]Padilla DeBorst, "Integral Mission Formation," 128.

[57]Padilla DeBorst, "Integral Mission Formation," 77; Daniel Salinas, *Latin American Evangelical Theology in the 1970's: The Golden Decade* (Leiden and Boston: Brill, 2009), 17-19.

[58]David C. Kirkpatrick, "C. René Padilla and the Origins of Integral Mission in Post-War Latin America," *Journal of Ecclesiastical History* 67, no. 2 (2016): 361-362.

[59]Kirkpatrick, "C. René Padilla," 364.

[60]Salinas, *Latin American Evangelical Theology*, 18.

[61]Kirkpatrick, "C. René Padilla," 361.

I found myself lacking a social ethic. My years of studies in the United States had not prepared me for the sort of theological reflection that was urgently needed in a revolutionary situation!"[62]

Samuel Escobar was born in Arequipa, Peru, in 1934. He completed his undergraduate studies at San Marcos University in Lima and his doctoral work at the Complutense University in Madrid, Spain.[63] Notably, Escobar's dissertation examined the life and teachings of Brazilian Christian social activist and educator Paulo Freire. Together with Padilla and Pedro Arana, Escobar founded the Latin American branch of IFES in 1958, and he also served as traveling and regional secretary for the organization.

As Padilla and his ministry partner Escobar read their Bibles, they came to understand the importance of distinguishing between what the Bible actually taught and the *ropa anglosajon*, or Anglo-Saxon cultural clothing of the gospel, which had been exported to Latin America from the United States.[64] Existing approaches to ministry, shaped primarily by foreign Western contexts, would not suffice for Latin American students who sought an indigenous expression of Christian faith that was relevant to their own experience and social conditions. Especially in the wake of the Cuban Revolution of 1953, many students gravitated toward justice protest and revolutionary struggle and sought a biblical understanding that would speak to matters of political and social liberation.[65] Drawing from their years of ministry experimentation with such socially conscious students, Samuel Escobar and René Padilla established the first Latin American justice-focused training for IFES university students in 1966 in Lima, Peru. This training integrated traditional discipleship and evangelism training with service projects in poor communities. The Lima course was also informed by the completion of Padilla's doctoral studies in Manchester under the famous evangelical biblical scholar F. F. Bruce.

---

[62]Kirkpatrick, "C. René Padilla," 361.
[63]Salinas, *Latin American Evangelical Theology*, 18.
[64]Padilla DeBorst, "Integral Mission Formation," 45.
[65]Kirkpatrick, "C. René Padilla," 361-62, 364-65.

Several years later, in December 1970, Padilla and Escobar met with twenty-three other Protestant church leaders in Cochabamba, Bolivia, to discuss the formation of a distinctly Latin American evangelical theology that addressed the poverty and oppression of Latin America. The attendees of the famous Cochabamba gathering were a diverse lot, representing twelve nationalities and nine denominations. The denominational and theological spectrum included Wesleyan, Nazarene, Anglican, Presbyterian, Baptist, Pentecostal, and Dispensationalist. In addition to pastors and theologians, the group included lay leaders, campus ministers, educators, seminary professors, evangelists, writers, and journal and magazine editors. The Bible and the authority of Scripture served as the point of consensus for this diverse community.[66]

The Latin American leaders convened at Cochabamba understood that the theological approaches and ministry methods of North America were insufficient for the contextual needs of Latin America. They were "tired of the evangelical power centers in North America telling us how to think, who to read, and what it meant to be evangelical," and they "decided it was time to start reflecting the faith as grownups and on our own."[67] In no uncertain terms, they rejected US "culture Christianity," which conflated the gospel with Western values and conformity with the status quo. According to this limited cultural expression of Christianity, "the racist can continue to be a racist, the exploiter can continue to be an exploiter." In the words of Escobar, moreover, US culture-Christians were the kind of people who "oppose the violence of revolution but not the violence of war" and "condemn all the sins that well-behaved middle class people condemn but say nothing about exploitation, intrigue, and dirty political maneuvering done by great multi-national corporations around the world."[68]

In response to these extreme blind spots of Western Protestant Christianity, those gathered at Cochabamba sought to reframe the gospel in a

---

[66]Salinas, *Latin American Evangelical Theology*, 96-97.
[67]Michael Clawson, "Misión Integral and Progressive Evangelicalism: The Latin American Influence on the North American Emerging Church," *Religions* 3, no. 3 (2012): 791.
[68]Padilla DeBorst, "Integral Mission Formation," 46.

fresh way that was faithful both to Scripture and the distinct Latin American cultural and historical context.[69] To achieve this goal and help foster productive theological discussion, Padilla and Escobar, together with Orlando Costas, Pedro Arana, Emilio Antonio Nuñez, Orlando Gutierrez, and Peter Savage, founded the Fraternidad de Teólogos Latinoamericanos. The name was soon changed to the Fraternidad Teológica Latinoamericana (FTL), the name it has retained to the present day.[70] The mission of the FTL included three major objectives: (1) "to foster reflection on the Gospel and its significance for the people and society in Latin America"; (2) "to become a platform for dialogue among thinkers who confess Jesus Christ as Lord and God, and who are willing to think in the light of the Bible in order to build a bridge between the gospel and the Latin American culture"; and (3) "to contribute to the life and mission of the Church of Christ in Latin America, not pretending to speak in the name of the church nor assuming to be the theological voice of the evangelicals in Latin America."[71] In subsequent decades, the FTL emerged as the leading Evangelical theological organization in Latin America.[72] It also inspired numerous missional initiatives and organizations, and helped train many who have gone on to be leaders in churches and the nonprofit sector.[73]

The greatest theological contribution of FTL and the radical evangélicos has been the framework of misión integral. According to the theology of misión integral, biblical mission must include "both proclamation and demonstration of the good news of the Reign of God through Christian teaching, presence, and social engagement for transformation."[74] Evangelism and social action are both integral to Christian mission and

---

[69]Padilla DeBorst, "Integral Mission Formation," 45-48.

[70]Clawson, "Misión Integral," 791; Padilla DeBorst, "Integral Mission Formation," 97.

[71]Salinas, *Latin American Evangelical Theology*, 25-26. Salinas's work represents the central historiography on the FTL. For a broader examination of the development of evangélico theology over the course of the twentieth century, see Salinas, *Taking Up the Mantle: Latin American Evangelical Theology in the 20th Century* (n.p.: Langham Global Library, 2017).

[72]Kirkpatrick, "C. René Padilla," 368.

[73]Padilla DeBorst, "Integral Mission Formation," 124.

[74]Padilla DeBorst, "Integral Mission Formation," 5.

cannot be artificially divided one from another. In 1969, Padilla, who is widely considered to be the "father" of integral mission declared:

> The proclamation of the gospel (*kerygma*) and the demonstration of the gospel that gives itself in service (*diakonía*) form an indissoluble (*indisoluble*) whole. One without the other is an incomplete, mutilated (*mutilado*) gospel and, consequently, contrary to the will of God. From this perspective, it is foolish to ask about the relative importance of evangelism and social responsibility. This would be equivalent to asking about the relative importance of the right wing and the left wing of a plane.[75]

To use another metaphor, mision integral declares that the gospel involves both vertical salvation (reconciliation of an individual with God through Christ) and horizontal engagement with the pressing social concerns of the day.[76] Like *harina integral* (whole wheat flour) or *arroz integral* (whole grain rice), biblical mission is all-encompassing and must entail both the verbal proclamation of the good news of Jesus and the practical expression of Christ's justice in the world.[77] Though this notion of a holistic gospel is somewhat common within Protestant evangelical circles today, what is much less known is that its origins lay in Latin America among radical evangélicos and the FTL. In fact, it has been said that the theological reintegration of evangelism and social action through misión integral has been "the most significant contribution which Latin American evangelicals have made internationally" to the global church. Since the 1970s, the global missions paradigm of misión integral has spread far beyond Latin America through the International Conference on World Evangelization held in Lausanne, Switzerland in 1974, the InterVarsity Urbana Missions Conference of 1970, and the International Fellowship for Mission as Transformation, Micah Global, and the Lausanne Movement.[78] Quite notably, the popular evangelical "missional church movement" has often neglected to credit Padilla and Escobar

---

[75]Kirkpatrick, "C. René Padilla," 368.
[76]Kirkpatrick, "C. René Padilla," 360.
[77]Padilla DeBorst, "Integral Mission Formation," 54.
[78]Padilla DeBorst, "Integral Mission Formation," 55, 57.

with the central theological framework that defines their ecclesiological method and practice. This is unacceptable cultural appropriation.[79]

The FTL continues to have a broad reach up into the present day through its convening of consultations and the CLADE Congresses (Congreso Latinoamericano de Evangelización), as well as through the proliferation of local and national chapters.[80] The FTL also promotes vibrant theological discussion through numerous written publications in the form of books, journals, and bulletins.

CONCLUSION

1968 was a defining moment in the history of the Brown Church. In that year, gathered in Medellín, Colombia, Roman Catholic bishops of Latin America "opted" to take the side of the poor who had been cast aside, *desachados*, for five hundred years. Since the Spanish conquest of 1492, those of Spanish descent had stolen and controlled the land and vast natural resources of Latin America at the expense of the indigenous peoples and created all manner of racist and inequitable socioeconomic and political structures to ensure their wealth and control. In addition, Afro-Latinas/os of Mexico, Central and South America, and the Caribbean had occupied an exploited racial class for as many years. Then, and to this day, those of indigenous and African descent in Latin America remain among the poorest and most disenfranchised. In 1968, in a deeply historic moment, Roman Catholic bishops gathered and said, "¡Ya basta! God takes the side of the poor, and so do we."

Liberation theologians of the Brown Church such as Gustavo Gutiérrez, Míguez Bonino, and Leonardo and Clodovis Boff, reminded not only Latin Americans—but the whole world—of the biblical preferential option for the poor. God loves all equally, but reserves a unique place of concern for all who are poor and ignored at the margins of society. In a sinful and broken world, they bear the brunt. The writings and teachings

---

[79]See, for example, John Stott, *Christian Mission in the Modern World* (Downers Grove, IL: Inter-Varsity Press, 2009).

[80]Padilla DeBorst, "Integral Mission Formation," 39-40.

of Latin American liberationists would go on to inspire many global expressions of Liberation Theology in the United States, Africa, Asia, and even the Pacific Islands.[81] Like all movements, Latin American Liberation Theology was diverse, and it had blind spots. Some of it leaned heavily Marxist, and a number of clergy departed from Jesus' teachings of nonviolence and, in the pattern of the Zealots, directly embraced the method of military confrontation. God knows. Él sabe. Let God be the judge.

Together with their Roman Catholic counterparts, Protestant Latin Americans pondered the same questions of social inequality and took a bold step: they "decolonized" their theology. Although in agreement with the core theocentric, bibliocentric, Christocentric, and pneumatological theological commitments of the evangelical church brought to Latin America by Euro-American missionaries, they protested the swaddling of the gospel in ropa anglosajon, or Anglo cultural clothing. Whereas many Anglo missionaries viewed their teaching as simply "biblical," Padilla, Escobar, and the leaders of the FTL understood that the theology that was transplanted to Latin America was deeply unbiblical insofar as it artificially divided the verbal proclamation of the gospel from the practical outworking of the gospel through social justice. In response, the FTL created its own local theology rooted in the Latin American history and context—misión integral. In reclaiming a holistic gospel, the FTL decolonized its faith. It also revolutionized the world of Protestant global missions by bringing it back to the core biblical teaching that faith without works is dead, and that true religion is loving widows, orphans, and the poor in their distress (Jas 1:27, 2:14-26). Eventually, misión integral would make its way to US Latinas/os through Fuller Theological Seminary and other institutions of Latina/o theological exploration. To this day, however, it has not been implemented en masse within the pews of the thousands of evangélico and Pentecostal churches in *el otro lado*.

---

[81]For an introduction to liberation theology of Oceania and the Pacific Islands, see Jonathan Blas Dias, *Towards a Theology of the Chamoru: Struggle and Liberation in Oceania* (Quezon City: Claretian Publications, 2010).

In the new theological world of liberation theology and misión integral of the 1960s–1980s, there were many—Catholic and Protestant—who felt uncomfortable taking a strong public stand against the status quo. Shaped by centuries of colonial Christianity, they did not feel it was their spiritual responsibility to do so, and they preferred a stance of neutrality in the face of racial oppression. As we will see in the next chapter, Archbishop Oscar Romero was for a time in this camp, but like Las Casas half a millennium earlier, he came to experience a radical conversion to the poor that would transform him into the most famous martyr of the Liberation Theology movement.

7

LIBERATION THEOLOGY IN PRACTICE

Archbishop Oscar Romero of El Salvador

No *TESTIMONIO* better captures the spirit of Liberation Theology than that of Archbishop Oscar Romero of El Salvador. Like Las Casas four centuries before, Romero's story is one of conscientization and conversion to the poor and a transformed understanding of Christ's teaching that the gospel is a proclamation of "good news" to the poor and all who have been cast aside. Ultimately, Romero's embodiment of this biblical truth led to his martyrdom after a short but powerful three years of prophetic ministry among the poor. It also led to his official canonization as a saint within the Roman Catholic Church on October 14, 2018.

Oscar Romero was born in 1917 to a humble family in Ciudad Barrios, San Miguel, in rural El Salvador.[1] Following his basic education and carpenter's apprenticeship, Romero attended seminary in San Salvador and San Miguel, and was ordained a Roman Catholic priest in 1942. For the first quarter-century of his religious vocation, Romero was known as a quiet, studious, social conservative who would not rock the boat nor challenge the conservative oligarchy.

---

[1] Marie Dennis, Renny Golden, and Scott Wright, *Oscar Romero: Reflections on His Life and Writings* (Maryknoll, NY: Orbis Books, 2000), 7; James R. Brockman, *Romero: A Life* (Maryknoll, NY: Orbis Books, 1990), 7-8, 24-25, 33.

Though initially skeptical of liberation theology, he privately and timidly challenged government violence against the rural poor and embraced some public works of compassion.[2] In February 1977, precisely because of his conservative reputation, Romero was installed as archbishop of San Salvador.[3] His appointment was hailed as a victory by the elites of the country because it was believed he would counter the movement of Liberation Theology among progressive priests and nuns. Among the latter, Romero's appointment was a huge disappointment. In the words of Jesuit liberation theologian Jon Sobrino, "We all thought we faced a very bleak future."[4]

All of that changed on March 12, 1977, with the murder of Romero's close friend, Jesuit priest Rutilio Grande.[5] Grande worked as a parish priest among the rural poor in Aguilares, and was murdered by government military forces for his support of the Liberation Theology movement. As a liberationist priest, Grande worked with a team of seminary students and catechists to establish Base Christian Communities among local residents. The goal of these religious communities was to raise the spiritual and political consciousness of their members and mobilize against government violence, poverty, and repression. As part of these efforts, Grande publicly denounced the landowning elite who monopolized agricultural landholdings to the detriment and suffering of the rural masses. In the face of mass poverty and human suffering, fourteen elite families controlled 60 percent of all arable land in the nation. These oligarchs, moreover, were supported by the military, police, elected officials, courts, and paramilitary forces. On March 12, 1977, Grande was gunned down while driving through tall sugar canes on his way to the celebration of evening Mass.

Grande's murder was the turning point of Romero's spiritual life and ministry—when the "scales fell from his eyes."[6] As recalled by Sobrino,

---

[2]Dennis, Golden, and Wright, *Oscar Romero*, 8, 9.

[3]Dennis, Golden, and Wright, *Oscar Romero*, 24-25; Brockman, *Romero*, 4.

[4]Dennis, Golden, and Wright, *Oscar Romero*, 25.

[5]Dennis, Golden, and Wright, *Oscar Romero*, 25-27.

[6]Dennis, Golden, and Wright, *Oscar Romero*, 27-28; Dermot Keogh, *Romero: El Salvador's Martyr* (Dublin: Dominican Publications, 1981), 60.

"I believe that the murder of Rutilio Grande was the occasion of the conversion of Archbishop Romero. . . . It was Rutilio's death that gave Archbishop Romero the strength for new activity . . . and the fundamental direction for his own life."[7] After that moment, Romero "opted" for the poor of El Salvador in their suffering and oppression. Like Las Casas five hundred years earlier, he became conscienticized.

As his first act of prophetic witness, Romero called for a single Mass to be held in all of San Salvador in honor of Father Rutilio Grande.[8] All other Masses in the archdiocese were canceled. In addition to announcing the single Mass, Romero also made the bold statement that he would boycott participation in official government affairs until the government ended repression of the clergy and the poor.[9] The unified Mass required rich urban elites and the rural poor to come together in an unprecedented religious gathering. Preaching to a captive audience, Romero condemned the murder of Father Grande at the hands of the landowning elite and corrupt government officials. He demanded repentance for this atrocious act, and called all into solidarity with the poor of El Salvador.

At that the Mass, he boldly declared,

> This is not the moment to speak about my personal relationship with Father Grande, but rather to gather from this cadaver a message for all of us who continue the pilgrimage. . . . Let us not forget. We are a pilgrim church, exposed to misunderstanding, to persecution; but a church that walks peacefully because we carry within us the force of love.[10]

To those who would dare repeat the murder of religious clergy, he also sternly warned, "Whoever touches one of my priests, touches me."[11]

For the next three years until his own martyrdom, Romero became a fierce public advocate for the poor in the name of Jesus, and called the

---

[7]Dennis, Golden, and Wright, *Oscar Romero*, 28.
[8]Dennis, Golden, and Wright, *Oscar Romero*, 31; Brockman, *Romero*, 14.
[9]Dennis, Golden, and Wright, *Oscar Romero*, 33.
[10]Dennis, Golden, and Wright, *Oscar Romero*, 32.
[11]Dennis, Golden, and Wright, *Oscar Romero*, 31.

rest of the church to do the same.[12] From that point on, Romero realized that neutrality in the face of murder and repression was no longer possible in El Salvador. Christ is the God of life, and so to follow him requires his followers—of all epochs and historical time periods—to struggle against the oppression of the poor: "We see with great clarity that here neutrality is impossible. . . . And here what is most fundamental about the faith is given expression in history: either we believe in a God of life, or we serve the idols of death."[13]

The following text, part of a modern-day epistle written to the churches of El Salvador in 1981, vividly describes the brutal murder and sexual violence perpetrated by death squads against the rural poor at the behest of the elite. It is disturbing and exemplifies the types of abuses which Romero, and Father Grande before him, gave their lives to denounce:

> One night, six men from the death squads came to her shack looking for guns. When they didn't find anything, they upset the sacks filled with corn shucks the family used to light their home during the long nights. They pointed their guns at Jacinta and told her not to move. Then they knocked her husband down in front of her, stepped on him and kicked him, breaking his neck.
>
> "God sees what you do," Jacinta told them, "and God will make you pay for this shameful act."
>
> "God is dead!" one of the men shouted. "We are the gods now."
>
> They dragged her two oldest daughters outside. Three men beat them, and then they raped each one. When they finished, Jacinta was forced to serve them water at gunpoint.
>
> "Don't tell anyone about this. If you do, we're going to come at night and kill everyone."[14]

During the 1970s and '80s, the Salvadoran military waged fierce war against the guerillas of the Farabundo Martí National Liberation Front (FMLN). In an attempt to squelch popular support for the FMLN, as

---

[12]Brockman, *Romero*, 62-63; 80-84.
[13]Dennis, Golden, and Wright, *Oscar Romero*, 53.
[14]Dennis, Golden, and Wright, *Oscar Romero*, 70, 71.

evidenced by this violent testimony, death squads targeted those who supported farming cooperatives, as well as priests, nuns, and all who were perceived as sympathetic to the FMLN.[15] Many priests, nuns, and religious workers were martyred in successive waves of violence. Graffiti in the capital of San Salvador declared, "Be a patriot, kill a priest." In 1977, Father Alfonso Navarro was murdered along with dozens of pastoral workers.[16] In 1978 and 1979, government forces and death squads continued their repression, and took the lives of Father Ernesto Barrera, Father Rafael Palacios, and Father Alirio Napoleón Macías Octavio Ortiz. In an astonishing act of cruelty, government forces murdered Father Octavio Ortiz and four youth while on a spiritual retreat.[17] American clergy were also targeted, and in December 1980, four American nuns and lay missioners were raped and murdered. Their names were Maura Clark (Maryknoll), Ita Ford (Maryknoll), Dorothy Kazel (Ursuline), and Jean Donovan (Cleveland lay missionary). One year later, close to one thousand people, primarily women and children, were massacred by the Salvadoran army at El Mozote.[18] In November 1989, El Salvadoran military forces continued their rampage and murdered six Jesuit priests and two of their female coworkers.

Between 1980 and 1992, the years spanning the El Salvadoran civil war, more than 75,000 people were killed.[19] Military and paramilitary forces conducted beheadings, skinned people alive, slit throats, and even ripped unborn children from their mother's wombs. Murdered corpses were dumped in village squares as warnings to potential sympathizers. This murderous activity of the Salvadoran government was funded by the United States. Moreover, it was led by officers and soldiers trained by the United States at the US Army School of the Americas.

---

[15]Dennis, Golden, and Wright, *Oscar Romero*, 10-11.
[16]Dennis, Golden, and Wright, *Oscar Romero*, 9, 10.
[17]Brockman, *Romero*, 54.
[18]Dennis, Golden, and Wright, *Oscar Romero*, 11.
[19]Dennis, Golden, and Wright, *Oscar Romero*, 10-11, 15.

Through weekly sermons broadcast over national radio, pastoral letters, and public talks, Romero decried the torture, murders, and disappearances of the El Salvadoran totalitarian state.[20] He did this with little support from the Vatican and in the face of opposition by many of his fellow bishops who accused him of mixing religion with politics. Invoking the spiritual truths of Liberation Theology, Romero embraced the doctrine of the preferential option for the poor and declared that it was unbiblical for the church in El Salvador to remain neutral in the face of the murder and repression of the poor.

Romero boldly proclaimed that the true church of Jesus Christ must take the side of the poor: "A church that does not join the poor, in order to speak out from the side of the poor against the injustices committed against them, is not the true church of Jesus Christ."[21]

Calling upon the scriptural authority of Matthew 25 and the biblical truth that all people are created in the image of God, Romero declared that Christ was present in the face of the rural poor of El Salvador. When they were tortured and abused, so was Christ; when children died of hunger, so did Christ; when they cried out to God and the church for liberation, so was Christ:

> The face of Christ is among the sacks and baskets of the farmworker; the face of Christ is among those who are tortured and mistreated in the prisons; the face of Christ is dying of hunger in the children who have nothing to eat; the face of Christ is in the poor who ask the church for their voice to be heard. How can the church deny this request when it is Christ who is telling us to speak for him?[22]

Romero also believed that it was the poor who should guide the church in justice, and that they should be the leaders and vanguard of their own spiritual and social liberation. It was the poor, because of their suffering and struggle, who teach the world the meaning of Christian

---

[20]Dennis, Golden, and Wright, *Oscar Romero*, 12, 16, 22, 36, 53, 86, 91.
[21]Dennis, Golden, and Wright, *Oscar Romero*, 65.
[22]Dennis, Golden, and Wright, *Oscar Romero*, 35.

love. Through entering into the world of the poor, all Christians come to a deepened faith in God and Jesus Christ. Indeed, for Romero, the poor were the image of Christ crucified for the world to see.[23]

The poor have shown the church the true way to go.[24]

The world of the poor teaches us what the nature of Christian love is, a love that certainly seeks peace, but also unmasks false pacifism—the pacifism of resignation and inactivity. It is a love that should certainly be freely offered, but that seeks to be effective in history. The world of the poor teaches us that the sublimity of Christian love ought to be mediated through the overriding necessity of justice for the majority. . . . The world of the poor teaches us that liberation will arrive only when the poor are not simply on the receiving end of handouts from governments or from the churches, but when they themselves are the masters and protagonists of their own struggle and liberation.[25]

In alignment with the teachings of Liberation Theology, Romero rejected a narrow Gospel that portrays salvation in a hyperindividualistic way and is focused only on life after death.[26] He dismissed a disembodied gospel that was not good news to the poor in this world, and any notion of the kingdom of God that did not promote justice in the present time. For Romero, our efforts toward justice have eternal value, and will be brought to ultimate fulfillment upon the return of Christ:

Unfortunately, brothers and sisters, we are the product of a spiritualized, individualistic education. We are taught: try to save your soul and don't worry about the rest. We told those who suffered: be patient, heaven will follow, hang on. No, that's not right, that's not salvation!

The great leader of our liberation is this Anointed One, the Lord who comes to announce the good news to the poor, to give liberty to the captives, to bear news of the disappeared to bring joy to so many homes that are in mourning, so that a new society may appear as in the sabbatical year

---

[23]Dennis, Golden, and Wright, *Oscar Romero*, 41, 51, 52.
[24]Dennis, Golden, and Wright, *Oscar Romero*, 65.
[25]Dennis, Golden, and Wright, *Oscar Romero*, 51.
[26]Dennis, Golden, and Wright, *Oscar Romero*, 65.

of Israel. . . . Christ has come precisely to announce the new society, the good news, the new times.[27]

For Romero, Christ was the very source of Liberation for El Salvador—the only country named after the Savior Himself. Justice and liberation could not come about through human effort alone, but through faith and hope in Christ, who gave his life to pay for the sin of injustice, and to open up the path toward human redemption:

> We human beings cannot produce our land's liberation.
> We Salvadorans are unable to save our country
> with our own human powers.
> But if we hope for a liberation to come from Christ,
> the Redeemer, then we can.
> This is the church's hope.
> This is why I preach much faith in Christ. He died to pay for all injustices
> and rose to bury in his tomb all evil
> and become the redemption of all those who suffer. He is hope and
>   eternal life.[28]

Christ inaugurated the kingdom of God two thousand years ago, and in so doing began a divine movement of justice, healing, and renewal that is to spread to every nation of the world. The kingdom of God has already begun, and with the empowerment of the Holy Spirit, it moves forward as an unstoppable force.

> With Christ, God has injected himself into history. With the birth of Christ, God's reign is now inaugurated in human time. . . .
> We recall that God's reign is now in this world and that Christ has inaugurated the fullness of time. His birth attests that God is now marching with us in history, that we do not go alone.[29]

The kingdom of God moves forward, moreover, in the model and example of Christ—with radical love and nonviolence, even toward our

---

[27]Dennis, Golden, and Wright, *Oscar Romero*, 78, 93.
[28]Oscar A. Romero, *The Violence of Love* (Maryknoll, NY: Orbis Books, 2004), 28.
[29]Romero, *Violence of Love*, 38.

enemies.[30] This love sent Jesus to die on a Roman imperial cross, and it is the path that enables our own transformation and the creation of universal sisterhood and brotherhood. In the words of Romero, the kingdom of God advances with "the violence of love":

> We have never preached violence,
> except the violence of love,
> which left Christ nailed to a cross,
> the violence that we must each do to ourselves to overcome our selfishness
> and such cruel inequalities among us.
> The violence we preach is not the violence of the sword, the violence of
>   hatred.
> It is the violence of love, of brotherhood,
> the violence that wills to beat weapons into sickles for work.[31]

In the end, Archbishop Oscar Romero was martyred for his prophetic Christian witness. In his last sermon before his death, Romero instructed members of the El Salvadoran military to disobey any orders requiring them to kill their fellow Salvadoran citizens.[32] He admonished them to seek their consciences before God and to obey God rather than corrupt military leadership. He called on them to end the brutal government repression that was sweeping the country.[33] Less than two months earlier, Romero had sent a letter to US president Jimmy Carter requesting that all military aid be stopped because it was being used to murder the Salvadoran people.[34]

Romero was assassinated on March 24, 1980, while administering Mass in the chapel of the Divina Providencia hospital.[35] Eerily, the Gospel reading for the day came from John 12:23-26, and foreshadowed Romero's imminent martyrdom:

---

[30]Brockman, *Romero*, 63.
[31]Romero, *Violence of Love*, 25.
[32]Keogh, *Romero, El Salvador's Martyr*, 2.
[33]Dennis, Golden, and Wright, *Oscar Romero*, 95.
[34]Dennis, Golden, and Wright, *Oscar Romero*, 94; Keogh, *Romero, El Salvador's Martyr*, 92; Brockman, *Romero*, 227.
[35]Dennis, Golden, and Wright, *Oscar Romero*, 97; Keogh, *Romero: El Salvador's Martyr*, 3, 99; Brockman, *Romero*, 244-245.

The hour has come for the Son of Man to be glorified. Very truly, I tell you, unless a grain of wheat falls into the earth and dies, it remains just a single grain; but if it dies, it bears much fruit. Those who love their life lose it, and those who hate their life in this world will keep it for eternal life. Whoever serves me must follow me, and where I am, there will my servant be also. Whoever serves me, the Father will honor.

Inspired by the teachings of Jesus, Archbishop Romero's last words beckoned his listeners to present their own lives as a sacrifice for others in the model of Christ. From the spiritual nourishment of the Eucharist, and Christian lives poured out in service, justice and peace would flow to the people of El Salvador:

Whoever offers their life out of love for Christ, and in service to others, will live like the seed that dies. . . . May this immolated body and this blood sacrificed for all nourish us so that we may offer our body and our blood as Christ did, and thus bring justice and peace to our people. Let us join together, then, in the faith and hope of this intimate moment of prayer . . . [36]

Six days later, 150,000 people assembled for the funeral Mass of Romero at the cathedral of San Salvador.[37] His eulogy was preached by Cardinal Corripio of Mexico. Government forces violently interrupted the peaceful funeral Mass with explosives and rifle fire, and thousands scattered.[38] In the midst of the chaos, Salvadoran snipers fired into the dispersing crowd. Thirty people were killed and four hundred injured.[39]

Following his murder and martyrdom, Romero became the most visible symbol of the Liberation Theology movement and one of the most prominent Christians in modern Latin American religious history. Echoing this sentiment, Gustavo Gutiérrez declared: "I think that we could say, without exaggeration, that the life and death of Monseñor Romero divides the recent history of the Latin American church into a before and after."[40] In

---

[36]Dennis, Golden, and Wright, *Oscar Romero*, 98.
[37]Dennis, Golden, and Wright, *Oscar Romero*, 104.
[38]Keogh, *Romero: El Salvador's Martyr*, 109-10; Brockman, *Romero*, 246-47, 249.
[39]Dennis, Golden, and Wright, *Oscar Romero*, 104.
[40]Dennis, Golden, and Wright, *Oscar Romero*, 105.

accordance with the promise of Jesus in John 12:26, Romero was honored by God through the institutional leadership of the global Catholic Church, and the popular masses from whom he learned. On February 3, 2015 he was declared a martyr by liberationist Pope Francis, and several months later, on October 14, 2018, Romero was declared a saint.

CONCLUSION

Archbishop Oscar Romero was one of those Latin American religious leaders who, at first, opted for political neutrality in the face of human suffering. Like Bartolomé de Las Casas five hundred years before him, Romero had a second conversion to the poor and became an unlikely historic leader, and martyr, of the Brown Church in Central America. Following the murder of friend and Jesuit priest Rutilio Grande, Romero came to understand that taking the side of the poor in their oppression was taking the side of Jesus, and that failing to act on their behalf was to ignore the suffering of Jesus himself. Romero became the public face of the Liberation Theology movement, and, together with Gutiérrez, Bonino, and the Boff brothers proclaimed a weighty gospel that challenges the sin of society and necessarily transforms the world:

> A church that doesn't provoke any crises, a gospel that doesn't unsettle, a word of God that doesn't get under anyone's skin, a word of God that doesn't touch the real sin of the society in which it is being proclaimed— what gospel is that? Very nice, pious considerations that don't bother anyone, that's the way many would like preaching to be. Those preachers who avoid every thorny matter so as not to be harassed, so as not to have conflicts and difficulties, do not light up the world they live in.[41]

---

[41]Romero, *Violence of Love*. It is significant to note that Romero's lived example of "the preferential option for the poor" inspired many from el otro lado. Among those touched by his message were the hundreds of thousands of Central American migrants, clergy, and allies who formed the Sanctuary Movement in the United States during the 1980s. For more on Latina/o leadership in the Sanctuary Movement, see Mario T. García, *Father Luis Olivares, A Biography: Faith, Politics and the Origins of the Sanctuary Movement in Los Angeles* (Chapel Hill: The University of North Carolina Press, 2018).

8

RECENT SOCIAL JUSTICE THEOLOGIES OF U.S. LATINAS/OS

*Latina/o Theology, Mujerista Theology,
and Latina/o Practical Theology*

INSPIRED **BY** Latin American liberation theologies, the Chicana/o and African American civil rights struggles, and the swell of diverse Latina/o communities in the United States, Latinas and Latinos began to self-theologize in the 1970s and '80s.[1] As Protestant and Roman Catholic, they rejected the racial paternalism of the Anglo religious community as well as the strategies of cultural assimilationism embraced by previous Latina/o generations.[2] They reflected on their unique experiences as Latinas and Latinos in light of Scripture, grassroots pastoral ministry, and formal theological education. The result was the creation of a new field of religious and theological inquiry in the United States known as Latina/o theology. According to religion scholar Edwin Aponte, this diverse discipline encompasses:

> The distinct theologies that emerge out of the social and cultural contexts
> of Latino/a peoples, which, nonetheless, have some shared characteristics.
> These common traits make Latino/a theology a communal undertaking that

---

[1]Justo González, email message to author, September 1, 2015.
[2]Miguel A. De La Torre and Edwin David Aponte, *Introducing Latino/a Theologies* (Maryknoll, NY: Orbis Books, 2001), 104.

is scholarly, pastoral, and organically connected to grassroots communities. Latino/a theology insists on doing theology in a relevant contextual way that is both in dialogue with the received dominant theological traditions as well as questioning of them and their claims of being standard.[3]

FORERUNNERS AND RECENT SHAPERS

Though formalized as an academic field of study in recent decades, Latina/o theology traces its heritage to both well-known Latin American historical figures such as Las Casas and Sor Juana and to grassroots Pentecostal and Roman Catholic leaders in the United States who have received little public recognition. Prophetic Pentecostal leaders of the Brown Church include Juan L. Lugo, Francisco Olazabal, Leoncia Rosada, and Santos Elizondo.[4] Born in Puerto Rico in 1890, Lugo experienced a radical Pentecostal conversion in 1913 while working as an immigrant laborer in Hawaii. Following his deep encounter with the Holy Spirit, he worked in ministry and church planting in San Francisco, Puerto Rico, and the northeastern United States. As a landmark accomplishment, Lugo founded in 1937 the Instituto Biblico Mizpa, a Pentecostal Bible college that drew students from throughout Puerto Rico and Latin America.

Like Lugo, Francisco Olazabal was a deeply influential Pentecostal evangelist of the early twentieth century, but in his case was noted for his work in the borderlands region of Mexico and Texas. Born in 1886, Olazabal led evangelistic endeavors during the Mexican Revolution, and also established the Latin American Council of Christian Churches (LACCC). The founding of the LACCC was an important historic act of cultural and political empowerment for Latina/o Christians in the United States, as it arose in response to Anglo racism within the Assemblies of God denomination. Through their collaborative efforts in Texas, California, and even Puerto Rico, Lugo and Olazabal helped foster an

---

[3]Edwin David Aponte and Miguel A. De La Torre, *Handbook of Latina/o Theologies* (St. Louis: Chalice Press, 2006), 1.

[4]De La Torre and Aponte, *Introducing Latino/a Theologies*, 98-101.

early sense of pan-Latina/o Pentecostal identity that transcended the normal ethnic and regional divisions of the day.

Born one generation after Lugo and Olazabal, Leoncia Rosado and Santos Elizondo were important Pentecostal female forerunners to Latina/o Theology. Known affectionately as "Mama Leo," Reverend Leoncia Rosado was born in Puerto Rico in 1912. Following an experience of baptism of the Holy Spirit in 1932, she became a pastor in New York City, and, together with her husband Reverend Francisco Rosado, founded the Damascus Youth Crusade and the Iglesia Cristiana Damasco. Long before its formal theological articulation, Mama Leo lived out the preferential option for the poor through her pastoral work among drug addicts and alcoholics. Santos Elizondo also acted on this theological commitment through the founding of a school, an orphanage, and a women's society in the borderlands of El Paso, Texas, and Juárez, Mexico. As a pastor within the Nazarene denomination, Elizondo drew opposition from Protestant missionaries for her role of female leadership, and also for her espousal of what was perceived to be heretical Nazarene doctrine.

Led by the Spirit and fueled by a distinct Latina/o Pentecostal theology and experience, Juan L. Lugo, Francisco Olazabal, Leoncia Rosada, and Santos Elizondo were important forerunners of the contemporary movement of Latina/o theology. At a time of virulent Jim Crow segregation in which Latinas/os experienced ethnic and racial discrimination both in society and in the institutional life of the Protestant church of the United States, they took bold stands, founding their own ecclesial communities and councils, creating culturally contextualized ministries and theologies, and caring for those cast to the margins of Anglo society. Insofar as they challenged the racism, paternalism, and assimilationist structures of mainstream denominations, they anticipated, and set the stage for the formal development of Protestant Latina/o theology in the 1960s–1980s.

In a similar manner, the Roman Catholic stream of Latina/o theology traces its origins to grassroots movements of Catholic clergy and laity in the 1960s.[5] Although the social justice of efforts Dolores Huerta and César Chávez are well documented, much less is known about the inter-related grassroots religious history of Padres Asociados para Derechos Religiosos, Educativos, y Sociales (PADRES) (Association of Fathers for Religious, Educational, and Social Rights), Las Hermanas (The Sisters), and Católicos por la Raza (Catholics for the Race).[6] Composed of Mexican American priests and nuns, PADRES and Las Hermanas deliberately and strategically confronted the racist institutional practices of the Roman Catholic Church in the United States.[7] As discussed by David Flores, these grassroots religious leaders challenged "longstanding discriminatory racial practices, such as segregated seating [in Mass], lack of respect for the Spanish language, poor representation of indigenous Chicana/o leadership [in Catholic institutions], and an unwillingness to support the United Farmworkers struggle."[8] In addition, PADRES and Las Hermanas questioned the lack of culturally relevant seminaries and Latina/o representation in the hierarchy of the Catholic Church.[9] Both organizations eventually expanded their membership ranks to include lay Catholics, and they constituted the first national religious associations of Latina/o Catholics.[10] As part of its specific goals, Las Hermanas networked Catholic women on a national basis to advocate for female ordination, and confronted the patriarchal structure of the Roman Catholic Church.[11] According to Flores, it may be said that PADRES and Las Hermanas represented a type of Chicana/o movement of social

---

[5]Felipe Hinojosa, "Católicos Por La Raza and the Future of Catholic Studies," *American Catholic Studies* 127, no. 3 (2016): 29. Lara Medina, *Las Hermanas: Chicana/Latina Religious-Political Activism in the U.S. Catholic Church* (Philadelphia: Temple University Press, 2004), 87-91. Richard Edward Martínez, *Padres: The National Chicano Priest Movement* (Austin: University of Texas, 2005), 102.

[6]De La Torre and Aponte, *Introducing Latino/a Theologies*, 104-5; Mario T. García, *Chicano Liberation Theology: The Writings and Documents of Richard Cruz and Católicos Por La Raza* (Kendall Hunt Publishing, 2009); David Jesus Flores, "The Chicana/o Movement and the Catholic Church," (Master's thesis; UCLA, 2017), 2.

[7]Martínez, *Padres*, 1-3; Medina, *Las Hermanas*, 1-5.

[8]Flores, "The Chicana/o Movement," 2.

[9]Martínez, *Padres*, 13-15; Medina, *Las Hermanas*, 75-78.

[10]De La Torre and Aponte, *Introducing Latino/a Theologies*, 104.

[11]Medina, *Las Hermanas*, 98-99, 102-3.

reform within the Catholic Church itself.[12] In describing its spiritual vision, Las Hermanas declared:

> *Hermanas* is an organization that wants to keep itself aware of the suffering of our Hispano people. By reason of our heritage, and in response to the mind of Vatican II and the encyclical *Populorum Progresio,* we feel obliged to be faithful to the Christian message of hopeful creation of a Christian humanism within the context and culture of the Hispano community.[13]

As reflected in this quote, Las Hermanas and PADRES seized on the spirit and rhetoric of Vatican Council II to challenge the exploitation and marginalization of Hispanos within the Roman Catholic Church.[14] Vatican II, and in particular its call for cultural contextualization, created an important opening for Mexican American clergy and laity "to announce their support for farmworkers, show solidarity with the Chicana/o community, and demand institutional change. The mid-1960s presented a social and political opportunity for direct action from Catholic Chicana/os."[15] Flowing from the efforts of Las Hermanas and PADRES came the founding of the Mexican American Cultural Center (MACC) in San Antonio, Texas, in 1972 as well as the creation of the Academy of Catholic Hispanic Theologians (ACHTUS) and the *Journal of Hispanic/Latino Theology.*[16] To this day, MACC, ACHTUS, and the *Journal of Hispanic/Latino Theology* remain central institutions of the Latina/o theology movement. The prophetic ministry of Las Hermanas and PADRES also spurred the proliferation of national religious conferences for Latina/o lay leaders under the auspices of Encuentro Nacional Hispano de Pastoral (National Hispanic Pastoral Encounter).

Whereas PADRES and Las Hermanas agitated the Catholic Church from within its own institutional ranks, an organization of Chicana/o

[12]Flores, "The Chicana/o Movement," ii.
[13]De La Torre and Aponte, *Introducing Latino/a Theologies*, 105.
[14]Martínez, *Padres*, 17-21; Medina, *Las Hermanas*, 19-25.
[15]Flores, "The Chicana/o Movement," 24.
[16]De La Torre and Aponte, *Introducing Latino/a Theologies*, 105, 106, 107; Martínez, *Padres*, 100-103; Medina, *Las Hermanas*, 99-102.

Roman Catholic activists, known as Católicos Por La Raza, sought to promote revolutionary change as institutional outsiders.[17] Católicos Por La Raza was founded in 1969 by Richard Cruz, Richard Martínez, and Joe Razo, as part of the merger of three civil rights organizations: The Chicano Law Students Association of Loyola Marymount University, United Mexican American Students of Los Angeles Community College, and a Los Angeles Chicana/o newspaper called *La Raza*.[18] Inspired by César Chávez, Dolores Huerta, and the Farmworkers movement, Cruz believed that "political revolt was itself a sacred action."[19] As Roman Catholic lay leaders inspired by the Chicana/o civil rights movement, Católicos Por La Raza agitated the Catholic Church in Los Angeles to increase its ministry presence in issues related to poverty, education, housing, and public heath, and also sought the increased representation of Mexican Americans in priestly roles and the institutional hierarchy.[20] Their famous protest of St. Basil's Cathedral on Christmas Eve 1969 left a landmark impression on both the Chicana/o movement and the Roman Catholic church in Los Angeles, and led to the hiring of the first Mexican American Catholic Bishop in Los Angeles history.[21] Unbeknownst to most, PADRES, Las Hermanas, and Católicos Por La Raza sowed the important *semillas* (seeds) that would come to sprout as the Latina/o Theology movement in the United States.

Since the 1980s, Latina/o theology and interdisciplinary research on the Brown Church has developed in three distinct stages that theologian Oscar Garcia-Johnson calls "founders," "builders," and "shapers."[22] Central figures in the initial development of Latina/o theology, or, "founders," include Methodist historical theologian Justo González,

---

[17]This argument is drawn from Flores, "The Chicana/o Movement," 2, 3; Hinojosa, "Católicos Por La Raza," 26.

[18]Flores, "The Chicana/o Movement," 25-27; Hinojosa, "Católicos Por La Raza," 26.

[19]Flores, "The Chicana/o Movement," 26.

[20]García, *Chicano Liberation Theology*, 21, 29, 30; Flores, "The Chicana/o Movement," 28-30.

[21]García, *Chicano Liberation Theology*, 53-55; Flores, "The Chicana/o Movement," 27, 30, 31, 36, 39; Hinojosa, "Católicos Por La Raza," 27.

[22]Oscar García-Johnson, *The Mestizo/a Community of the Spirit: A Postmodern Latino/a Ecclesiology*, Princeton Theological Monograph 105 (Eugene, OR: Wipf and Stock, 2009), 31-36.

Roman Catholic pastor and theologian Virgilio Elizondo, and American Baptist missiologist Orlando Costas.[23] Mario García stands out as the founder of Brown Church research within Chicana/o studies and Latina/o studies.[24] Elizabeth Conde-Frazier, Allan Figueroa Deck, Orlando Espín, María Pilar Aquino, and Eldin Villafañe are key figures of the "builders" stage. "Shapers" of Latina/o theology include Ada María Isasi-Díaz, Oscar García-Johnson, Edwin Aponte, Roberto Goizueta, Juan Martínez, Ruth Padilla-DeBorst, Miguel De La Torre, and Kay Higuera-Smith.[25]

HOW TO READ THE BIBLE

A central tenet of Latina/o theology is *teología en conjunto*, or, collaborative communal theology.[26] From a Latina/o perspective, theology is not a lone-ranger scholastic endeavor whose aim is individualistic academic acclaim. Rather, theology is a communal endeavor birthed from the

---

[23]See Justo González, *Mañana: Christian Theology from a Hispanic Perspective* (Nashville: Abingdon Press, 1990), 75; Justo González, *Santa Biblia: The Bible Through Hispanic Eyes* (Nashville: Abingdon Press, 1996); Virgilio Elizondo, *Galilean Journey: The Mexican-American Promise* (Maryknoll, NY: Orbis Books, 2005); Orlando E. Costas, *Christ Outside the Gate: Mission Beyond Christendom* (Maryknoll, NY: Orbis Books, 1993).

[24]Mario T. García, *Católicos: Resistance and Affirmation in Chicano Catholic History* (Austin: University of Texas Press, 2010); Mario T. García, *Father Luis Olivares, A Biography: Faith, Politics and the Origins of the Sanctuary Movement in Los Angeles* (Chapel Hill: The University of North Carolina Press, 2018); Mario T. García, *Chicano Liberation Theology: The Writings and Documents of Richard Cruz and Católicos Por La Raza* (Dubuque, IA: Kendall Hunt Publishing, 2009).

[25]To these lists could be added theologians and multidisciplinary scholars such as: M. Daniel Carroll, R., Fernando Segovia, Daisy Machado, Yolanda Tarango, Andrés Guerrero, Harold Recinos, Loida I. Martell-Otero, Arlene Sánchez-Walsh, Zaida Maldonado Pérez, Roberto Goizueta, Jeanette Rodriguez, Samuel Solivan, Ismael García, Daniel Ramírez, Gastón Espinosa, Ched Myers, Michelle A. González, Johnny Ramírez-García, Ismael García, Lara Medina, Richard Martínez, Gerardo Martí, Tony Tian-Ren Lin, Jacqueline M. Hidalgo, Gregory Lee Cuellar, Oscar Merlo, and Ondina E. González, among others. It is also critical to highlight the rising generation of Latina/o theologians and religious studies scholars who represent the avant-garde of the field. These up-and-coming scholars include Jonathan Calvillo, Sammy Alfaro, Sandra Maria Van Opstal, Lauren Guerra, Roberto Sirvent, Jules Martínez-Olivieri, Michelle C. Sánchez, Michael Jiménez, Elizabeth Tamez-Méndez, Nichole M. Flores, Elias Ortega-Aponte, Ann Hidalgo, Gabe Veas, Daniel Castelo, Rodolfo Estrada, Patrick Reyes, Yara González-Justiniano, and Grace Vargas. I should note that I have not included the names of scholars who have produced wonderful scholarship in Latina/o religious studies, but, as far as I am aware, have not publicly identified with the Christian tradition.

[26]Aponte and De La Torre, *Handbook*, 7.

firsthand experience of the grassroots Latina/o community itself. Teología en conjunto is produced from the mutual dialogue of pastors, theologians, and lay parishioners. From the start, Latina/o theology has also been ecumenical—Protestant and Catholic—as well as transdenominational—evangelical, mainline, and Pentecostal. Latina/o theology, moreover, emphasizes orthopraxis, or right action. Latina/o theologians insist that, just as faith without works is dead (Jas 2:14-26), so is theology dead if it does not engender the social and cultural uplift of the entire Latin/o community.[27]

Latina/o theology understands that all theology is contextual. Even though the Bible is God's inspired Word, all biblical interpretation is informed by the cultural context of the interpreter. All theologies are socially circumscribed, and we all approach our reading of the Bible from our distinct social location.[28] According to Latino theologian Miguel De La Torre, social location refers to "cultural experiences which influence a person's identity," and "these experiences define the meaning we give to the different symbols that exist in our lives, including whole texts [the Bible] or individual words that operate as a form of linguistic symbol." When individual Christians, or ethnic/racial communities of Christians, read the Bible, we do so in a way that is shaped by our own cultural context and autobiographical experiences.[29]

This is not necessarily a bad thing because it allows for meaningful and distinct cultural insights into the text of Scripture by different members of the body of Christ (Rom 12:4-5, 1 Cor 12:12-26). Seen in this light, God-given cultural diversity only reinforces unity in the church, because it encourages us to lean on one another in order to know God more fully. At the same time, the failure to recognize the important role

---

[27]This section is adapted from the essay "Toward a Perspective of 'Brown Theology'" by Robert Chao Romero, from *Evangelical Theologies of Liberation and Justice*, edited by Mae Elise Cannon and Andrea Smith (Downers Grove, IL: IVP Academic, 2019), 75-95.

[28]Loida I. Martell-Otero, Zaida Maldonado Pérez, and Elizabeth Conde-Frazier, *Latina Evangélicas: A Theological Survey from the Margins* (Eugene, OR: Cascade Books, 2013), 19; Miguel De La Torre, *Reading the Bible from the Margins* (Maryknoll, NY: Orbis Books, 2013), 2.

[29]De La Torre, *Reading the Bible from the Margins*, 2-3.

of ethnic culture and experience in shaping biblical interpretation can produce damaging results because it can lead a culturally dominant community to insist that its own interpretations of the Bible are "objective" and "official" to the exclusion of all others. The end result is the tribalization of Jesus and the circumscription of God within the narrow cultural understanding of a single ethnic or racial community. Such biblical nationalism is idolatry, and it has historically led to biblical interpretations that have oppressed Latinas/os, blacks, Native Americans, Asian Americans, and other people of color in the United States. This is what American and European colonization did for five hundred years, and what certain pockets of Western Christianity continue to insist on.

In recognition of the value of cultural context in interpreting Scripture, Justo González has introduced the concept of "reading the Bible in Spanish," or with "Hispanic eyes."[30] By this, he does not mean reading the Bible in a Spanish translation, but rather, reading Scripture in light of the distinct, and diverse, historical experiences of Latinas/os in the United States. "If it is true that we bring a particular perspective to history and to theology, then we must also bring a particular perspective to the interpretation of Scripture. And, once again, it may be that this perspective will prove useful not only to us but also to the church at large."[31] "Hispanic eyes," according to González, "is the perspective of those who claim their Hispanic identity as part of their hermeneutical baggage, and also read the Scripture within the context of a commitment to the Latina/o struggle to become all that God wants us and all of the world to be—in other words, the struggle for salvation/liberation."[32] Reading the Bible through Hispanic eyes has led many Latina/o theologians to focus their reflection on the themes of marginality, poverty, mestizaje/mulatez (European, indigenous, and African cultural mixture), exile, and communal/familial solidarity.[33]

---

[30]González, Mañana:, 75; González, Santa Biblia, 28.
[31]González, Mañana, 75.
[32]González, Santa Biblia, 28-29.
[33]González, Santa Biblia, 31, 57, 77, 91, 103.

Miguel De La Torre has advocated for an approach of reading the Bible from the perspective of the oppressed and those on the margins of society—what Gustavo Gutierrez has called "a militant reading" of Scripture.[34] In this way, the Bible is viewed as much more than just a text for scholarly analysis, but rather as a "text of hope" that seeks to "grasp God in the midst of struggle and oppression."[35] A militant reading of Scripture liberates the Bible from colonial interpretations that oppress and sideline Latinas/os and other people of color and, instead, contemplates the Bible as a source of Christ's love and hope for all peoples, beginning with those living on the margins of society. Drawing from these paradigms, Latina/o theologians have produced important analyses of the biblical significance of Galilee and the theological framework of lo cotidiano.

Latino authors such as Virgilio Elizondo and Orlando Costas have highlighted the fact that Jesus was raised in Galilee, selected Galileans as his first disciples, and performed most of his public ministry in Galilee. As noted in Scripture:

> Now after John was arrested, Jesus came to Galilee, proclaiming the good news of God, and saying, "The time is fulfilled, and the kingdom of God has come near; repent, and believe in the good news." As Jesus passed along the Sea of Galilee, he saw Simon and his brother Andrew casting a net into the sea—for they were fishermen. And Jesus said to them, "Follow me and I will make you fish for people." (Mk 1:14-17)

In his pathbreaking book, *The Galilean Journey: The Mexican-American Promise*, Elizondo argues that the Galilean roots of Jesus point to God's preferential option for those of marginalized communities.[36] In Jesus' day,

---

[34]De La Torre, *Reading the Bible from the Margins*, 4.
[35]De La Torre, *Reading the Bible from the Margins*, 4.
[36]Virgilio Elizondo, *Galilean Journey: The Mexican-American Promise* (Maryknoll, NY: Orbis Books, 2005), 91. It is significant to note that Puerto Rican missiologist Orlando Costas came to a similar theological understanding of "Galilee," independent of Elizondo, also in the early 1980s. See Costas, *Christ Outside the Gate*, 6; Orlando Costas, "Evangelism from the Periphery: A Galilean Model," *Apuntes* 2, no. 3 (1982): 52-54.

Galilee was a symbol of multiple rejection.[37] Whereas Jerusalem was the center of Jewish religious, economic, and political life, Galilee was looked down on as a cultural backwaters—"the hood" of its day. And if Galilee in general was "the hood," then Jesus' hometown of Nazareth in Galilee was "the hood of the hood"—perhaps similar to the way in which popular culture (wrongly) refers to Compton, California. And so quipped Nathanael, "Can anything good come out of Nazareth?" (Jn 1:46).

Galileans were mostly poor peasant farmers, and they spoke both Greek and Aramaic with an accent.[38] Galileans were also looked on with suspicion by their compatriots in Jerusalem because they lived in a multicultural borderlands region that was a crossroads of Jewish, Roman, and Greek society, and noted for its mestizaje.

Based on his understanding of Galilee as a marginalized sociogeographic location in the biblical narrative, Elizondo articulates the "Galilee principle": *What human beings reject, God chooses as his very own.*[39] When God became human in Jesus Christ, God chose to be embodied as a socially, economically, and politically insignificant Galilean. He did not choose to be born into a rich and prestigious royal family from the capital, but chose to be raised and formed as a Galilean from the despised town of Nazareth. And when it came time to proclaim the good news of the arrival of the kingdom of God, Jesus began in Galilee and dedicated most of his public ministry to the oppressed community that raised him.

The Galilee principle gives great hope to Latinas/os in the United States because we know what it is like to be marginalized by those from the Jerusalems of our day. When people look down on us for being from East or South Los Angeles, for being culturally mestizos and mulatos, and for speaking with an accent, we say, "¿Y qué? So was our Lord."

---

[37]Elizondo, *Galilean Journey*, 50-53.
[38]Ched Myers, *Binding the Strongman: A Political Reading of Mark's Story of Jesus* (Maryknoll, NY: Orbis Books, 2012), 49, 53; Elizondo, *Galilean Journey*, 52.
[39]Elizondo, *Galilean Journey*, 91.

Though the world may reject and stereotype us as uneducated, working class, and undocumented, we give thanks to Jesus that he calls us his very own. We give praise, for when the good news of salvation was brought to the world, it was preached initially to those like us. We also rejoice that when Jesus announced the kingdom of God, he did not select the rich and educated from influential families to lead his movement. Rather, he chose working class fishermen, farmers, and mestizo Galileans to be his first disciples—the "Latinas/os" of his day. Though the gospel is for all, it came first to us.

According to Puerto Rican missiologist Orlando Costas, Christ not only lived his life in the metaphorical margins of Galilee, but also suffered "outside the gate" of the institutional powers of Jerusalem. According to Hebrews 13:11-14 (emphasis added):

> For the bodies of those animals whose blood is brought into the sanctuary by the high priest as a sacrifice for sin are burned outside the camp. Therefore Jesus also suffered *outside the city gate* in order to sanctify the people by his own blood. Let us then go to him outside the camp and bear the abuse he endured. For here we have no lasting city, but we are looking for the city that is to come.

For Costas, Christ's suffering outside the city gate of Jerusalem signifies God's close identification with all who are disenfranchised and cast aside by society. "Jesus Christ is today one with the outcast and oppressed of the earth. Wherever there is oppression, there is the Spirit of Christ incarnated in the *experience* of the oppressed; there is God contextualized in the present history of the nonpersons of society."[40] Christ suffers with, and accompanies, the poor who suffer outside the gate of privileged, middle and upper class society. Indeed "he is one of them."[41] In order to be faithful to Jesus, Christians must "go to him outside the camp" to meet him in the face of the downtrodden who are the heralds of God's good news of salvation in contrast with the wise and mighty of this world. In

---

[40]Costas, *Christ Outside the Gate*, 13.
[41]Costas, *Christ Outside the Gate*, 13.

addition, in the model of Christ, followers of Jesus must deny themselves, take up their cross, and serve others.[42]

As one who suffered outside the gate, Jesus modeled a different kind of leadership from that of Caesar, Herod, and the religious establishment of his day. The rule and reign of Christ is founded on service, liberation, and sacrificial love. According to Costas, Jesus

> does not rule as a despot or oppressor, but as a liberating servant. The lordship of Christ is not grounded on military might, but on sacrificial love. It is not oppressive and emasculating, but creating and liberating. It is not totalitarian, but communal and fraternal. It facilitates the formation of a new world community on the basis of love and service.[43]

This Christ of history and the Bible is not the same Christ propagated by colonial and oppressive world powers, and it is the duty of Christians to discern between the true Jesus who suffers and identifies with the poor of the world and the false imperial messiahs who hide the real identity of Christ from millions of Christians throughout the globe. Indeed, for the gospel to be true, it must result in the transformation of the suffering and social conditions of those who are oppressed.[44]

MUJERISTA THEOLOGY

Latina theologians have extended the principle of God's preferential option for the marginalized to women.[45] Roman Catholic theologian Ada María Isasi-Díaz developed the term "mujerista" to describe a person who makes a preferential option for Latina women and their struggle for liberation.[46] Isasi-Díaz, moreover, dedicated her life to developing a "mujerista theology" from the perspective of Latina women. Mujeristas

---

[42]Costas, *Christ Outside the Gate*, 12, 14.

[43]Costas, *Christ Outside the Gate*, 8, 9.

[44]Costas, *Christ Outside the Gate*, 14-16.

[45]This section is adapted from the essay "Toward a Perspective of 'Brown Theology'" by Robert Chao Romero, 75-95.

[46]*Mujerista* can be translated "womanist." Ada María Isasi-Díaz, *Mujerista Theology: A Theology for the Twenty-First Century* (Maryknoll, NY: Orbis Books, 2005), 60.

celebrate and lay claim to the distinct image of God in women, and support a "process of enablement for Latina women which insists on the development of a strong sense of moral agency and clarifies the importance and value of who we are, what we think, and what we do."[47] Mujerista theology calls out the oppressive patriarchal and racist structures that subjugate Latinas, and it promotes the process of liberation from internalized oppression.

A central concept of mujerista theology is that of lo cotidiano, or the daily lived experience of Latinas.[48] Mujerista theology dignifies the lived experiences of Latinas in work, family, and society. Whereas majority white culture often shuns the Latina immigrant/working class reality, mujerista theology privileges lo cotidiano as an important source of theologizing, knowledge, and understanding. Though many may look down on our mothers, tías, and abuelas for their daily commutes on the bus, travails in domestic and factory work, exhausting familial responsibilities, and faithful church participation, mujerista theology declares that it is precisely in the daily rhythm and grind of lo cotidiano that unique theological and epistemological understandings flow. As Latinas/os we say: "Your mom may have a law degree from Stanford, but my mom has a PhD in life from the school of Lo Cotidiano." In the words of Isasi-Díaz:

> Therefore, lo cotidiano, the daily experience of Hispanic women, not only points to their capacity to know but also highlights the features of their knowing. Lo cotidiano is a way of referring to Latinas' efforts to understand and express how and why their lives are the way they are, how and why they function as they do.[49]

PENTECOSTAL LATINA/O THEOLOGY

"Latina evangélicas" Loida I. Martell-Otero, Zaida Maldonado-Pérez, and Elizabeth Conde-Frazier have built on, and contextualized, these notions

---

[47]Isasi-Díaz, *Mujerista Theology*, 1, 2, 62, 63.
[48]Isasi-Díaz, *Mujerista Theology*, 66.
[49]Isasi-Díaz, *Mujerista Theology*, 68.

of lo cotidiano within an evangelical and Pentecostal framework.[50] In their recent pathbreaking work, *Latina Evangélicas: A Theological Survey from the Margins*, Martell-Otero, Maldonado-Perez, and Conde-Frazier contemplate a distinct Latina evangelical identity and theology based on the perspective of Latina Protestants in the United States:

> The contributors to this book are grateful for the rich theological lode provided by such notable scholars as Ada María Isasi-Díaz, Jeannette Rodríguez, Maria Pilar Aquino, and a host of others with whom we have collaborated in the past; but we also recognize a need to provide a voice that is distinctively Protestant, or evangélica.[51]

Latina evangélica theology is distinguished by its triple emphasis on the importance of the Holy Spirit, soteriology, and Scripture.[52] According to evangélicas, the Holy Spirit empowers women and legitimizes their calling in the face of patriarchal and racist social and ecclesial structures. It is the Holy Spirit who personally guides and empowers Latinas in the daily struggle of lo cotidiano. Recovering the feminine gender of the word *ruach*, or, "spirit," found in the Hebrew text of the Old Testament, Maldonado-Pérez refers to the Holy Spirit as "she." Maldonado-Pérez declares poetically that the Holy Spirit is the "wild child" of the Godhead who emboldens and inspires Latinas in their quotidian struggles:

> I love the Holy Spirit. She is like the wild child of the Trinity, anywhere and everywhere moving, calling forth, and stirring things up. She is wonderfully illusive yet also fully present. She is untamable, full of possibilities and creative potential. She is the salsa beat in our daily foxtrot and the un-dos-tres-bachata in our electric slide. . . . She is life-giving breath, wind, and fire. She is the ruach [feminine Hebrew word for Spirit] elohim, the flaming divine pneuma that is always "going native" because she wants to be encountered by all. . . . Filled, inspired, and moved by the Holy Spirit,

---

[50]This section is adapted from the essay "Toward a Perspective of 'Brown Theology'" by Robert Chao Romero, 75-95.
[51]Martell-Otero, Perez, and Conde-Frazier, *Latina Evangélicas*, 18.
[52]Martell-Otero, Perez, and Conde-Frazier, *Latina Evangélicas*, 30, 31, 35.

evangelicas engage life from the perspective of the One who is able to move over chaos, nothingness, and death, speaking life into death-bearing situations and being midwives to hope. The Holy Spirit emboldens us, even through the shadow of death, to fight the good fight on behalf of those gripped by despair.[53]

Latina evangélica theology complements Mujerista theology not only in terms of its focus on the active role of the Holy Spirit, but also insofar as it emphasizes both the personal and communal salvation of Jesus in the context of lo cotidiano. In Christ, Latinas experience salvation as beloved daughters of God, despite their rejection by American society as *satas* (mongrels or mutts) and *sobraja* (worthless).[54] Salvation, moreover, is not just heaven when we die, as important as that may be, but also God's salvation experienced in the here and now, and the messiness of life—lo cotidiano. "The Spirit is the One who heals personally and communally (katartismos) in light of institutional injustice" and "Jesus is the divine sato jíbaro (mutt or country peasant) who lives to bring life to communities crushed by death-dealing powers."[55]

In contrast with Ada María Isasi-Díaz, who claimed that the Bible plays a minimal role among Catholic Latinas, Latina evangélicas assert that Scripture is central for Christian practice and belief. It is within the Bible that Latinas find hope and wisdom for the daily realities and hardships of life, and in the Scriptures that they encounter the living God who brings liberation.[56] According to Elizabeth Conde-Frazier, the Bible is a living and dialogic text of liberation: "While using the resources available to them as scholars, clergy, or laity, [Latina evangélicas] read for liberation. . . . The women read the text from the context of their lives so that they establish a dialogue between the sacred text and the text of their lives."[57]

---

[53]Martell-Otero, Perez, and Conde-Frazier, *Latina Evangélicas*, 43, 44, 46, 47.
[54]Martell-Otero, Perez, and Conde-Frazier, *Latina Evangélicas*, 32, 87, 88.
[55]Martell-Otero, Perez, and Conde-Frazier, *Latina Evangélicas*, 32.
[56]Martell-Otero, Perez, and Conde-Frazier, *Latina Evangélicas*, 35, 36.
[57]Martell-Otero, Perez, and Conde-Frazier, *Latina Evangélicas*, 192, 193.

Following the admonition of Conde-Frazier, an emerging generation of Latina evangélicas are continuing the project of exegeting
Scripture through the lens of their own experience. Sandra Maria Van
Opstal, Karen González, Natalia Kohn Rivera, Noemi Vega Quiñones,
and Kristy Garza Robinson have recently published a trinity of books
that, from diverse Latina perspectives, plumb the Bible for practical
insight into topics such as worship, immigration, and leadership. In
The Next Worship: Glorifying God in a Diverse World, Colombian
American Sandra Van Opstal tackles the increasingly important
question: How do we lead worship in communities that are growing
increasingly diverse?[58] Drawing from two decades of pastoral and
worship ministry experience with InterVarsity, the Christian Community Development Association, and the Evangelical Covenant and
Christian Reformed denominations, Van Opstal asserts that "multiethnic worship acknowledges and honors the diversity of people in the
local and global church, and teaches congregations to understand and
honor that same diversity."[59] Moreover, according to Van Opstal,
through multicultural worship the Holy Spirit brings us into solidarity
and communion with global communities we may never meet, and
"enable[s] prophetic imagination in which people can see the future
reality of God's kingdom breaking into the present."[60]

As a Latina immigrant, pastor-theologian, and immigration law
practitioner, Karen González supplies unique biblical and legal perspective on immigration. In *The God Who Sees: Immigrants, the Bible,
and the Journey to Belong*, González deftly weaves together original
biblical exegesis, tear-jerking personal narratives of her family's own
immigrant journey, and analysis of US immigration law and policy.[61]
As poignant examples, she demonstrates that, based upon existing law,

[58]Sandra Maria Van Opstal, *The Next Worship: Glorifying God in a Diverse World* (Downers Grove:
IVP Books, 2016), 17.
[59]Van Opstal, *The Next Worship*, 16.
[60]Van Opstal, *The Next Worship*, 15, 22.
[61]Karen González, *The God Who Sees: Immigrants, the Bible, and the Journey to Belong* (Harrisonburg, VA: Herald Press, 2019).

Ruth and Abraham would not be allowed entry into the United States today because the former was an economic migrant and the latter a criminal immigrant.

Finally, in *Hermanas: Deepening Our Identity and Growing Our Influence*, Kohn Rivera, Vega Quiñones, and Garza Robinson provide a discipleship and leadership development resource for Latina women based upon the narratives of twelve biblical women, including Esther, Rahab, Ruth, Deborah, and Mary.[62] The authors exegete their own experiences as Latinas within the Scriptures, and frame compelling biblical themes such as the worker and bridal paradigms, mija leadership, atrevida leadership, and grief as intimacy.[63]

In addition to inspiring the writings of a new generation of Latina evangélicas, the pioneering work of Loida I. Martell-Otero, Zaida Maldonado-Pérez, and Elizabeth Conde-Frazier stands at the forefront of what Sammy Alfaro calls "liberating Pentecostal theologies."[64] According to Sammy Alfaro, Latin American and US Latina/o Pentecostal pastors and theologians over the past twenty years have sought their distinctive theological voice within the broader context of the Latin American and Latina/o experience, as well as the global Pentecostal church, which tends towards spiritualized understandings that are detached from social liberation.[65] Drawing from Jesus' messianic manifesto in Luke 4:18-19, Alfaro and others see Spirit baptism as intrinsically connected to the holistic liberation of oppressed communities:

The Spirit of the Lord is upon me,
   because he has anointed me
      to bring good news to the poor.

---

[62]Natalia Kohn Rivera, Noemi Vega Quiñones, and Kristy Garza Robinson, *Hermanas: Deepening Our Identity and Growing Our Influence* (Downers Grove, IL: InterVarsity Press, 2019).

[63]*Mija* means "my daughter"; *atrevida* refers to a woman who is bold or daring.

[64]Sammy Alfaro, "Liberating Pentecostal Theologies: A View from the Latina/o and Latin American Pentecostal Contexts," in *Global Renewal Christianity: Spirit-Empowered Movements Past, Present, and Future*, vol. 2, *Latin America*, ed. Vinson Synan, Amos Yong, and Miguel Alvarez (Lake Mary, FL: Charisma House, 2016), 355-70.

[65]Alfaro, "Liberating Pentecostal Theologies," 359.

He has sent me to proclaim release to the captives

    and recovery of sight to the blind,

        to let the oppressed go free,

   to proclaim the year of the Lord's favor. (Lk 4:18-19)

According to this passage, the Spirit came upon Jesus to anoint him as the Christ who would bring the good news of God's kingdom and liberation precisely to the poor and oppressed.[66] As discussed by Latin American theologian Dario López Rodríguez, this passage extends the biblical notion of Jubilee to encompass the holistic nature of Christ's message and a preferential option for the marginalized of society:

> For that reason, it is no accident the Lukan Jesus preferentially opts for the excluded and the nobodies of society. It is no accident why precisely the messianic platform espoused in the synagogue of Nazareth indicates that the liberating mission of Jesus had in its horizon to revert the destiny of the poor and the marginalized.[67]

Building on these Lukan understandings of the mission of Jesus, López Rodríguez and Daniel Chiquete critique traditional Pentecostal interpretation of Acts 2 and the pouring out of the Spirit on Pentecost:

> When the day of Pentecost had come, they were all together in one place. And suddenly from heaven there came a sound like the rush of a violent wind, and it filled the entire house where they were sitting. Divided tongues, as of fire, appeared among them, and a tongue rested on each of them. All of them were filled with the Holy Spirit and began to speak in other languages, as the Spirit gave them ability. Now there were devout Jews from every nation under heaven living in Jerusalem. And at this sound the crowd gathered and was bewildered, because each one heard them speaking in the native language of each. Amazed and astonished, they asked, "Are not all these who are speaking Galileans? And how is it that we hear, each of us, in our own native language?" (Acts 2:1-8)

---

[66]Alfaro, "Liberating Pentecostal Theologies," 363.
[67]Alfaro, "Liberating Pentecostal Theologies," 363.

According to classical Pentecostal theology, speaking in tongues is important as physical evidence that a person has experienced baptism of the Holy Spirit. Extending this traditional understanding, Chiquete and López argue for a communal and culturally contextualized interpretation of this passage.[68] For Chiquete, this central biblical text underscores the significance of multiculturalism in the church because the events of Pentecost signaled the unthinkable expansion of the Jewish religious community to include Gentile believers. Viewed from this lens, speaking in tongues is not simply an ecstatic personal experience, but "a missional and liberative experience for those who heard of the mighty deeds of God in their own languages."[69] In a further hermeneutical step, Chiquete links Peter's subsequent sermon in the same chapter of Acts to the prophetic proclamations of Joel and Amos demanding justice for the poor, and announcing woes upon the rich and overindulgent:

Thus says the Lord:

For three transgressions of Israel,
    and for four, I will not revoke the punishment;
because they sell the righteous for silver,
    and the needy for a pair of sandals—
they who trample the head of the poor into the dust of the earth,
    and push the afflicted out of the way. (Amos 2:6-7)

Alas for those who lie on beds of ivory,
    and lounge on their couches,
and eat lambs from the flock,
    and calves from the stall;
who sing idle songs to the sound of the harp,
    and like David improvise on instruments of music;
who drink wine from bowls,
    and anoint themselves with the finest oils,
    but are not grieved over the ruin of Joseph!

---

[68] Alfaro, "Liberating Pentecostal Theologies," 364.
[69] Alfaro, "Liberating Pentecostal Theologies," 364-65.

Therefore they shall now be the first to go into exile,

and the revelry of the loungers shall pass away. (Amos 6:4-7)

Thus, the Spirit of God was poured out on Pentecost "on all flesh," "even on the male and female slaves" (Joel 2:28-29), not simply as a doctrinal statement that speaking in tongues was evidence of baptism in the Spirit, but rather as invocation, and invitation to embody the social program of liberation heralded by Joel and Amos.[70] Viewed in this light, speaking in tongues and baptism of the Spirit are spiritual encounters that lead one to multicultural community, proclamation of good news to the poor, and the enactment of justice for all who are oppressed.

Contemporary Latina/o Pentecostal theologizing of social justice has been shaped fundamentally by Eldin Villafañe and his path-breaking book, *El Espiritu Liberador: Hacia una Etica Social Pente-costal Hispanoamericana.*[71] First published in 1992, this work repre-sents the first articulation of a Latina/o Pentecostal social ethics framework. According to Villafañe, the ethical conduct of Latina/o Pentecostals, on both an individual and social level, should stem from the guidance of the Holy Spirit. If we live in the Spirit, then we will also walk in the Spirit in terms of our ethical principles and practices (Gal 5:25). Our social ethics and practices, moreover, flow from fol-lowing in the Spirit's historic project of the kingdom of God. "In the Spirit, who is the mediator of the resurrected Christ, the kingdom has been universalized."[72] In addition, to take part in the kingdom of God is to participate in the power of the coming age, through the Holy Spirit, and, because Christ is king of this world, there is no area of life where the kingdom of God is not at work. As a profound implication of the all-encompassing scope of Christ's reign, Villafañe asserts that to participate in the kingdom of God requires Christians to fight injustice

---

[70] Alfaro, "Liberating Pentecostal Theologies," 365.

[71] Eldin Villafañe, *El Espiritu Liberador: Hacia una Etica Social Pentecostal Hispanoamericana* (Grand Rapids: Eerdmans, 1997). Also in English, *The Liberating Spirit: Toward an Hispanic American Pentecostal Social Ethic* (Grand Rapids: Eerdmans, 1993).

[72] Villafañe, *El Espiritu Liberador,* 168, 169; translation mine.

through the political process. An important task of the Latina/o Pentecostal church of the United States is therefore to discern where the Spirit is working to break the chains of exploitation and oppression, and to partner with God in those liberative efforts.[73]

In order to join the liberationist leading of the Spirit, Villafañe further argues that Pentecostals must be able to see with new eyes the "signs of the kingdom," which are present in Latina/o culture, society, and religious practices.[74] He identifies five "signs" or themes that must be discerned in order for the Latina/o Pentecostal church to effectively carry out its unique kingdom calling:

1. Mestizaje (cultural mixture): The Iglesia Pentecostal Hispana reflects the profound cultural mixture of Latin America. As "la Raza Cósmica," Latinas/os are a mixed race people of Spanish, African, Asian, and indigenous roots.[75] As a sign of the kingdom, the multicultural Latina/o Pentecostal church embodies the racial shalom that God intends for the world.

2. La Morenita (La Virgen de Guadalupe): Although Pentecostal Christians do not typically embrace La Virgen de Guadalupe as part of its religious constructs, Villafañe asserts that it is fitting to affirm the positive image of femininity that La Virgen represents, as part of the process of social liberation.

3. Migración (migration): Latinas/os have been a migratory people since the US-Mexico War of 1848. We are a pilgrim people, and our migratory experience makes us "bridge people" capable of mediating between the rich and influential of North America and the poor and exploited of Latin America. This is part of the unique mission of the Latina/o church, and it requires that we continue to be both bilingual and bicultural.

---

[73]Villafañe, *El Espiritu Liberador*, 169-70.
[74]Villafañe, *El Espiritu Liberador*, 171.
[75]See José Vasconcelos, *The Cosmic Race / La raza cosmica* (Baltimore: Johns Hopkins University Press, 1997).

4. Menesterosos (poor and oppressed): The Pentecostal church has been a refuge for poor and working-class Latinas/os. The Pentecostal church must be a space where they can continue to be affirmed in their human dignity and find holistic liberation. .

5. Modelos sociales (the Hispanic church as a model): The Hispanic Pentecostal church should be a model of the kingdom of God to the broader Latina/o community. It should be known as a site of spiritual revelation, cultural preservation, communal liberation, and reconciliation, as well as serve as a training ground for emerging leaders.[76]

According to Villafañe, these distinct signs of the kingdom within the Latina/o Pentecostal church reflect the work of the Holy Spirit in the world. Recognizing these signs, the church must partner with the Spirit to restrain evil and help create a more just and peaceful society—all as a sign of the new order of the kingdom of God. Seen in this light, all social and cultural institutions are fallow grounds for the manifestation of the grace of God through the church. "The work of the church (the koinonia) consists of discerning the presence of God, and following the mobilization orders of the Spirit, who goes before us in the battle."[77] In following the Spirit, the church confronts structural evil and sin with the strategy of love and justice.[78]

Fusing Villafañe's vision of the Spirit as Liberator and Costas' Christological framework of Christ Outside the Gate, Oscar García-Johnson presents a pneumatological vision of the Holy Spirit as decolonizing force.[79] According to García-Johnson, the Spirit of God was moving outside the "gate" of institutional Western Christianity in Latin America before the European conquest. This dignifies the indigenous and African descent peoples and cultures of the Americas and rebukes the colonial

---

[76]Villafañe, El Espiritu Liberador, 171-72.

[77]Villafañe, El Espiritu Liberador, 172; translation mine.

[78]Villafañe, El Espiritu Liberador, 173, 181.

[79]Oscar García-Johnson, Spirit Outside the Gate: Decolonial Pneumatologies of the American Global South (Downers Grove, IL: IVP Academic, 2019).

notion that natives and Africans were subhuman pagans requiring the civilizing hand of Christian Europeans. Unlike Juan Ginés de Sepulveda and other colonial theologians, García-Johnson asks, How was the Spirit of God at work among indigenous peoples prior to the Spanish conquest? How did the Spirit draw native communities to the Creator through native religions? According to García-Johnson,

> Such hermeneutical-pneumatological openness is set to cross the boundaries of the canonical imagination of the West in the search for its own canonical imagination, the creative invisible, where it seeks to engage with and identify the Holy Spirit, the Grand Spirit, and spirits and powers operating in the pre-/post-Columbian religious imagination of the Americas.[80]

García-Johnson also argues that the Spirit of God, as "Decolonial Healer," continues to work in the Global South to reveal Jesus to subjugated peoples despite the grave misrepresentations of Christian colonialism. The Spirit is the "Decolonial Healer of the wounded lands, cultures, and peoples of the colonized South and minoritized populations of the North."[81] The Holy Spirit is presently healing the "colonial wound" of Latin America through the religious imaginaries and practices of native communities. One major aspect of the colonial wound, according to Garcia-Johnson, is the sense of racial inferiority internalized by many Latin Americans based on their non-European cultural heritage.

The colonial wound, moreover, is perpetuated by a "coloniality of belief" comprising three main misconceptions, or "pillars" of misunderstanding.[82] This misunderstanding sustains and multiplies racial injustice in Latin America, especially among indigenous peoples:

1. *"Latin American suffering is a historical reality determined by God, as illustrated by the success of the European conquest."* García-Johnson asserts that this deeply rooted spiritual belief is used to justify the brutal genocide of indigenous peoples and feeds an

---

[80]García-Johnson, *Spirit Outside the Gate*, 168.
[81]García-Johnson, *Spirit Outside the Gate*, 3-4.
[82]García-Johnson, *Spirit Outside the Gate*, 71-72.

overriding sense of fatalism in Latin America. It also breeds reluc-
tance to challenge evil and oppression.

2. *"Christ is the representation of tragedy (which is inscripted in our
   brown bodies and histories) and invites us to contemplate suffering
   (and almost worship it) in daily life."* This faulty Christology further
   justifies the social oppression of indigenous peoples as it casts Jesus
   as the role model of a "conquered Amerindian" who lives his life
   in the reticence of abject poverty.

3. *"God blesses the foreigner-in-power and tolerates the use of imperial
   violence to accomplish his purposes in our lands and with our people."*
   This deeply entrenched belief has made Latin Americans passive
   in the face of five hundred years of colonial oppression at the hands
   of Spaniards, Portuguese, French, British, and various other
   colonial oppressors.[83]

According to García-Johnson, these underlying theological presup-
positions have nurtured a disempowering coloniality of belief, and left a
deep psychological imprint on the wounded psyche of Latin America.
These beliefs, moreover, have been exploited by a wide variety of colonial
regimes, dictators, oppressive governments, and even Christian leaders,
throughout the history of Latin America up until the present moment.[84]
It may equally be said that these pillars of colonial belief have been internalized by many US Latinas/os, and led to exploitation by charismatic
religious and political leaders—both Anglo and Latina/o.

In the face of such coloniality of belief and imperial governance,
García-Johnson powerfully presents the Holy Spirit as Liberator.[85] The
Holy Spirit is working in, with, and beneath, marginalized Latin
American and US Latina/o religious communities to heal the colonial
wound.[86] As Liberator, the Spirit of God guides us in the process of

---

[83]García-Johnson, *Spirit Outside the Gate*, 71-72.
[84]García-Johnson, *Spirit Outside the Gate*, 72.
[85]García-Johnson, *Spirit Outside the Gate*, 156-59.
[86]García-Johnson, *Spirit Outside the Gate*, 140, 201, 208.

spiritual and structural decolonization—both on an individual and corporate level. Moreover, the Spirit is moving outside the gates of traditional colonial religious institutions—i.e., the white evangelical church and Anglo American Catholicism—and bringing liberation through popular, grassroots expressions of Christianity.

To conclude this discussion of key works on Latina/o missiology and pneumatology, it is important to highlight recent Trinitarian accounts that attend to the matter of God acting in Christ through the Spirit in the enactment of liberation. In *A Visible Witness: Christology, Liberation, and Participation*, Puerto Rican theologian Jules A. Martínez-Olivieri offers the first monograph-length work on Christology in Latin America written from a Protestant perspective.[87] In this pathbreaking book, Martínez-Olivieri traces the development of a distinct Latin American Christology through the writings of José Míguez-Bonino, Nancy Bedford, Guillermo Hansen, Antonio Gonzales, and David del Salto. He also builds theological bridges between Catholic liberationist and Protestant traditions in Latin America by highlighting the common emphasis on the praxical nature of theology, Christology, and soteriology. Martínez-Olivieri uniquely proposes "a Trinitarian or theodramatic Christology: an account of Jesus of Nazareth, the Son of God, in light of the communicative interactions of God the Father and God the Holy Spirit in the economy of history," an "account [that] ground[s] the Christian notion of salvation as liberation and the church's participation in the experience of redemption."[88] Inspired by the Theater of the Oppressed in Latin America and by Kevin J. Vanhoozer's notion of the drama of doctrine, Martínez-Olivieri presents the church as a "theater of liberation," "a community that rehearses life in the social imagery of redemption."[89] As the body of Christ, empowered by the Spirit, the church is both recipient of

---

[87]Jules A. Martinez-Olivieri, *A Visible Witness: Christology, Liberation, and Participation* (Minneapolis: Fortress Press, 2016).

[88]Martinez-Olivieri, *A Visible Witness*, 204-5.

[89]Martinez-Olivieri, *A Visible Witness*, 193.

liberation and a participant in the formation of a liberated humanity.[90] "As a company of actors, the ecclesia performs the drama of the eschaton: it is a communal witness to the reality that another world is possible, characterized by justified people acting justly, thereby being visible 'spec-actors' of God's justice-making activity."[91]

LATINA/O PRACTICAL THEOLOGY

Shaped and influenced by Latina/o theology, Latina/o activists and community development practitioners have recently begun publishing books that represent a new genre of practical theology. Drawing on decades of experience in community organizing and Christian community development, Alexia Salvatierra, Noel Castellanos, and Ray Rivera have published books that offer biblical frameworks for the pursuit of social justice, as well as practical models for social engagement.

In *Faith-Rooted Organizing: Mobilizing the Church in Service to the World*, Alexia Salvatierra presents an original framework of community organizing that is "shaped and guided in all ways by our faith," and that draws the unique gifts and resources of the church into broader multi-sectoral movements for social justice.[92] A "Luther-costal" minister, Salvatierra is the leading Christian voice on immigration advocacy and reform in the United States, and her book is based on her four decades of community organizing and pastoral experience in the United States, Mexico, Central America, and the Philippines. Faith-rooted organizing (FRO) complements secular Alinsky-based approaches employed by labor unions and other community organizations, and is "designed to enable the faith 'sector' to give its best to the whole."[93] FRO views as its core goal the establishment of the Beloved Community of peoples of all cultural and ethnic backgrounds, and draws from Scripture to define its

---

[90]Martinez-Olivieri, *A Visible Witness*, 189.
[91]Martinez-Olivieri, *A Visible Witness*, 192-93.
[92]Alexia Salvatierra, *Faith-Rooted Organizing: Mobilizing the Church in Service to the World* (Downers Grove, IL: InterVarsity Press, 2014), 9-10.
[93]Salvatierra, *Faith-Rooted Organizing*, 10.

values, tools, and methods. Drawing from the inspiration of Latina/o Theology, FRO understands the human Christ to have been a poor Jewish peasant who challenged the injustice of the Roman Empire. Flowing from this understanding, FRO privileges the perspective of the poor in its analysis of structural inequality. Rather than "deciding" issues based on the common self-interest of organizational members, FRO seeks to discern the *kairos*—divinely orchestrated—moments of God. A kairos issue reveals "the deeply held lies that justify a pattern of injustice and opens up a space for God's truth to combat those lies directly."[94] FRO also relies upon the Spirit of God to transform oppressors and social structures through both "dove power"—nonviolent love in the model of César Chávez, Martin Luther King, Jr., and Mahatma Gandhi—and "serpent power"—the use of wealth, social influence, and numbers.[95] Serpent power responsibly wields tools of worldly power for the purposes of the kingdom of God. Finally, faith-rooted organizing unleashes the prophetic authority of religious symbols and traditions such as prayer, song, Santa Cena, pilgrimage, and healing services, as strategies of public communication.[96]

Building on the similar theme of Christ as marginalized Galilean, Noel Castellanos applies principles of Brown Theology to the framework of Christian community development. In *Where the Cross Meets the Street: What Happens to the Neighborhood When God Is at the Center*, he tells his own journey of faith and concientization, from the son of Mexican migrant farmworkers, to pastor of La Villita Church in Chicago, to the leadership of the CCDA.[97] Notably, Castellanos speaks of the important influence of many of the same Brown theologians discussed in this book. He writes of Orlando Costas, Gustavo Gutiérrez, and Virgilio Elizondo, and draws poignant connections between the Galilean

---

[94]Salvatierra, *Faith-Rooted Organizing*, 65, 66.

[95]Salvatierra, *Faith-Rooted Organizing*, 74, 78.

[96]Salvatierra, *Faith-Rooted Organizing*, 105, 124, 126.

[97]Noel Castellanos, *Where the Cross Meets the Street: What Happens to the Neighborhood When God Is at the Center* (Downers Grove, IL: InterVarsity Press, 2015).

and mestizo origins of Jesus and the holistic approach of Christian community development. These authors gave Castellanos the theological language to understand his own life history and ministry journey. They made him "woke":

> I was beginning to read and understand the story of Jesus from the margins of the barrio, and I was overwhelmed by the realization that Jesus launched his kingdom ministry to the entire world with a ragtag team of Galilean men and women from a mestizo and marginalized reality. While I was tempted to conclude that Jesus was part Mexican, I was more certain than ever that he was not the white version I had always pictured. . . . In that context, it was unmistakable that Jesus of Nazareth identified with the marginalized, the oppressed and the vulnerable—and I was determined to do the same in my ministry.[98]

According to Castellanos, the "cross meets the streets" in Jesus' prayer, "Thy kingdom come, Thy will be done in earth, as it is in heaven" (Mt 6:10 KJV).[99] The kingdom of God is a present, not just future reality, and Christians are called to be Christ's instruments of justice and redemption now. The kingdom of God comes alive in urban communities when our ministries embrace a holistic approach, which includes "incarnation, proclamation and formation, demonstration of compassion, restoration and development, and the confrontation of injustice."[100] On the contrary, most US churches are hindered from effective ministry among the poor because our privilege and wealth keeps us from relationship and proximity to the poor, and our Western mindset uplifts personal comfort, expects quick results, and devalues suffering and perseverance.

Raymond Rivera offers a unique contribution to the nascent literature of Latina/o social justice practical theology from a Nuyorican, Pentecostal perspective. A forty-five-year urban ministry veteran, Rivera is well known for his apostolic giftings and his founding of the

---

[98]Castellanos, *Where the Cross Meets the Street*, 80-81.
[99]Castellanos, *Where the Cross Meets the Street*, 74.
[100]Castellanos, *Where the Cross Meets the Street*, 74.

Latino Pastoral Action Center in New York City. In *Liberty to the Captives: Our Call to Minister in a Captive World*, Rivera presents theologies of captivity and calling, and offers four paradigms of ministering in captivity.[101] Inspired by Orlando Costas and Gustavo Gutiérrez, Rivera asserts that the fall produced a state of human separation from God and bondage to self. This captivity is brutal and dehumanizing, and has led to spiritual and civic decay, and all manner of social injustice. It has produced machísmo and sexism and has invaded all social institutions and human relationships:

> Captivity seeped into the totality of human existence, encompassing the social, economic, political, and spiritual realms. Abusers, adulterers, thieves, murderers, dictators, and terrorists are easy to point out. But captivity surrounds us everywhere we go. It is present in our families, churches, and schools. It permeates our workplaces. It has a seat at the boardrooms of businesses and corporations. Even the community-based organization across the street, with all the good it does, is not exempt from captivity. It is present in our foster care system and other social safety nets. It certainly permeates every level of government. It affects our healthcare and welfare systems. Our military and prison complexes cannot escape it either. Nothing exists or is produced without being impacted by captivity.[102]

In refreshing Latina/o Pentecostal fashion, Rivera unabashedly declares that it is Christ who frees us from our individual and social captivity. Through his death and resurrection, Christ brought about our redemption from sin and captivity, and calls us into relationship with himself. In turn, Jesus calls us to be ministers in captivity. Notably, Rivera shares the powerful story of his own calling to Christ and ministry while a youth in the rough and tumble streets of Ocean Hill/Brownsville. His *testimonio* pierces the veil of Latina/o Pentecostal Christianity for the reader who may be unfamiliar, and details

---

[101]Raymond Rivera, *Liberty to the Captives: Our Call to Minister in a Captive World* (Grand Rapids: Eerdmans, 2012).

[102]Rivera, *Liberty to the Captives*, 9-10.

charismatic experiences of healing and deliverance that have long
been familiar to the Brown Church.

> But on this fateful day, when I was on my knees and repeated the utter-
> ances of praise to God that the guest speaker asked my friends and me to
> repeat, I knew my life had changed. Like Jesus (Matthew 3:16) and Paul
> (Acts 9:17), I had been baptized with the Holy Spirit![103]

Flowing from an understanding of the indelible personal transformation that is the result of God's call, Rivera presents four paradigms of
ministering in captivity. These include

1. Engage Your Community: we are to engage our community as instruments of God's healing, and should do this in a holistic fashion
   that addresses both the spiritual and physical needs of individuals,
   and the community at large.[104]

2. Confront Your Community: like John the Baptist, God calls us to
   prophetically confront members of our own religious community
   over issues of social injustice. This may involve both the religious
   and political arenas, and often becomes necessary because of the
   preaching of a "truncated" gospel that concerns itself with personal
   salvation but ignores broader racial and social realities.[105]

3. Engage the Powers: as followers of Jesus, we are sometimes called
   to engage non-Christians and non-Christian institutions in partnership, in order to create solutions for social problems. Like Ne-
   hemiah who engaged the king of Persia, it is sometimes appropriate for us to solicit support from government entities and our
   elected representatives as a means of advancing kingdom values,
   peace, and justice.[106]

4. Confront the Powers: in the spirit of César Chávez, Martin Luther
   King, Jr., Frederick Douglass, Charles Finney, and Lucretia Mott,

---

[103]Rivera, *Liberty to the Captives*, 38.
[104]Rivera, *Liberty to the Captives*, 43-45.
[105]Rivera, *Liberty to the Captives*, 72, 77.
[106]Rivera, *Liberty to the Captives*, 93, 94.

the Christian church must confront government powers and business interests over the abuse of immigrants, children, the poor, and all who are marginalized.[107]

In *Liberty to the Captives,* Rivera reminds us of these four critical tenets, which have been part of the prophetic witness of the Brown Church for five hundred years.

CONCLUSION

Unknown to most scholars and students of ethnic studies, as well as to most within the Latina/o religious community itself, Latina/o theologians have engaged in decolonial and culturally contextualized self-reflection since the 1970s. Inspired by Latin American liberation theologies, the civil rights movement, and the growth of diverse Latina/o communities in the United States, Latina/o theology stands on its own as a distinct and eminently valuable theological voice and academic discipline. It must no longer be ignored by ethnic studies, or viewed askance by the discipline of religious studies, or Christian colleges, seminaries, and universities. Latina/o theology embodies the spiritual treasure of the US Latina/o community. To reject it, is to reject *us.*

Rooted in the five-hundred-year experience of Latin Americans and US Latinas/os as a colonized people, Latina/o theologians identify closely with the marginal Galilean roots of Jesus and his suffering outside the institutional gates of empire. Like Jesus, Latina/o theologians represent a voice of a minority community perennially overlooked, and repeatedly colonized—first by the Spanish and then as an internal colony of the United States for the past 150 years. In response, and as result, Latina/o theologians seek solidarity beyond the confines of Latin American nationalism and historic denominational divides, and create interwoven theologies of racial justice in community, or *en conjunto.*

As a crucial corrective to the early literature of the field, Latina theologians such as Ada María Isasi-Díaz, Jeannette Rodríguez, Maria Pilar

---

[107]Rivera, *Liberty to the Captives,* 41-42, 118-19.

Aquino, Elizabeth Conde-Frazier, and Loida I. Martell-Otero have offered liberative voices that challenge the patriarchy still firmly rooted in Latin American and US Latina/o culture and society. They have reclaimed lo cotidiano as a vital space of theological and pastoral imagination for the mujeres who lead our community, and by extension, for the rest of us.

As a growing and thriving spiritual home for millions of Latinas/os, the *Iglesia Pentecostés* has given rise to some of the most creative and dynamic expressions of Latina/o theology in recent years. Pentecostal theologians such as Conde-Frazier, Maldonado-Pérez, Villafañe, and García-Johnson present compelling portraits of the Liberating Spirit, the "wild child of the Trinity," who is active in the day-to-day lives of believers, and who anoints us unto the preaching of good news to the poor, and freedom to all who are oppressed. Drawing from this same Pentecostal lineage, Alexia Salvatierra, Noel Castellanos, and Ray Rivera, among others, have translated the insights of Latina/o theology into impactful community organizations and practical models for social engagement.

CONCLUSION

The Brown Church Today and Tenets
of a "Brown Christian" Identity

MARIA WAS A STUDENT in my class last year. Toward the end of the term she came to me with a request. She asked if I would share with her my lecture slides from the past three classes. "Sure," I replied. "What's the matter?" Maria told me she had missed class because her mother had been wrongfully arrested and detained by immigration authorities. Her mom had "papers," but she had been swept up in an immigration raid because she was Latina—because she was "brown." Maria had to return home to watch her siblings so that her father could find her mother. It took four days before they were able to locate Maria's mom and rescue her from wrongful detention. Four days.

A five-alarm fire is raging through the Latina/o immigrant community. Millions are impacted. And yet, relatively few outside of our community—and very few within the evangelical community—seem to care. In fact, through their xenophobic rhetoric many are intentionally stoking the flames without regard to the many lives being consumed.

The recent executive orders on immigration in the United States are spreading deep fear and terror throughout immigrant communities, and families like Maria's are being torn apart. Why? Because these executive orders have expanded the definition of "criminal" so broadly that it sweeps up all eleven million undocumented immigrants as priorities for deportation. Arrests of immigrants with no criminal records have tripled.[1] Under the previous American administration (which was no friend of immigrants, to be sure), perpetrators of serious crimes, at least in theory, were prioritized for deportation. Families and those without criminal records were relegated to the end of the line.

The new immigration guidelines have led to unconscionable arrests, deportations, and enforcement tactics in recent months, including the separation of children from their parents at the border and their imprisonment in cages,[2] the deportation of parents without proper due process, and the placement of their children in US foster care—a modern day form of child trafficking by the US government. These horrific practices also include the arrest and detention of a ten-year-old girl with cerebral palsy who had just left the hospital after receiving emergency gall bladder surgery,[3] an undocumented mother who was hospitalized with a brain tumor,[4] an undocumented father who was dropping his child off at school, another who was driving his pregnant wife to the hospital to give birth,[5] and a victim of domestic violence who was testifying in court.[6]

---

[1]Portions of this chapter are adapted from the essay "Immigration and the Latina/o Community" by Robert Chao Romero, from *Still Evangelical?*, edited by Mark Labberton (Downers Grove, IL: InterVarsity Press, 2018), 66-80. Ben Leonard, "Under Trump Arrests of Undocumented Immigrants with No Criminal Record Have Tripled," NBC News, August 13, 2018, www.nbcnews.com /politics/immigration/under-trump-arrests-undocumented-immigrants-no-criminal-record -have-tripled-n899406.

[2]David Sim, "Children Crying at U.S. Border and Sitting in Cages: Trump's Separation Policy in Pictures," *Newsweek*, June 20, 2018.

[3]Marwa Eltagouri, "A 10-Year-Old Immigrant Was Rushed to the Hospital in an Ambulance. She Was Detained on the Way," *Washington Post*, October 27, 2017.

[4]Chris Sommerfeldt, Erin Kurkin, and Nancy Dillon, "Undocumented Woman with Brain Tumor Seized by Federal Agents at Texas hospital, Family Fears She Will Die," *Daily News*, February 24, 2017, www.nydailynews.com/news/national/undocumented-woman-brain-tumor-removed -hospital-lawyer-article-1.2979956.

[5]Jade Hernandez, "Undocumented Dad Taken by ICE While Dropping Kids Off at School," ABC Eyewitness News, March 3, 2017, https://abc7chicago.com/news/undocumented-dad-taken-by -ice-while-dropping-kids-off-at-school/1783028.

[6]Jonathan Blitzer, "The Woman Arrested by ICE in a Courthouse Speaks Out," *The New Yorker*, February 23, 2017, www.newyorker.com/news/news-desk/the-woman-arrested-by-ice-in-a -courthouse-speaks-out.

Equally unconscionable is the repeal of Deferred Action for Childhood Arrivals (DACA), which has served as a life raft for more than 800,000 undocumented young adults and their families.[7] This executive action was implemented in 2012 after Congress failed to pass the Dream Act. DACA shielded undocumented youth from deportation and granted them a work permit. Though it was imperfect and never intended to be a permanent solution, it gave hope to millions of undocumented youth and their family members.

Pastor Noe Carias's story also clearly illustrates how immigrant families are being inhumanely targeted by the recent executive orders. Pastor Noe is a minister in the Assemblies of God denomination and has lived in the United States for more than two decades. At the age of eight, during the civil war in Guatemala, he was kidnapped by guerillas. After five years in captivity he escaped and fled to the United States as a child refugee. Pastor Noe eventually married a US citizen and became the father of two children who are US citizens. He has no criminal record. And yet, in July 2017, he was arrested and detained by Immigration and Customs Enforcement (ICE) during a periodic check-in with immigration officials.[8]

The Brown Church of the United States has arisen to challenge its persecution at the hands of a twenty-first-century Pharaoh named Donald Trump. Like the Israelites three thousand years ago, the Latina/o community has been scapegoated by the majority culture and cast as a foreign military threat in a time of war. We are exploited for our cheap labor and vast economic contributions to the Gross Domestic Product of the United States ($428 billion annually) as well as for our additional billion dollar contributions to federal, state, and local taxes.[9] In the

---

[7] Vanessa Romo, Martina Stewart, Brian Naylor, "Trump Ends DACA, Calls On Congress to Act," NPR, September 5, 2017.

[8] Kyung Lah, "California Pastor Caught in Immigration Enforcement Net," CNN, August 7, 2017, www.cnn.com/2017/08/07/us/california-pastor-ice-detainee-noe-carias/index.html.

[9] Robert Chao Romero, "Migration as Grace," *International Journal of Urban Transformation* 1 (October 2016): 11-30; Travis Loller, "Many Illegal Immigrants Pay Up at Tax Time," *USA Today*, April 11, 2008; "At Tax Time, Illegal Immigrants Are Paying, Too," Associated Press, April 10, 2008, www.nbcnews.com/id/24054024/ns/business-personal_finance/t/tax-time-illegal-immigrants -are-paying-too.

same breath, we are blamed for the economic and national security woes of the country by wily politicians eager for the power of elected office. Led by the president, these politicians manipulate sinful human nature and our fallen tendency to hate those who are not like us, in the name of nationalism. Their racist rhetoric and conservative media performances can be compared to political "soft porn" that titillates a wide range of voters—from neo-Nazis donning khakis and torches, to disaffected working class white voters in Red States, to conservative fundamentalist Christians who would never consider themselves racist, and yet have never severed their colonial ties with the destructive ideology of Manifest Destiny. Such xenophobic rhetoric has inspired numerous hate crimes and acts of physical violence against immigrants, including the El Paso massacre—the worst mass slaughter of Latinas/os in modern times. In the meantime, our immigrant mothers, fathers, sisters, brothers, friends, tías, tíos, and abuelitas and abuelitos are told to continue their same intensive labor production "without straw for bricks"(Ex 5:6-18)—without the basic necessities for work and life, such as employment visas, access to healthcare and transportation, affordable housing, and quality education for their children.

The Brown Church is rising up against these injustices in the name of Jesus, the Savior from Galilee, who takes the side of the oppressed and most vulnerable, and who has walked with us through the evils of conquest, colonialism, segregation, exploitation, and violent military interventions in the lands of our mothers and fathers. This time is no different.

Like Moses, Miriam, and Aaron, we are standing up together to challenge the oppression of empire. Seeing ourselves in the Exodus narrative, we apply the biblical text to our present experience and declare:

> Afterward the Brown Church went to Donald Trump and said, "Thus says the LORD, the God of Israel, 'Let my people go, so that they may live lives of shalom and abundance in the land that was once theirs.'"
>
> But Donald Trump said, "Who is the LORD that I should heed him and let the Hispanics go? I worship the God of Make America Great Again,

Manifest Destiny, and America First. I do not know about the Christianity of which you speak—this Jesus of Galilee and the God of the Oppressed." . . . But the president of the United States said to them, "Brown Church, why are you taking the people away from their work? Get to your labors!" (Ex 5:1-4 Contemporary Chicana/o Version)

We, the Brown Church, say "¡No! ¡Ya basta!" We are grounded in the love of Christ, the power of the Holy Spirit, and more than five hundred years of communal struggle and community cultural wealth. From La Virgen and Las Casas, to the multicultural voices of Guáman Poma, Sor Juana, and Garcilaso de la Vega, to the Chicana/o civil rights movement of Dolores Huerta and César Chávez, to San Oscar Romero and the historic and contemporary sanctuary movements, spiritual capital has been a central component of our Latina/o community cultural wealth. As an outgrowth of our prophetic advocacy efforts and praxis, moreover, we have developed Brown Theology: a unique and consistent body of social justice theology based on the Bible. Over the past century, pastors, priests, and theologians such as Gustavo Gutiérrez, René Padilla, Ada María Isasi-Díaz, Virgilio Elizondo, Justo González, and Elizabeth Conde-Frazier have taught us to think about God en conjunto, and have framed foundational concepts such as the preferential option for the poor, misión integral, mujerista theology, the Galilee principle, and Latina evangelica theology.

Rooted in this tradition, the Brown Church also has a rising generation of young leaders like Kari:

The dream began with my parents, two young warriors, determined to escape a world of poverty in search for a future in a country where rumor had it, dreams came true. They sacrificed everything they held dear so I could carry on with their dreams. America has seen me grow, cry, hurt, laugh, and fight for twenty-four years since I migrated at eight months old from Oaxaca. The sobering truth about what it means to be undocumented in this country wounded my validity and identity. The limitations, persecution of undocumented communities, and the fear of separation from my family pushed me into coping with art, music, and smoking. I held a great grudge against God for years. But in 2012, I received a wonderful gift in this country—the salvation, grace, and love from Jesus Christ. I realize Jesus brought me to this country as a foreigner to understand vulnerability and marginalization to be more like him. When I had to pay $5,000 out-of-pocket to pay for UCLA because undocumented students didn't get financial aid, he provided. He knew my desire to become an educator and made the way with DACA. Now I stand as a kinder/first grade Special Education teacher completely in love with serving the children of this community. My identity and citizenship are found in Christ, and no human law will change this. I rest in his love knowing that he too was despised and rejected but he loves with an unfailing love. My dream and purpose in this country is to be a fountain of his love and grace.

Kari is not alone, and she stands at the vanguard with other rising leaders.[10]

In addition to the cutting edge leadership of Christians from the rising generation, we have the wise, collective leadership of elders who have tread this path for many decades before us, and for whom this is not their first fight. We have Pope Francis, the first Latin American leader of the 1.2 billion member Roman Catholic Church, from which the Brown Church descends. We have "La Madrina,"[11] Rev. Dr. Alexia Salvatierra, who has fought racial battles of injustice in the name of Jesus on four continents and pioneered the development of faith-rooted organizing. The Brown Church also celebrates within its ranks Latina/o elders who lead a wide variety of national organizations focused upon advocacy, community development, and higher education. These include: Rev. Dr. Raymond Rivera and Rev. Susana Rivera Leon of the Latino Pastoral Action Center;

---

[10]Influential millennial leaders include Grecia and Josh López Reyes, Esperanza Gene, David Jaimes, Sandy Ovalle, Juan Martínez, Nancy Negrete, and Siobe and Gabriel López of the Brown Ecclesial Network. Sandra Maria Van Opstal, Marcos Canales, Inés Velásquez-McBride, Jeremy Del Rio, Karen González, Alejandra Geonetta-Trihus, José Humphreys, Gabe Veas, Glafira Lopez, Jaime Jorge, Noemi Vega, Natalia Kohn Rivera, Kristy Robinson, Marlena Graves, José Serrano, Vanessa Martinez, Jennifer Guerra, Rosa Ramirez, and J.C. Arce also lead diverse and dynamic pastoral ministries.

[11]"The Godmother."

Rev. Mayra Nolan, Rev. Michael Mata, and Rev. Rudy Carrasco of the Christian Community Development Association; Ava Steaffens of World Relief; Rev. Dr. Gabriel Salguero, Rev. Walter Contreras, and Rev. Dr. Elizabeth Ríos of the National Latino Evangelical Coalition; Rev. Dr. Oscar García-Johnson, Director, Fuller Seminary's Centro Latino; Rev. Luís Cortes and Judith Torres-Lynch of Esperanza; Rev. Dr. Melvin Valiente and Rev. Ada Valiente of Mateo 25/We Care; Rev. Dr. Edward Fraijo Delgado and Rev. Dr. Elizabeth Conde-Frazier of Asociación para la Educación Teológica Hispana (AETH). Finally, as executive director of the Louisville Institute and president of Ashland Theological Seminary, respectively, Dr. Edwin Aponte and Dr. Juan Martínez steward leading theological institutions serving multicultural constituencies.

The Revolution is bubbling. *Está subiendo La Raza.*[12] Can you see it? We just need to find each other. Listen closely, and you will hear the cheers of the great cloud of witnesses encouraging us forward: Sor Juana, Las Casas, Montesinos, Guaman Poma, Garcilaso de la Vega, Catarina de San Juan, Padre Martínez de Taos, Alonso Perales, Cleofas Calleros, Archbishop Oscar Romero, César Chávez, Mama Leo, Santos Elizondo, Francisco Olazabal, Juan Lugo, and Orlando Costas. They are now with Jesus *y ellas/ellos están gritando. Con Cristo, ellos están llamando.*[13] Calling us forward. Cheering us on. It is time for La Raza to come together, to step up—no longer divided.

Jesus is calling us to a new movement and new wineskins for the new work of *Espíritu Liberador* among us. A revolution of Latina/o followers of Jesus—Mexicana/o, Peruviana/o, Chilena/o, Hondureña/o, Salvadoreña/o, Tica/Tico, Cubana/o, Dominicana/o, Puerto Riqueña/o, Argentina/o, y de Paraguay, Uruguay, Colombia, Brazil, Nicaragua, Belize, Bolivia, Venezuela, Ecuador, Guatemala, Panama. Transdenominational, *también—Evangélico, Católico, Protestante.* Transgenerational—*los viejos como los jóvenes—unidas/os en Cristo, nuestro Señor y Vida.* And everyone

---

[12]"The Race is rising up."
[13]"They are now with Jesus and they are shouting. With Christ, they are calling."

else is welcome, too, because our goal is the Beloved Community. *Ven y
únete a nosotros. Somos familia.* And as familia, we know that women and
men must hold equal leadership and authority in our midst. Machísmo
is a dark legacy of our colonial past: *no es bienvenido.*[14]

Jesus of Galilee. Jesus who heals the colonial wound. The Spirit of Jesus
who meets us in the Christian-Activist borderlands, decolonizes our
churches and institutions, and yet who also calls us into reconciliation
with one another and our historic oppressors. Not a cheap grace and
reconciliation that glosses over five hundred years of violence and racism
that have killed, segregated, deported, and left hungry. No, a Spirit-led
process of naming, resonating, repenting, decolonizing, and healing. For,
as the Brown Church, we do not wage war as the world does (2 Cor
10:3-5), not even as do our secular allies, no matter how well-intentioned
they may be. Our goal is no less than the loving and liberating reign of
the kingdom of God, the good news of Jesus of Galilee. In the words, and
example, of Christ our Savior,

> The Spirit of the Lord is upon me,
>> because he has anointed me
>>> to bring good news to the poor.
> He has sent me to proclaim release to the captives
>> and recovery of sight to the blind,
>>> to let the oppressed go free,
> to proclaim the year of the Lord's favor. (Lk 4:18-19)

As Brown Christians, we claim a social identity that encompasses our
love for Jesus, our rich and diverse God-given cultural heritage(s), and
our passion for justice and liberation. We no longer leave any of it outside
the colonizer's door. In response to the question, "¿Quién soy yo?," the
Brown Christian responds:

---

[14]"Transdenominational, also—Evangelical, Catholic, Protestant. Transgenerational—the old and
the young—united in Christ, our Lord and Savior. And everyone else is welcome, too, because
our goal is the Beloved Community. Come and join us. We are family. And as family, we know
that women and men must hold equal leadership and authority in our midst. Sexism is a dark
legacy of our colonial past: it is not welcome."

1. I am the Brown Church.

2. *God calls me "Míja/o" (Daughter/Son).* I am Abba's child because Jesus gave his life for me. As God's child, I uniquely reflect my Father's image to the world.

   I reflect the image of my Father, holistically, in terms of my: (1) individual personality, gifts, talents (Ps 139:13-16); (2) rich, distinct, and diverse Latina/o cultural heritage, and other cultural heritages I may possess (Rev 21:26); and (3) gender (Gen 1:27).

3. *My Latina/o culture is a gift from God.* My Latina/o culture, in all of its diversity, is a treasure from God (Rev 21:26). I celebrate it in all of its rich "mestizaje" (cultural mixture). All of its components—indigenous, African, European, Jewish, Asian, Middle Eastern, and whatever else there may be—are equally a gift from God.

   At the same time, I realize that all ethnic cultures, including Latina/o culture, have been infected and distorted by sin (Rom 3:23; Rom 5:12; Rev 21:27). Machísmo and anti-indigenous prejudice are prime examples. I look to Christ to sanctify both myself, and my culture(s) (Rom 6:6; 1 Cor 6:11; Gal 2:20). Through God's Word, I can recognize the difference (Jn 17:17; 2 Tim 3:16-17).

4. *Concientización.* My historical consciousness has been raised, and I am aware that Latinas/os have experienced deep personal and structural racism and injustice over the past five hundred years. In the United States, our peculiar experience of racism has been betwixt and between that of "black" and "white"—it has been "Brown." Such discrimination is sin and displeases God (Mk 12:31; Mt 25:31-46; Is 10:1-3; Ps 12:5; Jer 22:3; Ex 22:21; Lev 19:33-34; Jer 22:3-5; Prov 17:5).

5. *Commitment to social justice in discipleship.* As a follower and student of Jesus Christ, I possess a biblical duty to love, care, and advocate for all who are marginalized and oppressed of every cultural back-

ground, including Latinas/os (Mt 25:31-46; Prov 31: 8-9; Ps 146:7-9; Is 58:6-11). Social justice and compassion for the marginalized is a central emphasis of the kingdom of God (Lk 4:16-18; Lk 6:20-26; Lk 16:19-31; Mt 25:31-46).

This action and commitment is guided and empowered by my daily walk of discipleship with Jesus Christ. Such discipleship is the most critical aspect of life in the kingdom of God. I do this in the large footsteps of Bartolomé de Las Casas, Sor Juana Inés de la Cruz, César Chávez, Archbishop Oscar Romero, and the Mothers and Fathers of Latin American Liberation Theology, misión integral, and Latina/o theology. Christian discipleship is founded on love, and transforms all aspects of my personal life, shaping me daily, more and more into the character of Christ (Lk 9:23-24; 2 Cor 3:17-18; Jn 3:16-17). Social justice is a natural outflow of my personal transformation (1 Jn 3:14, 16-18). Like two wings of a plane, my personal discipleship is inseparable from my commitment to social justice for all.

6. *God's Word.* The Scriptures are the inspired Word of God and my guide for life, and personal and social transformation (2 Tim 3:16-17; 2 Pet 1:20-21; Ps 119:105). The Bible is a treasure, and God meets us, and speaks to us, through it (Mt 13:52; Heb 4:12; Ps 119:72, 81, 98). It is sweeter than honey to the taste, and it brings peace, hope and wisdom (Ps 119:103, 130, 165). The word of God will never fail (Lk 1:37; Josh 21:45). Social and political doctrines may change with time, but God's Word remains my authority (Mt 24:35).

7. *Love and nonviolence.* In the example of Jesus, Dolores Huerta, César Chávez, and Archbishop Oscar Romero, I believe that if we resist injustice firmly, peacefully, and with love, then God will intervene in our cause and bring social change. Filled with the inestimable power of the Holy Spirit who raised Jesus from the

dead, my method of social change is nonviolence of heart and external action. I believe that "love is the most powerful organizer." In the words of Jesus, who himself lived and gave his life in the context of empire: "You have heard that it was said, 'You shall love your neighbor and hate your enemy.' But I say to you, Love your enemies and pray for those who persecute you, so that you may be children of your Father in heaven" (Mt 5:43-45).

8. *The Beloved Community.* Social justice is not an end in itself. In the words of our brother Rev. Dr. Martin Luther King Jr., the goal of social justice is not social justice, but the "beloved community." Done in the spirit of love and the empowerment of Jesus Christ, social justice leads to the reconciliation of all people from every cultural and ethnic background (Col 1:17-20; Gal 3:28-29; Rev 5:6-10, 7:9-10, 21:26-27). My discipleship and activism celebrate and embrace my God-given cultural heritage(s), but it is not ethnocentric. The Brown Church welcomes all. I seek the shalom and reconciliation of all of humanity in Jesus Christ. We are one familia.

9. *The Church.* I pursue justice and the Beloved Community in spiritual communion with the local church and the global body of Christ. Together with the apostle Paul, I recognize that I cannot long be a follower of Jesus outside of the church because, by God's design, we need one another, and belong to each other (1 Cor 12:18-21; Rom 12:5). The church has been uniquely entrusted with the keys of the kingdom of God, and even the gates of Hades will not prevail against it (Mt 16:18). In the words of César Chávez, "When we refer to the Church we should define the word a little. We mean the whole Church, the Church as an ecumenical body spread around the world. . . . That Church is one form of the Presence of God on earth, and so naturally it is powerful. It is a powerful moral and spiritual force which cannot be ignored by any movement."

As Brown Christians, Rosa, Carlos, Edwin, you, and I, now have a home. For years we have wandered in the "spiritual borderlands" of Christianity and activism, longing for an identity and community which encompassed our love for Jesus, our rich, God-given cultural heritage, and our passion for social justice. Welcome home. You now belong.

We are the Brown Church!

BIBLIOGRAPHY

Acuña, Rudy. *Occupied America: A History of Chicanos.* New York: Pearson, 2014.

Afro America: La Tercera Raíz. CONACULTA/Gobierno Federal Veracruz. Instituto Veracruzano de la Cultura, 2010.

Alfaro, Sammy. *Divino Compañero: Toward a Hispanic Pentecostal Christology.* Princeton Theological Monograph Series 147. Eugene, OR: Pickwick, 2010.

———. "Liberating Pentecostal Theologies: A View from the Latina/o and Latin American Pentecostal Contexts." In *Global Renewal Christianity: Spirit-Empowered Movements Past, Present, and Future.* Vol. 2, *Latin America.* Edited by Vinson Synan, Amos Yong, and Miguel Álvarez, 355-70. Lake Mary, FL: Charisma House, 2016.

Anzaldúa, Gloria. *Borderlands/La Frontera: The New Mestiza.* San Francisco: Aunt Lute Books, 2012.

———, ed. *Making Face, Making Soul: Creative and Critical Perspectives by Women of Color.* San Francisco: Aunt Lute Books, 1990.

Aponte, Edwin David. *¡Santo! Varieties of Latino/a Spirituality.* Maryknoll, NY: Orbis Books, 2012.

Aponte, Edwin David, and Miguel A. De La Torre. *Handbook of Latina/o Theologies.* St. Louis: Chalice Press, 2006.

Aquino, Maria Pilar. "Directions and Foundations of Hispanic/Latino Theology: Toward a Mestiza Theology of Liberation." *Journal of Hispanic/Latino Theology* 1, no. 1 (1993): 5-21.

Aquino, Maria Pilar, Daisy L. Machado, and Jeanette Rodriguez, eds. *A Reader in Latina Feminist Theology: Religion and Justice.* Austin: University of Texas Press, 2002.

Bailey, Gauvin Alexander. "A Mughal Princess in Baroque New Spain: Catarina de San Juan (1606–1688), the China Poblana." *Anales del Instituto de Investigaciones Estéticas* 19, no. 71 (1997): 37-73.

Bardacke, Frank. *Trampling Out the Vintage: César Chávez and the Two Souls of the United Farm Workers.* Brooklyn: Verso Books, 2012.

Bell, Rob. *Velvet Elvis: Repainting the Christian Faith.* New York: HarperCollins, 2005.

Bellah, Robert N., and Phillip E. Hammond. *Varieties of Civil Religion.* San Francisco: Harper & Row, 1980.

Betancur, Belisario, and Reinaldo Figueredo Planchart. "From Madness to Hope: the 12-Year War in El Salvador: Report of the Commission on the Truth for El Salvador." Accessed October 5, 2018. www.usip.org/sites/default/files/file/ElSalvador-Report.pdf.

Boff, Leonardo, and Clodovis Boff. *Introducing Liberation Theology*. Maryknoll, NY: Orbis Books, 2005.

Bradford Burns, *The Poverty of Progress: Latin America in the Nineteenth Century*. Berkeley: University of California Press, 1983.

Brockman, James R. *Romero: A Life*. Maryknoll, NY: Orbis Books, 1990.

Brown v. Board of Education of Topeka, 347 U.S. 483.

Bruns, Roger. *César Chávez: A Biography*. Westport, CT: Greenwood Press, 2005.

Buergenthal, Thomas. "The United Nations Truth Commission for El Salvador." *Vanderbilt Journal of Transnational Law* 27, no. 3 (1994): 497-544.

Calvillo, Jonathan, and Stanley R. Bailey. "Latino Religious Affiliation and Ethnic Identity." *Journal for the Scientific Study of Religion*, 54, no. 1 (2015): 57-78.

Canning, Raymond. "Christ's Self-identification with 'The Least of Mine' (Matthew 25:40, 45) According to Augustine: 'Is This the Humility of God?'" *Australian eJournal of Theology* 15 (2010). Accessed October 12, 2018. http://aejt.com.au/__data/assets/pdf _file/0009/225387/Canning_Christs_self_identification_GH.pdf.

Carrasco Juarez, Veronica. "Give Until It Hurts: The Speeches and Letters of Mother Teresa," Master's Thesis, Texas Tech University, 2007.

Carrera, Magali M. "Locating Race in Late Colonial Mexico," *Art Journal* 57, no. 3 (1998): 36-45.

Carroll R., M. Daniel. *Christians at the Border: Immigration, the Church, and the Bible*. Grand Rapids: Baker Academic, 2008.

Castellanos, Noel. *Where the Cross Meets the Street: What Happens to the Neighborhood When God Is at the Center*. Downers Grove, IL: InterVarsity Press, 2015.

Castelo, Daniel, and Elaine Health. *Pentecostalism as a Christian Mystical Tradition*. Grand Rapids: Eerdmans, 2017.

Castleman, Bruce A. "Social Climbers in a Colonial Mexican City: Individual Mobility Within the Sistema de Castas in Orizaba, 1777–1791." *Colonial Latin American Review* 10, no. 2 (2001): 229-49.

Cavanaugh, William T. "The Ecclesiologies of Medellín and the Lessons of the Base Communities." *CrossCurrents* 44, no. 1 (1994): 67-84.

Chávez, Leo R. *The Latino Threat: Constructing Immigrants, Citizens, and the Nation*. Stanford: Stanford University Press, 2008.

Clawson, Michael. "Misión Integral and Progressive Evangelicalism: The Latin American Influence on the North American Emerging Church." *Religions* 3 (2012): 790-807.

Conde-Frazier, Elizabeth. *Hispanic Bible Institutes: A Community of Theological Construction*. Scranton, PA: University of Scranton Press, 2004.

Cone, James H. *Martin & Malcolm & America: A Dream or a Nightmare*. Maryknoll, NY: Orbis Books, 2012.

Conference of Latin American Bishops. "Medellin 1968 (excerpts)." www.geraldschlabach .net/medellin-1968-excerpts.

Costas, Orlando. *Christ Outside the Gate: Mission Beyond Christendom.* Maryknoll, NY: Orbis Books, 1982.

———. "Evangelism from the Periphery: A Galilean Model." *Apuntes* 2, no. 3 (1982): 51-59.

———. "Hispanic Theology in North America." In *Struggles for Solidarity: Liberation Theologies in Tension,* edited by Lorine M. Getz and Ruy O. Costa, 63-74. Minneapolis: Fortress Press, 1992.

Cox, Victoria. *Guaman Poma de Ayala: Entre los Conceptos Andino y Europeo de Tiempo.* Cuzco, Peru: Centro de Estudios Regionales Andinos Bartolomé de Las Casas, 2002.

Cuellar, Gregory Lee. *Voices of Marginality: Exile and Return in Second Isaiah 40-55 and the Mexican Immigrant Experience.* New York: Peter Lang, 2008.

Cunningham, Hilary. *God and Caesar at the Rio Grande: Sanctuary and the Politics of Religion.* Minneapolis, MN: University of Minnesota Press, 1995.

Curran, Charles E. *Catholic Social Teaching, 1891–Present: A Historical, Theological, and Ethical Analysis.* Washington, DC: Georgetown University Press, 2002.

Dalton, Frederick John. *The Moral Vision of César Chávez.* Maryknoll, NY: Orbis Books, 2003.

Daniels, Roger. *Coming to America: A History of Immigration and Ethnicity in American Life.* New York: Perennial, 2002.

Davidson, David M. "Negro Slave Control and Resistance in Colonial Mexico, 1519-1650." *Hispanic American Historical Review* 46, no. 3 (1966): 235-253.

De Aragon, Ray John. *Padre Martinez and Bishop Lamy.* Las Vegas, NM: The Pan-American Publishing Company, 1978.

De La Torre, Miguel. *Doing Christian Ethics from the Margins.* Maryknoll, NY: Orbis Books, 2014.

———. *The Politics of Jesús: A Hispanic Political Theology.* Lanham, MD: Rowman & Littlefield, 2015.

———. *Reading the Bible from the Margins.* Maryknoll, NY: Orbis Books, 2013.

De La Torre, Miguel, and Edwin David Aponte. *Introducing Latino/a Theologies.* Maryknoll, NY: Orbis Books, 2001.

De la Vega El Inca, Garcilaso. *Comentarios Reales de los Incas.* Lima, Peru: Fondo Editorial Universidad Inca Garcilaso de la Vega, 2016.

———. *Royal Commentaries of the Incas and General History of Peru, Abridged.* Translated by Harold V. Livermore. Edited by Karen Spalding. Indianapolis: Hackett Publishing Company, 2006.

De Las Casas, Bartolomé. *History of the Indies.* Edited by Andrée Collard. New York: Harper Torchbooks, 1971.

———. *In Defense of the Indians.* DeKalb: Northern Illinois University Press, 1992.

———. *A Short Account of the Destruction of the Indies.* Edited by Nigel Griffin. London: Penguin Books, 1992.

Deck, Allan Figueroa. *The Second Wave: Hispanic Ministry and the Evangelization of Cultures.* New York: Paulist Press, 1989.

Del Castillo Grajeda, Bachiller José. *Compendio de la Vida y Virtudes de la Venerable Catarina de San Juan*. Mexico: Ediciones Xochitl, 1946.

Delgado Bernal, D. "Using a Chicana Feminist Epistemology in Educational Research." *Harvard Educational Review* 68, no. 4 (1998): 555-79.

Dennis, Marie, Renny Golden, and Scott Wright. *Oscar Romero: Reflections on His Life and Writings*. Maryknoll, NY: Orbis Books, 2000.

Dias, Jonathan Blas. *Towards a Theology of the Chamoru: Struggle and Liberation in Oceania*. Quezon City, Philippines: Claretian Publications, 2010.

Doss v. Bernal et al. (1943), Superior Court of the State of California, Orange County, no. 41466.

"El Plan Espiritual de Aztlán." MECha of Central Washington University. Accessed September 18, 2018. www.cwu.edu/~mecha/documents/plan_de_aztlan.pdf.

Elizondo, Virgilio. *Galilean Journey: The Mexican-American Promise*. Maryknoll, NY: Orbis Books, 2005.

———. *Guadalupe: Mother of the New Creation*. Maryknoll, NY: Orbis Books, 1997.

———. *La Morenita: Evangelizer of the Americas*. San Antonio, TX: Mexican American Cultural Center, 1980.

Escobar, Samuel. *En Busca de Cristo en América Latina*. Buenos Aires, Argentina: Ediciones Kairós, 2012.

———. *La Fe Evangélica y las Teologías de la Liberación*. El Paso, TX: Casa Bautista de Publicaciones, 1987.

———. *In Search of Christ in Latin America: From Colonial Image to Liberating Savior*. Downers Grove: IVP Academic, 2019.

———. *A Time for Mission: The Challenge of Global Christianity*. Leicester: Inter-Varsity Press, 2003.

Espín, Orlando. "Grace and Humanness: A Latino/a Perspective." In *We Are a People! Initiatives in Hispanic American Theology*, edited by Roberto S. Goizueta, 133-64. Minneapolis, MN: Fortress Press, 1992.

Espinosa, Gastón. *Latino Pentecostals in America: Faith and Politics in Action*. Cambridge, MA: Harvard University Press, 2014.

Espinoza, Gastón, and Mario T. García, eds. *Mexican American Religions: Spirituality, Activism, and Culture*. Durham, NC: Duke University Press, 2008.

Estrada, Rodolfo. "The Spirit as an Inner Witness in John 15.26." *Journal of Pentecostal Theology* 22, no. 1 (2013): 77-94.

Flores, David Jesus. "The Chicana/o Movement and the Catholic Church." MA thesis, UCLA, 2017.

Flores, Nichole M. "'Our Sister, Mother Earth': Solidarity and Familial Ecology in Laudato Si." *Journal of Religious Ethics* 46, no. 3 (2018): 463-78.

Foos, Paul. *A Short, Offhand Killing Affair: Soldiers and Social Conflict During the Mexican-American War*. Chapel Hill, NC: University of North Carolina Press, 2002.

Freire, Paulo. *Pedagogy of the Oppressed*. New York: Continuum, 2005.

Friede, Juan, and Benjamin Keen, eds. *Bartolomé de Las Casas in History: Toward an Understanding of the Man and His Work*. DeKalb, IL: Northern Illinois University Press, 1971.

García, Ignacio M. *White but Not Equal: Mexican Americans, Jury Discrimination, and the Supreme Court*. Tucson, AZ: University of Arizona Press, 2009.

García, Ismael. *Dignidad: Ethics Through Hispanic Eyes*. Nashville, TN: Abingdon, 1997.

García, Mario T. *Católicos: Resistance and Affirmation in Chicano Catholic History*. Austin, TX: University of Texas Press, 2010.

———. *Chicano Liberation Theology: The Writings and Documents of Richard Cruz and Católicos Por La Raza*. Dubuque, IA: Kendall Hunt Publishing, 2009.

———. *Father Luis Olivares, A Biography: Faith, Politics and the Origins of the Sanctuary Movement in Los Angeles*. Chapel Hill, NC: The University of North Carolina Press, 2018.

———. *The Gospel of César Chávez: My Faith in Action*. Lanham, MD: Sheed & Ward, 2007.

García, Matthew. *From the Jaws of Victory: The Triumph and Tragedy of César Chávez and the Farm Worker Movement*. Berkeley, CA: University of California Press, 2014.

García-Johnson, Oscar. *The Mestizo/a Community of the Spirit: A Postmodern Latino/a Ecclesiology*. Princeton Theological Monograph 105. Eugene, OR: Wipf and Stock, 2009.

———. *Spirit Outside the Gate: Decolonial Pneumatologies of the Global American South*. Downers Grove, IL: IVP Academic, 2019.

García-Johnson, Oscar, and William A. Dyrness. *Theology Without Borders: An Introduction to Global Conversations*. Grand Rapids: Baker Academic, 2015.

Garza, Edward D. *LULAC: League of United Latin-American Citizens*. Master's thesis, Southwest Texas State Teachers College, 1951.

Gaspar de Alba, Alicia. *Sor Juana's Second Dream: A Novel*. Albuquerque, NM: University of New Mexico Press, 1999.

———. *[Un]framing the "Bad Woman": Sor Juana, Malinche, Coyolxauhqui, and Other Rebels with a Cause*. Austin, TX: University of Texas Press, 2014.

Goizueta, Roberto. *Caminemos Con Jesús: Toward a Hispanic/Latino Theology of Accompaniment*. Maryknoll, NY: Orbis, 1995.

Gómez, Laura E. *Manifest Destinies: The Making of the Mexican American Race*. New York: New York University Press, 2007.

———. "Off-White in an Age of White Supremacy: Mexican Elites and the Rights of Indians and Blacks in Nineteenth-Century New Mexico." In *"Colored Men" and "Hombres Aquí": Hernandez v. Texas and the Emergence of Mexican-American Lawyering*, edited by Michael A. Olivas, 1-40. Houston, TX: Arte Público Press, 2006.

Gonzales, Rodolfo. "I Am Joaquin." https://www.latinamericanstudies.org/latinos/joaquin.htm.

González, Gilbert. *Labor and Community: Mexican Citrus Worker Villages in a Southern California County, 1900-1950*. Chicago: University of Illinois Press, 1994.

González, Justo. *Mañana: Christian Theology from a Hispanic Perspective*. Nashville: Abingdon Press, 1990.

———. *The Mestizo Augustine: A Theologian Between Two Cultures*. Downers Grove, IL: InterVarsity Press, 2016.

———. *Santa Biblia: The Bible Through Hispanic Eyes*. Nashville, TN: Abingdon Press, 1996.

———. *The Story of Christianity: The Early Church to the Present Day*. Peabody, MA: Prince Press, 2005.

González, Karen. *The God Who Sees: Immigrants, the Bible, and the Journey to Belong*. Harrisonburg, VA: Herald Press, 2019.

González, Michelle A. *A Critical Introduction to Religion in the Americas: Bridging the Liberation Theology and Religious Studies Divide*. New York: New York University Press, 2014.

González, Ondina E. and Justo L. González. *Christianity in Latin America: A History*. Cambridge: Cambridge University Press, 2008.

———. *Nuestra Fe: A Latin American Church History Sourcebook*. Nashville, TN: Abingdon Press, 2014.

Grant, Ulysses S. "Personal Memoirs. 1885–86. Chapter III. Army Life—Causes of the Mexican War—Camp Salubrity." Accessed September 28, 2018. www.bartleby.com /1011/3.html.

Griswold del Castillo, Richard, and Richard A. García. *César Chávez: A Triumph of Spirit*. Norman, OK: University of Oklahoma Press, 1997.

Griswold del Castillo. *The Treaty of Guadalupe Hidalgo: A Legacy of Conflict*. Norman, OK: University of Oklahoma Press, 1990.

Guaman Poma de Ayala, Felipe. *The First New Chronicle and Good Government*. Translated by David Frye. Indianapolis: Hackett, 2006.

Guerra, Lauren. "Beautified by the Spirit: Community Murals as a Liberative Source for Constructive Pneumatology." PhD diss., Graduate Theological Union-Berkeley, 2016.

Guerrero, Andrés. *A Chicano Theology*. Maryknoll, NY: Orbis Books, 1987.

Gutiérrez, David G. *Walls and Mirrors: Mexican Americans, Mexican Immigrants, and the Politics of Ethnicity*. Berkeley: University of California Press, 1995.

Gutiérrez, Gustavo. *The God of Life*. Maryknoll, NY: Orbis Books, 1991.

———. *Gustavo Gutiérrez: Essential Writings*. Edited by James B. Nickoloff. Minneapolis, MN: Fortress Press, 1996.

———. *A Theology of Liberation*. Maryknoll, NY: Orbis Books, 2012.

Haines, Michael, and Richard Steckel, eds. *A Population History of North America*. Cambridge: Cambridge University Press, 2000.

Haney-Lopez, Ian. *White by Law: The Legal Construction of Race*. New York: New York University Press, 2006.

Hanke, Lewis. *All Mankind Is One: A Study of the Disputation Between Bartolomé de Las Casas and Juan Ginés de Sepúlveda on the Religious and Intellectual Capacity of the American Indians*. DeKalb, IL: Northern Illinois University Press, 1974.

———. *The Spanish Struggle for Justice in the Conquest of America.* Dallas, TX: First Southern Methodist University Press, 2002.

Hanks, Angela, Danyelle Solomon, and Christian E. Weller, "Systematic Inequality: How America's Structural Racism Helped Create the Black-White Wealth Gap." Center for American Progress. February 21, 2018. www.americanprogress.org/issues /race/reports/2018/02/21/447051/systematic-inequality.

Heaney, Sharon. *Contextual Theology for Latin America: Liberation Themes in Evangelical Perspective.* Eugene, OR: Wipf & Stock, 2008.

Heizer, Robert F., and Alan J. Almquist. *The Other Californians: Prejudice and Discrimination Under Spain, Mexico, and the United States to 1920.* Berkeley, CA: University of California Press, 1977.

Hidalgo, Ann. "¡Ponte a Nuestro Lado! Be on Our Side! The Challenge of the Central American Liberation Theology Masses." In *Liturgy in Postcolonial Perspectives: Only One Is Holy*, edited by C. Carvalhaes, 125-34. New York: Palgrave Macmillan, 2015.

Hidalgo, Jacqueline. *Revelation in Aztlán: Scriptures, Utopias, and the Chicano Movement.* New York: Palgrave Macmillan, 2016.

Higginbotham, F. Michael. *Race Law: Cases, Commentary, and Questions.* Durham, NC: Carolina Academic Press, 2010.

Hill, Jonathan. *The History of Christian Thought: The Fascinating Story of the Great Christian Thinkers and How They Helped Shape the World as We Know It Today.* Downers Grove, IL: InterVarsity Press, 2004.

Hinojosa, Felipe. "Católicos Por La Raza and the Future of Catholic Studies." *American Catholic Studies* 127, no. 3 (2016): 26-29.

Huber, Lindsay Pérez. "Challenging Racist Nativist Framing: Acknowledging the Community Cultural Wealth of Undocumented Chicana College Students to Reframe the Immigration Debate." *Harvard Educational Review* 79, no. 4 (2009): 704-30.

Hurtado, Aída, and Patricia Gurin. *Chicana /o Identity in a Changing U.S. Society.* Tucson, AZ: University of Arizona, 2004.

Isasi-Díaz, Ada Maria. *En La Lucha/In the Struggle: Elaborating a Mujerista Theology.* Minneapolis, MN: Fortress, 1993.

———. *Mujerista Theology: A Theology for the Twenty-First Century.* Maryknoll, NY: Orbis Books, 2005.

———. "Mujeristas: A Name of Our Own!!" Religion Online. Accessed September 18, 2018. www.religion-online.org/article/mujeristas-a-name-of-our-own.

Jiménez, Michael. *Remembering Lived Lives: A Historiography from the Underside of Modernity.* Eugene, OR: Cascade Books, 2017.

Keating, AnaLouise. "'I'm a Citizen of the Universe': Gloria Anzaldúa's Spiritual Activism as Catalyst for Social Change." *Feminist Studies* 34, no. 1/2, The Chicana Studies Issue (2008): 53-69.

Keene, Benjamin. *A History of Latin America: Volume I.* Boston, MA: Houghton Mifflin Company, 1992.

Keogh, Dermot. *Romero: El Salvador's Martyr*. Dublin: Dominican Publications, 1981.

Kirk, Pamela. *Sor Juana Ines de la Cruz: Religion, Art, and Feminism*. New York: Continuum, 1998.

Kirkpatrick, David C. "C. René Padilla and the Origins of Integral Mission in Post-War Latin America." *Journal of Ecclesiastical History* 67, no. 2 (2016): 351-71.

———. *A Gospel for the Poor: Global Social Christianity and the Latin American Evangelical Left*. Philadelphia: University of Pennsylvania, 2019.

Kohn Rivera, Natalia, Noemi Vega Quiñones, and Kristy Garza Robinson. *Hermanas: Deepening Our Identity and Growing Our Influence*. Downers Grove: InterVarsity Press, 2019.

Krogstad, Jens Manuel, and Mark Hugo Lopez. "Hispanic Immigrants More Likely to Lack Health Insurance Than U.S.-born." *Pew Research Center*. September 26, 2014. www.pewresearch.org/fact-tank/2014/09/26/higher-share-of-hispanic-immigrants-than-u-s-born-lack-health-insurance.

"Laws of Burgos" text. Southern Methodist University. Accessed September 20, 2018. http://faculty.smu.edu/bakewell/BAKEWELL/texts/burgoslaws.html.

Lee, Hak Joon. *We Will Get to the Promised Land: Martin Luther King, Jr.'s Communal-Political Spirituality*. Cleveland, OH: The Pilgrim Press, 2006.

Lee, Sang Hyun. *From A Liminal Place: An Asian American Theology*. Minneapolis, MN: Fortress Press, 2010.

León, Luis D. *The Political Spirituality of César Chávez*. Berkeley, CA: University of California Press, 2015.

Levy, Jacques E. *César Chávez: Autobiography of La Causa*. Minneapolis, MN: University of Minnesota Press, 2007.

Lin, Tony Tian-Ren. "The Best of Both Worlds: The Role of Word of Faith Pentecostalism in Assimilating Latino Immigrants." PhD diss., University of Virginia, 2010.

Lincoln, Abraham. "Spot Resolutions." December 22, 1847. www.digitalhistory.uh.edu/disp_textbook.cfm?smtid=3&psid=3672.

———. "The War with Mexico: Speech in the United States House of Representatives." January 12, 1848. http://teachingamericanhistory.org/library/document/the-war-with-mexico-speech-in-the-united-states-house-of-representatives.

Livermore, Abiel Abbott. *The War with Mexico Reviewed*. Boston, MA: American Peace Society, 1850.

Lloyd-Moffett, Stephen R. "The Mysticism and Social Practice of César Chávez." In *Latino Religions and Civic Activism in the United States*, edited by Gaston Espinosa, Virgilio Elizondo, and Jesse Miranda, 35-52. Oxford: Oxford University Press, 2005.

Lopez v. Seccombe. 71 F. Supp. 769 (S.D. Cal. 1944).

Mares, E.A., Bette S. Weidman, Thomas J. Steele, Patricia Clark Smith, and Ray John Aragon. *Padre Martinez: New Perspectives from Taos*. Taos, NM: Millicent Rogers Museum, 1988.

Martell-Otero, Loida I., Zaida Maldonado Pérez, and Elizabeth Conde-Frazier. *Latina Evangélicas: A Theological Survey from the Margins*. Eugene, OR: Cascade Books, 2013.

Martí, Gerardo. *Worship Across the Racial Divide: Religious Music and the Multiracial Congregation*. Oxford: Oxford University Press, 2017.

Martínez, George A. "Legal Indeterminacy, Judicial Discretion, and the Mexican-American Litigation Experience, 1930-1980." *UC Davis Law Review* 27, no. 3 (1994): 557-618.

Martínez, Juan Francisco. *The Story of Latino Protestants in the United States*. Grand Rapids: Eerdmans, 2018.

———. *Walk with the People: Latino Ministry in the United States*. Eugene, OR: Wipf and Stock, 2016.

Martínez, Richard Edward. *Padres: The National Chicano Priest Movement*. Austin: University of Texas, 2005.

Martínez, Roberta H. *Latinos in Pasadena*. Mount Pleasant, SC: Arcadia Publishing, 2009.

Martinez-Olivieri, Jules. *A Visible Witness: Christology, Liberation, and Participation*. Minneapolis, MN: Fortress Press, 2016.

McGrath, Alistair E. *Historical Theology: An Introduction to the History of Christian Thought*. Oxford: Blackwell Publishers, 1998.

———. *Theology: The Basic Readings*. Oxford: Blackwell Publishing, 2008.

Medina, Lara. *Las Hermanas: Chicana/Latina Religious-Political Activism in the U.S. Catholic Church*. Philadelphia: Temple University Press, 2004.

Mendez v. Westminster 161 F.2d 774 (9th Cir. 1947).

Merlo, Oscar. "Impactando las Generaciones Emergentes (Impacting the Emerging Generations)." Volume 3. Edited by Lucas Leys, Hector Torres, Marcos Barrientos, and Pedro Eustache. Santa Ana, CA: Kerygma, 2014.

Miller, Robert J., Jacinta Ruru, Larissa Behrendt, and Tracy Lindberg. *Discovering Indigenous Lands: The Doctrine of Discovery in the English Colonies*. Oxford: Oxford University Press, 2012.

Muñoz, José Esteban. "Preface: Fragment from the Sense of Brown Manuscript." *GLQ: A Journal of Lesbian and Gay Studies* 24, no. 4 (2018): 395-97.

Myers, Ched. *Binding the Strongman: A Political Reading of Mark's Story of Jesus*. Maryknoll, NY: Orbis Books, 2012.

National Center for Children in Poverty, "Poverty by the Numbers: By Race, White Children Make Up the Biggest Percentage of America's Poor." Accessed September 18, 2018. www.nccp.org/media/releases/release_34.html.

National Public Radio. "Now Counted by Their Country, Afro-Mexicans Grab Unprecedented Spotlight." All Things Considered. February 6, 2016. www.npr.org/2016/02/06/465710473/now-counted-by-their-country-afro-mexicans-grab-unprecedented-spotlight.

Op, Andrew Hofer. "Matthew 25:31-46 as an Hermeneutical Rule in Augustine's *Enarrationes in Psalmos*." *The Downside Review* 126, no 445 (2008): 285-300.

Orosco, José-Antonio. *César Chávez and the Common Sense of Nonviolence*. Albuquerque, NM: University of New Mexico Press, 2008.

Ortega-Aponte, Elias and Catherine Keller. *Common Goods: Economy, Ecology, and Political Theology*. New York: Fordham University Press, 2015.

Padilla, C. René, "Integral Mission and its Historical Development." In *Justice, Mercy and Humility: Integral Mission and the Poor*, edited by Tim Chester, 42-58. Carlisle: Paternoster, 2002.

———, ed., *Misión Integral y Pobreza: El Testimonio Evangélico Hacia el Tercer Milenio: Palabra, Espíritu y Misión*. Buenos Aires, Argentina: Ediciones Kairós, 2001.

———. "My Theological Pilgrimage." In *Shaping a Global Theological Mind*, edited by Darren Marks, 127-38. Hampshire, UK: Ashgate, 2008.

———. *¿Qué es la Misión Integral?* Buenos Aires, Argentina: Ediciones Kairós, 2006.

Padilla, René and Tetsunao Yamamori. *The Local Church, Agent of Transformation: An Ecclesiology for Integral Mission*. Buenos Aires: Ediciones Kairós, 2004.

Padilla DeBorst, Ruth Irene. "Integral Mission Formation in Abya Yala (Latin America): A Study of the Centro de Studios Teológicos Interdisciplinarios (1982-2002) and Radical Evangélicos." PhD diss., Boston University, 2016.

———. "An Integral Transformation Approach: Being, Doing and Saying." In *The Mission of the Church: Five Views in Conversation*, edited by Craig Ott, 41-67. Grand Rapids: Baker Academic, 2016.

Perea, Juan F., Richard Delgado, Angela P. Harris, Stephanie M. Wildman, and Jean Stefancic. *Race and Races: Cases and Resources for a Diverse America*. St. Paul, MN: West Group, 2000.

Pew Research Center: Religion and Public Life. "The Shifting Religious Identity of Latinos: Nearly One in Four Latinos Are Former Catholics." May 7, 2014. www.pewforum .org/2014/05/07/the-shifting-religious-identity-of-latinos-in-the-united-states.

Plessy v. Ferguson. 163 U.S. 537 (1896).

Pubols, Louise. *The Father of All: The de la Guerra Family, Power, and Patriarchy in Mexican California*. San Marino: Huntington-USC Institute on California and the West, 2009.

"Quadragesimo Anno: On Reconstruction of the Social Order." Encyclical of Pope Pius XI. May 15, 1931. http://w2.vatican.va/content/pius-xi/en/encyclicals/documents/hf_p -xi_enc_19310515_quadragesimo-anno.html.

Ramírez, Daniel. *Migrating Faith: Pentecostalism in the United States and Mexico in the Twentieth Century*. Chapel Hill, NC: University of North Carolina Press, 2015.

Ramírez-Johnson, Johnny. *An Ethnography of Social Mobility: Immigrant Membership in a Seventh-day Adventist Puerto Rican Ethnic Church*. Lewiston, NY: Edwin Mellen Press, 2008.

Recinos, Harold J. *Good News from the Barrio: Prophetic Witness for the Church*. Louisville, KY: Westminster John Knox, 2006.

"Requerimiento, 1514." NC State University. Accessed September 20, 2018. https://faculty
.chass.ncsu.edu/slatta/hi216/require.htm.

"Rerum Novarum: On Capital and Labor." Encyclical of Pope Leo XIII. May 15, 1891.
http://w2.vatican.va/content/leo-xiii/en/encyclicals/documents/hf_l-xiii_enc_1505
1891_rerum-novarum.html.

Reyes, Patrick. *Nobody Cries When We Die: God, Community, and Surviving to Adulthood.*
St. Louis, MO: Chalice Press, 2016.

Richmond, Douglas. "The Legacy of African Slavery in Colonial Mexico, 1519-1810," *The
Journal of Popular Culture* 35, no. 2 (2001): 1-16.

Rivera, Raymond. *Liberty to the Captives: Our Call to Minister in a Captive World.* Grand
Rapids: Eerdmans, 2012.

Romero, Oscar A. *The Violence of Love.* Maryknoll, NY: Orbis Books, 2004.

Romero, Robert Chao. *The Chinese in Mexico, 1882-1940.* Tucson, AZ: University of Arizona Press, 2010.

———. *Jesus for Revolutionaries: An Introduction to Race, Social Justice, and Christianity.*
Los Angeles, CA: Christian Ethnic Studies Press, 2013.

———. "Migration as Grace," *International Journal of Urban Transformation* 1 (2016): 10-35.

Romero, Robert Chao, and Luis Fernando Fernandez. "Doss v. Bernal: Ending Mexican
Apartheid in Orange County." *UCLA CSRC Research Report* no. 14 (February 2012).

Roten, Johann. "Nican Mopohua: The Story of Our Lady of Guadalupe in Nahuatl." University of Dayton, Ohio. Accessed September 20, 2018. https://udayton.edu/imri/mary/n
/nican-mopohua.php.

Rothenberg, D. *Memory of Silence: The Guatemalan Truth Commission Report.* London:
Palgrave Macmillan, 2016.

Rouse, Irving. *The Tainos: Rise and Decline of the People Who Greeted Columbus.* New
Haven, CT: Yale University Press, 1993.

Ruiz, Vicki. *From Out of the Shadows: Mexican Women in Twentieth Century America.*
Oxford: Oxford University Press, 2008.

Rustomji-Kerns, Roshni. "Mirrha-Catarina de San Juan: From India to New Spain." *Am-
erasia Journal* 28, no. 2 (2002): 28-37.

Salinas, J. Daniel. *Latin American Evangelical Theology in the 1970's: The Golden Decade.*
Leiden and Boston: Brill, 2009.

———. *Taking Up the Mantle: Latin American Evangelical Theology in the 20th Century.*
Langham Global Library, 2017.

Salvatierra, Alexia. *Faith-Rooted Organizing: Mobilizing the Church in Service to the
World.* Downers Grove, IL: InterVarsity Press, 2014.

Salyer, Lucy E. *Laws Harsh as Tigers: Chinese Immigrants and the Shaping of Modern
Immigration Law.* Chapel Hill, NC: The University of North Carolina Press, 1995.

San Miguel, Guadalupe, Jr. "The Impact of Brown on Mexican American Desegregation
Litigation, 1950s to 1980s." *Journal of Latinos and Education* 4, no. 4 (2005): 221-36.

Sánchez, George. *Becoming Mexican American: Ethnicity, Culture and Identity in Chicano Los Angeles, 1900-1945.* Oxford: Oxford University Press, 1993.

Sánchez, Michelle C. "Calvin and the Two Bodies of Christ: Fiction and Power in Dogmatic Theology." *Political Theology* 19, no. 5 (2018): 439-56.

Sánchez-Walsh, Arlene. *Latino Pentecostal Identity: Evangelical Faith, Self, and Society.* New York: Columbia University Press, 2003.

Sandoval, Moises. *The Mexican American in the Church: Reflection on Identity and Mission.* New York: Sadlier Books, 1983.

Scott, Nina M. "Sor Juana Inés de la Cruz: 'Let Your Women Keep Silence in the Churches . . .'" *Women's Studies International Forum* 8, no. 5 (1985): 511-19.

Segovia, Fernando F. "In the World but Not of It: Exile as Locus for Theology of the Diaspora." In *Hispanic/Latino Theology: Challenge and Promise*, edited by Ada María Isasi-Díaz and Fernando Segovia, 195-217. Minneapolis: Fortress Press, 1996.

Sirvent, Roberto. *Embracing Vulnerability: Human and Divine.* Eugene, OR: Pickwick Publications, 2014.

Sirvent, Roberto, and Danny Haiphong. *American Exceptionalism and American Innocence: The Fake News of U.S. Empire.* New York: Skyhorse Publishing, 2019.

Slack, Edward R. Jr. "The Chinos in New Spain: A Corrective Lens for a Distorted Image." *Journal of World History* 20, no. 1 (2009): 35-67.

Smallwood, E. Mary. "High Priests and Politics in Roman Palestine." *The Journal of Theological Studies* 13, no. 1 (1962): 14-34.

Smith, Kay Higuera, Jayachitra Lalitha, and L. Daniel Hawk. *Evangelical Postcolonial Conversations: Global Awakenings in Theology and Praxis.* Downers Grove, IL: InterVarsity Press Academic, 2014.

Smith, Nicholas. "Aristotle's Theory of Natural Slavery." *Phoenix* 37, no. 2 (1983): 109-22.

Solórzano, Daniel and Tara Yosso. "Critical Race Methodology: Counter-Storytelling as an Analytical Framework for Education Research." *Qualitative Inquiry* 8, no. 1 (2002): 23-44.

Sor Juana Inés de la Cruz. "Answer by the Poet to the Most Illustrious Sister Filotea de la Cruz." Translated by William Little. 2008. http://dept.sfcollege.edu/hfl/hum2461/pdfs /sjicanswer.pdf.

Stott, John. *Christian Mission in the Modern World.* Downers Grove, IL: InterVarsity Press, 2009.

Strum, Philippa. *Mendez v. Westminster: School Desegregation and Mexican-American Rights.* Lawrence, KS: University Press of Kansas, 2010.

Tamez-Méndez, Elizabeth. "Rethinking Latino Youth Ministry: Frameworks That Provide Roots and Wings for Our Youth." *Apuntes: Theological Reflections from the Hispanic-Latino Context* 37, no. 2 (Summer 2017): 42-91.

T-Races, Testbed for the Redlining Archives of California's Exclusionary Spaces, Los Angeles. Accessed October 12, 2018. http://salt.umd.edu/T-RACES/demo/demo.html.

"Treaty with the Republic of Mexico." The Library of Congress. February 2, 1848. https://memory.loc.gov/cgi-bin/ampage?collId=llsl&fileName=009/llsl009.db&recNum=982.

Trinidad, Saúl, and Juan Stam. "Christ in Latin American Protestant Preaching." In *Faces of Jesus: Latin American Christologies*, edited by José Míguez Bonino, 39-45. Maryknoll, NY: Orbis Books, 1985.

United States Conference of Catholic Bishops. "Saints Who Were Great Evangelizers." Accessed September 20,2018. www.usccb.org/prayer-and-worship/prayers-and-devotions/saints/evangelizing-saints.cfm.

United States Conference of Catholic Bishops. "Seven Themes of Catholic Social Teaching." Accessed October 2, 2018. www.usccb.org/beliefs-and-teachings/what-we-believe/catholic-social-teaching/seven-themes-of-catholic-social-teaching.cfm.

United States State Department, Office of the Historian. "The Immigration Act of 1924 (The Johnson-Reed Act)." Accessed October 1, 2018. https://history.state.gov/milestones/1921-1936/immigration-act.

University of Washington, Seattle Civil Rights & Labor History Project. "Racial Restrictive Covenants." Accessed October 1, 2018. http://depts.washington.edu/civilr/covenants.htm.

Van Opstal, Sandra Maria. *The Next Worship: Glorifying God in a Diverse World*. Downers Grove, IL: InterVarsity Press, 2016.

Vargas, Zaragosa. *Crucible of Struggle: A History of Mexican Americans from the Colonial Period to the Present Era*. Oxford: Oxford University Press, 2010.

Vasconcelos, José. *The Cosmic Race / La Raza Cosmica*. Baltimore: Johns Hopkins University Press, 1997.

Veas, Gabe. "From Awareness to Transformation: The Necessity of Leaders and Institutions to Embody Moral Courage for Racial Conciliation." *The International Journal of Urban Transformation* 2 (2017): 124-60.

Velasco-Márquez, Jesús. "A Mexican Viewpoint on the War with the United States." Accessed September 28, 2018. www.pbs.org/kera/usmexicanwar/prelude/md_a_mexican_viewpoint.html.

Veracini, Lorenzo. *Settler Colonialism: A Theoretical Overview*. London: Palgrave Macmillan, 2010.

Vickery, Paul. *Bartolomé de las Casas: Great Prophet of the Americas*. Mahwah, NJ: Paulist Press, 2006.

Villafañe, Eldin. *El Espiritu Liberador: Hacia una Etica Social Pentecostal Hispanoamericana*. Grand Rapids: Eerdmans, 1997.

———. *The Liberating Spirit: Toward an Hispanic American Pentecostal Social Ethic*. Grand Rapids: Eerdmans, 1993.

Wells, Ronald A. "César Chávez's Protestant Allies: The California Migrant Ministry and the Farmworkers." *Journal of Presbyterian History* (2009): 5-16. https://libraries.ucsd.edu/farmworkermovement/essays/essays/cec.pdf.

Willard, Dallas. *The Divine Conspiracy: Rediscovering Our Hidden Life in God*. New York: HarperCollins, 1998.

Wilson, Samuel. *Hispaniola: Caribbean Chiefdoms in the Age of Columbus*. Tuscaloosa, AL: University of Alabama Press, 1990.

Wright, N.T. *The Challenge of Jesus: Rediscovering Who Jesus Was and Is*. Downers Grove, IL: InterVarsity Press, 1999.

——. *Jesus and the Victory of God*. Minneapolis, MN: Fortress Press, 1996.

——. *Simply Jesus: A New Vision of Who He Was, What He Did, and Why He Matters*. New York: HarperOne, 2011.

Yoder, John Howard. *The Priestly Kingdom: Social Ethics as Gospel*. South Bend, IN: University of Notre Dame Press, 1985.

Yosso, Tara J. "Whose Culture Has Capital? A Critical Race Theory Discussion of Community Cultural Wealth." *Race Ethnicity and Education* 8, no. 1 (2005): 69-91.

Yosso, Tara J., and Daniel G. Solórzano. "Leaks in the Chicana and Chicano Educational Pipeline." Latino Policies and Issues Brief, no. 13. (March 2006). www.chicano.ucla.edu /files/LPIB_13March2006.pdf.

Yugar, Theresa A. *Sor Juana Inés de la Cruz: Feminist Reconstruction of Biography and Text*. Eugene, OR: Wipf & Stock, 2014.

AUTHOR AND SUBJECT INDEX

SCRIPTURE INDEX

C|C CHRISTIAN COMMUNITY
D|A DEVELOPMENT ASSOCIATION

The Christian Community Development Association (CCDA) is a network of Christians committed to engaging with people and communities in the process of transformation. For over twenty-five years, CCDA has aimed to inspire, train, and connect Christians who seek to bear witness to the Kingdom of God by reclaiming and restoring under-resourced communities. CCDA walks alongside local practitioners and partners as they live out Christian Community Development (CCD) by loving their neighbors.

CCDA was founded in 1989 under the leadership of Dr. John Perkins and several other key leaders who are engaged in the work of Christian Community Development still today. Since then, practitioners and partners engaged in the work of the Kingdom have taken ownership of the movement. Our diverse membership and the breadth of the CCDA family are integral to realizing the vision of restored communities.

The CCDA National Conference was birthed as an annual opportunity for practitioners and partners engaged in CCD to gather, sharing best practices and seeking encouragement, inspiration, and connection to other like-minded Christ-followers, committed to ministry in difficult places. For four days, the CCDA family, coming from across the country and around the world, is reunited around a common vision and heart.

Additionally, the CCDA Institute serves as the educational and training arm of the association, offering workshops and trainings in the philosophy of CCD. We have created a space for diverse groups of leaders to be steeped in the heart of CCD and forge lifelong friendships over the course of two years through CCDA's Leadership Cohort.

CCDA has a long-standing commitment to the confrontation of injustice. Our advocacy and organizing is rooted in Jesus' compassion and commitment to Kingdom justice. While we recognize there are many injustices to be fought, as an association we are strategically working on issues of immigration, mass incarceration, and education reform.

To learn more, visit www.ccda.org/ivp

Finding the Textbook You Need

The IVP Academic Textbook Selector
is an online tool for instantly finding the IVP books
suitable for over 250 courses across 24 disciplines.

ivpacademic.com